Albania
the Master Key
to the Near East

Albania
The Master Key to the Near East

Christo A. Dako

Original introduction by Prof. Richard Gottheil
of Columbia University

First published in 1919

Republished on the centennial anniversary
of the Paris Peace Conference

Compiled with preface by David Hosaflook

Albania, the Master Key to the Near East

Originally published in 1919 (Boston: E. L. Grimes Company)

This compiled edition with historical preface copyright © 2020 David Hosaflook

All rights reserved. No part of this book may be reproduced in any form without permission in writing from the copyright holder, except by reviewers, who may quote brief passages in a review.

ISBN 978-1-946244-29-1 (paperback edition)
ISBN 978-1-946244-30-7 (electronic edition)

Cataloging in Publication Data:

Dako, Christo A., 1876–1941
    Albania : the master key to the Near East / Christo A. Dako ; introduction by Richard Gottheil ; compiled with preface by David Hosaflook.
    p. : ill., maps, facsims. ; cm.
    Includes maps, illustrations, appendices, bibliographical references, and index.

Library of Congress Control Number: 2020916399

Subject: HIS010010 HISTORY / Europe / Eastern
1.7.1.0.0.0.0 Albania, 949.65

Front cover image from: Dako, Sevasti D. "Albania's Rights, Hopes and Aspirations," *Yll'i Mëngjezit (The Morning Star)*, ed. Miss Paraskevi D. Kyrias (Boston), vol. 3, no. 7, November 1918.

Institute for Albanian and Protestant Studies
Tirana, Albania
Longwood, FL

www.instituti.org

PREFACE

DAVID HOSAFLOOK, 2019

One hundred years ago, the world went to Paris. The Great War (1914–1918) had ended, two vast empires had dissolved (Ottoman and Austro-Hungarian), and the Great Powers were gathered to redraw the map of the world. For six months in Paris, leaders of the victorious Allied powers wrestled with the question of how best to effect world peace in the aftermath of world war. Delegates and petitioners from across the globe flooded into Paris to seek the best possible outcomes for their own nations and peoples, appealing especially to the so-called "Big Four": United States President Woodrow Wilson, British Prime Minister David Lloyd George, French Prime Minister Georges Clemenceau, and Italian Prime Minister Vittorio Emanuele Orlando.

It was hoped that the Paris Peace Conference of 1919–1920 would bring an end to war. It did not. "The Great War" became known as "World War *One*." This is not to suggest that the Peace Conference was a failure or that the peacemakers did less than was humanly possible. Historians agree that there were many successes; but the task—fixing the entire world—proved too big even for the "Big Four." Clemenceau admitted as much with candor and clarity, stating: "It is much easier to make war than peace."[1]

---

[1] Ribot, A. *Journal d'Alexander Ribot et correspondances inédites, 1914–1922*. London, 1933, 255.

In the vacuum left by the Ottoman Empire's dissolution, the political boundaries of two particularly fragile regions would have to be decided: the Middle East and the Near East (an expression then denoting the Balkan Peninsula). The First World War had started in the Balkans, it was therefore of paramount importance to get the Balkans right. This was complicated on account of the many nationalities in Southeastern Europe who all seemed to espouse over-optimistic territorial ambitions and touted self-serving narratives about the region's history. They all sought to convince the key decision makers of their rights, to debunk the claims being made by their regional rivals, and to ensure favorable outcomes for their own national aspirations. The old cliché about the Balkans was foreboding: "Too much history; not enough geography." So well known was the region for its proclivity to conflict that a new word was invented in 1919—*Balkanize*—meaning "to break up into smaller and often hostile units."

Might little Albania hold the key to promoting peace, or at least to avoiding another war in the Balkans? The Albanian educator and national figure Christo Dako thought so. In 1919 he published a book (this book) to argue such a case. He aimed to influence the plenipotentiaries in Paris, or at least to influence their influencers, especially the Americans, who were on the rise as a global power and whose president had pledged his commitment to uphold the rights of smaller nations. In January of 1918, Woodrow Wilson gave his famous "Fourteen Points" speech, outlining his plan to end the war and promote world peace. At least three of the fourteen points affected Albania directly, making nationality a valid basis for self-determination (XI), assuring autonomous development (XII), and guaranteeing political independence and territorial integrity to both large and small states alike (XIV). None of the fourteen points, however, named Albania specifically.

Christo Dako began writing this book in 1913, in the context of the Balkan Wars, the London Conference of Ambassadors (which proposed to decide Albania's fate as a nation), and shortly after Albania's proclamation of independence in November, 1912. The Albanians were largely unknown in the world, and even less understood. For several centuries, Muslim Albanians had been considered Turks and Orthodox Albanians had been considered Greeks. In 1913 Albania's political borders were established (corresponding to today's borders), but the Albanians were frustrated that Kosovo, Chameria and other territories with large Albanian populations were ceded to their neighbors. Nor were those neighbors content, for they continued to pursue aggressive territorial expansion which could only be realized at Albania's further expense. In 1917, shocking news was leaked by the Bolsheviks about a secret pact made in 1915 in London between the Russian Empire, the United Kingdom, the French Republic, and the Kingdom of Italy, in which most Albanian territories would eventually be divided between Italy, Greece, Serbia, and Montenegro. This revelation outraged the Albanians, and Dako found fresh motivation to continue writing his treatise.

After World War One, Greece intensified its claims on Anatolia, Cyprus, and the southern Balkans (this was known as the *Megali Idea*). Although the Great Powers generally considered this idea as an exercise in megalomania, Greece had a favorable bargaining position. First, it had fought on the winning side of the war. Second, it could provide an ally in the Near East, especially to Great Britain, who needed regional influence in a post-Ottoman world. Third, and most momentous, Greece had a larger-than-life, persuasive prime minister in the person of Eleftherios Venizelos, who put in long hours at the Paris Peace Conference lobbying for his cause. In the wake of 500 years of Ottoman rule and under imminent threat from their expansionist neighbors, Albania's position seemed impossible, as noted by the Canadian scholar and Oxford University professor, Margaret MacMillan:

> Poor little Albania, with such powerful enemies and so few friends. It had almost no industry, little trade, no railways at all and only about two hundred miles of paved road. Albania emerged just before the war, created out of four districts of the Ottoman Empire. Few outsiders ever visited it; little was known about its history or its people.[2]

Little, indeed, was known about Albania. To address this in the run-up to Paris in 1918, various pamphlets began to emerge from the Albanian community in the United States, with titles such as: "The Albanian Question" by Mehmet Konitza; "Albania's Rights, Hopes, and Aspirations" by Sevasti Kyrias Dako and Dhimitri Bala; and "Memorandum on Albania" by Fan Stylian Noli (published in the periodical *The Adriatic Review*, itself a platform for promoting awareness about Albania). These pamphlets and articles were sent to the U.S. State Department and to President Wilson himself, but did not suffice to counterbalance the claims Albania's rivals were making in intellectual and political circles. In Paris, for example, Venizelos not only presented inflated

---

[2] MacMillan, Margaret. *Paris 1919: Six Months that Changed the World.* New York: Random House, 2002, 357–358.

population statistics about Greek majorities in Southern Albania, but he also argued that the Albanians were an inferior civilization, unable to govern themselves (much less any Greek minorities), and should considered themselves fortunate to be incorporated into an enlarged postwar Greece.[3]

To counter these notions, two educated Albanians published scholarly books, written to inform outsiders about Albania's rich history and its freedom-loving people.[4] These were the first comprehensive histories of Albania to be published in English. They included maps, indexes, and copious references. Constantine Chekrezi, a Harvard-educated Albanian, was the first to publish in 1919. It was a 255-page volume with an introduction by Charles D. Hazen, professor of Modern History at Columbia University. The book was entitled, rather generically, *Albania, Past and Present*.[5]

The second book was by Christo Dako, also published in 1919, six years after he began writing. It contained 290 pages with an introduction by a different Columbia University professor, Richard Gottheil. Dako's title was more intentional, pragmatic and strategic than the previous books and pamphlets: *Albania: the Master Key to the Near East*. Even if overstated, this title had the power to attract the attention of those deciding the fate of the Balkans. The book was beautifully bound, in hopes of being noticed. It was crimson red, like Albania's flag, with gold lettering. Unlike Chekrezi's work, Dako's book included photographs, thirty of them,

---

[3] Stickney, Edith P. *Southern Albania or Northern Epirus in European International Affairs, 1912 – 1923*. Stanford University Press, 1926, 79.

[4] *The Albanian Struggle in the Old World and New*. Boston: The Writer, Inc., 1939, 62.

[5] Chekrezi, Constantine. *Albania, Past and Present*. New York: MacMillian, 1919.

strategically chosen to portray educated Albanian men and women, children in traditional costumes, national political gatherings, a modern musical band, and influential foreigners supporting Albania. Dako knew the power of images and sound-bites in a context of international information overload. He knew that the elite audience he hoped to reach might only take time to skim his masterpiece, so he embedded his core message into the very title. Albania, he argued, was "the master key" to the Balkans. This title expressed hope but also sounded a warning. The implication was this: "Albania can be a powerful ally for peace, but neglect it at the world's peril."

Christo Dako (1876–1941) was born in Kortcha and moved to Bucharest at the age of twelve. Later, while a student of mathematics at the University of Bucharest, he became active in an Albanian nationalist group which was arguably the most active and influential of the many such groups outside Albania. Its purpose was "the liberation of Albania from the Turkish yoke and its freedom from under the dominance of the Greek clergy." As a young man Dako was elected secretary and thus "came into contact and intimate association with many of the sturdy pioneers of the Albanian National Movement" (page 207).

One such pioneer was Miss Sevasti Kyrias (Qiriazi), the first Albanian woman to receive a high school and college diploma and the first principal of the Albanian Girls' School in Kortcha, a Protestant-based school founded in 1891 that struggled to survive amidst political, ecclesiastical and social opposition. Ottoman law and the Greek church had forbidden teaching the Albanian language, and there were almost no Albanian textbooks available, other than the copies the school staff printed in secret on hectograph machines.

In 1905 Sevasti visited Bucharest, met Christo, and secured his help in preparing Albanian language math, geometry, and algebra textbooks. When completed, they would have to find creative ways to smuggle them to the school girls at Kortcha. Both recognized a kindred spirit in the other. They were both intelligent and educated, both from Kortcha, both from Orthodox backgrounds, both converts to Protestantism, and both consumed with emancipating their fellow Albanians.

In 1907 Christo Dako went to the United States to study at Oberlin College's Graduate School of Theology and "prepare himself for preaching the Gospel to his native people."[6] He was firmly committed to return to his homeland to promote education. Meanwhile, back in Kortcha, an American missionary couple, Phineas and Violet Kennedy, had arrived to assist Sevasti and her colleagues in the Girls' School and to expand the Evangelical church ministry. (This work had been founded in 1890 by Sevasti's late brother, Gerasim Kyrias.) In March of 1909, Dako's American sponsor, S. Arthur Baldwin, wrote to Kennedy: "[Christo] is a dear consecrated spirit and one of the brainiest Albanians as well as truest spirits that I ever met. We love him like a son."[7] Baldwin suggested that Dako might begin working with Kennedy and the mission after he earned his degree. In April, however, Dako interrupted his studies in response to a call by the Albanian national club to return to Bucharest. They needed his counsel and experience in light of the suppression of Albanian nationalist activities by the Young Turks government. Baldwin was impressed with Dako's

---

[6] S. Arthur Baldwin to Rev. P. B. Kennedy, May 12, 1909. Institute for Albanian and Protestant Studies, Edwin Jacques Archive (IAPSEJ). See also page 208 of this book.

[7] S. Arthur Baldwin to Rev. P. B. Kennedy, Feb. 15, 1909, IAPSEJ.

principled decision, especially since he had been offered a position in a Protestant mission working with Romanians and Albanians in the USA, for triple the salary he could earn in the Balkans.[8]

In her memoirs, Sevasti Kyrias described how her ambitions, hopes, and longings for the future aligned so well with Christo's, making marriage seem "predestined" and "inevitable."[9] Their plans for marriage in the early summer of 1910 were delayed, however, when Christo was arrested in Elbasan and imprisoned in Monastir for writing an article in the periodical *Bashkimi i Kombit* in which he protested against atrocities committed by Turkish soldiers on an Albanian woman.[10] Dako described hearing about the incident from an eyewitness and feeling compelled to respond. He wrote, "I could not, myself, avenge the murder of this brave woman with deeds of arms, and could but resort to my pen" (211). Unbeknownst to Dako, the press of Europe reprinted his story. In Germany, affiliates of the Young Turks discovered the article, complained to their superiors and called for his arrest. After several weeks of harsh treatment, he was released. Wasting no time, on July 10, 1910, he married Sevasti Kyrias and took her to Bucharest.

In October the newlyweds returned to Monastir, Sevasti's home town. Their future was uncertain. The Balkan Wars were yet to erupt, but the threat of war was growing louder. Albania's future as an autonomous province was under threat, leading to an increase in Albanian uprisings

---

[8] S. Arthur Baldwin to Rev. P. B. Kennedy, May 12, 1909, IAPSEJ.

[9] Kyrias-Dako, Sevasti. *My Life: the Autobiography of the Pioneer of Female Education in Albania*. Tirana: Institute for Albanian and Protestant Studies, 2016.

[10] Dako, Kristo. *Bashkimi i Kombit*, no. 37, May 20, 1910.

and Turkish reprisals. The Dakos had to work with utmost caution. They quietly prepared Albanian textbooks and wrote memos to the Great Powers about the political situation. Christo traveled to Kortcha to defend the beleaguered Girls' School, where he learned even more about the Greek threat to southern Albania. It was hard for Christo and Sevasti to imagine a positive outcome or, more practically, to decide where to live and how to best invest their energies for the greatest benefit of their people.

Then, in May, 1911, an unexpected stranger appeared at the Dakos' door in Monastir. Charles Crane, a wealthy American businessman and philanthropist with significant political influence and global awareness, wanted to meet them. Among his friends was the former president of Princeton University, now the governor of New Jersey, Woodrow Wilson. Crane was on his way to speak at Sevasti's alma mater, the American College for Girls at Constantinople, where he served on the Board of Trustees. Desiring to learn all he could about the Middle East and Eastern Europe, he wanted to know more about Albania. An Oberlin College professor on the Board of Trustees of the Girls' School in Kortcha had told Crane about Christo and Sevasti. Assured that the Dakos were educated, trustworthy, and well-connected, Crane stopped off in Monastir to meet them and to plan a tour of Albania. Sevasti described her first impressions of Mr. Crane: "Our meeting was very informal. I felt as though I had known him always and that he was already our friend."[11] Albania needed such a friend at such a time.

---

[11] Kyrias-Dako, *My Life*, 167–168.

Later that month, Christo Dako and Charles Crane, with an escort of twenty-four mounted troops, set off from Monastir. They visited Resna, Ohrid, Qukes, and Elbasan. They traversed the Krrabë mountain pass to Tirana, visited Kruja, then went to Durres and Shkodra. Along the journey they met prominent Albanian patriots and national leaders.[12] They witnessed extreme poverty and acts of cruelty. They heard the distant gunfire of Albanian insurgents. They experienced the hostility of local authorities. In Shkodra, their books and papers were confiscated and Dako was arrested. Crane protested with great vehemence. While he waited for a resolution, he visited the British anthropologist Edith Durham in Podgorica and the refugees she was helping, then went on to Cetinje and met Ismail Qemali and other Albanian leaders (who would proclaim Albania's independence within months). After nine days of imprisonment, Dako was released and rejoined Crane in Cetinje, where they traveled on together to Vienna to debrief.

The significance of Crane's journey with Dako is comparable to Edith's Durham's first tour of Albania in 1904 with the Albanian Bible distributor Thanas Sina—a tour from Leskovik to Shkodra that acquainted her with the Albanian national awakening and compelled her to advocate for Albania's human and political rights. Like Durham, Crane was also moved to action by what he had seen. He immediately sent money to finance the college education of twelve Albanians, six men and six women, at the American

---

[12] Among those Crane met were Fehim Bey Zavalani, George Kyrias, Izet Bey Zavalani, Hamdi Bey, Akif Pasha, Shefket Bey, Fuat Bey Toptani, Hysen Bey Vrioni, Ismail Qemali, and Luigj Gurakuqi.

mission colleges in Istanbul, and he began to exert his political influence on Albania's behalf.

The Crane family and the Dako family maintained their friendship for many years. In 1912 Christo returned to Oberlin to complete his degree, joined by Sevasti's sister, Paraskevi Kyrias, who began her own course of study at Oberlin and became the first Albanian woman to earn a Masters degree. The same year, a presidential election consumed American politics. Crane's friend Woodrow Wilson became the Democratic Party's nominee, and Charles Crane supported his campaign generously. When Wilson won, Crane's potential influence increased dramatically, but it would be several years before the Albanians understood Wilson's significance.

Christo Dako, though not a historian by profession, proved a careful researcher and was uniquely qualified to write about Albanian matters. Not only was he well connected in Bucharest, Macedonia and Albania, but he also became active with Albanian patriotic societies in New England. In 1913 he was elected both president of the Albanian Vatra Federation and editor of the Boston weekly *Dielli*. He maintained those positions briefly, however, with Fan Noli asserting more control over Vatra.[13] Over the next years Dako traveled widely on both sides of the Atlantic meeting various nationalist groups, and he "gradually developed a plan for the coordination of all patriotic societies on both sides of the Atlantic."[14]

Between 1917–1920 Christo Dako assisted Paraskevi Kyrias in the publication of *Yll'i Mëngjezit* (Morning Star),

---

[13] *The Albanian Struggle in the Old World and New*. Boston: The Writer, Inc., 1939, 53.

[14] Ibid., 56.

a semi-monthly English-Albanian periodical published in Boston. The periodical focused on history, literature, biographical material, life in America, and even political insights. In 1918 Dako formed the Albanian National Party in Worcester, Massachusetts. Ismail Qemali (modern Albania's founding father and first prime minister) was its chief agent, and Mrs. Sevasti Kyrias-Dako was its president.[15]

Christo Dako did not attend the Paris Peace Conference, for he was working feverishly to complete his book and get it distributed. In his place, he sent his sister-in-law, Paraskevi Kyrias, to represent the Albanian National Party, one of several Albanian delegations to Paris, all with slightly different ideas of how to protect Albania's sovereignty and, if possible, to win back the Albanian-majority regions the Great Powers had excluded from them in 1913 in London. Paraskevi was the only female representative from Albania, indeed one of the few females from *any* country sent to Paris in official capacity. She was a gifted communicator, a formidable debater, and a charming media presence. She made it a point to sign her official memorandums to foreign powers as "Miss Paraskevi Kyrias," emphasizing her gender. The presence of a progressive, fearless Albanian female in a male-dominated conference greatly undermined the Greeks' portrayal of the Albanians as a backward, inferior civilization.

Although Christo Dako was not in Paris, he kept abreast of the developments by telegram, and played as active a role as possible from the United States. One example of this regarded a memorandum President Wilson issued in April about Italian claims, in which he allowed Italy to retain Vlora,

---

[15] Ibid., 60.

the city where Albania's independence had been declared.[16] Paraskevi sent a telegram to Christo, who immediately responded by telegram with a protest to President Wilson. He also wrote Charles Crane, begging him to exert his political influence to effect a policy reversal. He prepared a press pack concerning Vlora for Charles Crane, sending it personally through his son Richard Crane, who happened to be on his way to Paris to visit his father.

When *Albania: The Master Key to the Near East* was published in the spring of 1919, reviews began to appear in the newspapers. One called it "a great aid to the right understanding of European problems."[17] Another claimed: "The whole purview of the book shows the craftsmanship of the genuine scholar, writing proudly about his own people and their cause and thus attaining a production that far outshines the compilations of the car window observers."[18] Not surprisingly, the book was dedicated to Mr. and Mrs. Charles Crane, Albania's most influential friends who, it seems, attempted to convince President Wilson why it made sense to defend Albania's borders. Dako wrote: "We really owe more to Mr. Crane than to any other individual outside of our own nation" (255).

The first copies of the book arrived in Paris in May of 1919. Paraskevi Kyrias wrote in her diary that when she read

---

[16] "Memorandum Concerning the Question of Italian Claims on the Adriatic," presented by President Wilson to the Italian delegation, April 14, 1919, cited in Congressional Record—Senate, May 30, 1919 (Vlora is spelled incorrectly as "Volna," a symbolic example of the world's unfamiliarity with Albania).

[17] Book review in the *Jamestown Evening Journal*, cited in *Yll'i Mëngjezit*, December 1919, 289.

[18] Book review in the *Pittsburgh Dispatch*, cited in *Yll'i Mëngjezit*, December 1919, 289.

it, she valued it as a treasure the likes of which the Albanians had never seen. She and the Albanian petitioners began delivering the book by hand to influential people. In June, the periodical *Albania* reported that 250 copies had been distributed to key delegates and influencers in Paris.[19] On June 9, Paraskevi mailed a copy to the most powerful man in Paris, President Wilson.

We do not know how much attention President Wilson paid to Dako's book, but we do know that after its publication, the tide of United States support began to turn in Albania's favor. More influential delegates and intellectuals began to defend Albania's interests and to question the claims of its neighbors. Still, Albania was on the chopping block. On January 14, 1920, the British, French and Italian prime ministers—in the absence of the United States representative—presented a proposal giving Vlora to Italy, Shkodra and other parts of Northern Albania to Yugoslavia, and Gjirokastër and Kortcha to Greece. The United States government did not receive this news well. The prime ministers of Britain and France did all they could to persuade Wilson, but his rejection of the proposal was resolute. On March 6, 1920, the United States unequivocally rejected any plan that deprived Albania of its borders established in 1913. Thus, "President Wilson and the American delegation in Paris did more in favor of Albania than any other Power to save the country from the danger of partition."[20]

Woodrow Wilson is still revered in Albania, Kosovo, and North Macedonia. Each of those countries has issued

---

[19] "Një vepër kombëtare e cquar". *Albania*, 5 June 1919.

[20] Pearson, Owen. *Albania and King Zog: Independence, Republic and Monarchy, 1908-1939.* London: I. B. Tauris, 2004, 142.

postage stamps in his honor. Boys, bars, streets, and schools are named after him. In 1992, on the 100th anniversary of Albania's independence, one of Tirana's main squares was renamed "Wilson Square" (in Albanian, "Sheshi Uillson"), and a full statue of America's twenty-eighth president was unveiled. Whereas, in 2019, for the 100th anniversary of the Peace Conference, a bust of a smiling Wilson with his top hat was ceremoniously unveiled in the Albanian district of Skopje, North Macedonia, in front of the main offices of the Čair Municipality. The unveiling was attended by the mayor of Staunton, Virginia (Wilson's birthplace) and included a symbolic sister city accord between Staunton and Čair. Because Mother Teresa—an ethnic Albanian—was born in Skopje, the two cities cited solidarity in both being humble birth places of two of the world's foremost Nobel laureates.

Christo Dako went on to accept several roles in the new Albanian government. He was appointed the General Superintendent of Public Education, elected a member of the House of Representatives, and then appointed Minister of Education and Finance.[21] He is perhaps best known for his work in relocating the Kortcha Girls School to Kamëz, near the capital Tirana, and remaking it as the Kyrias Institute for girls and women, a national school representing all districts, classes, and religious beliefs. It opened its doors in the Fall of 1922 and was widely praised by Albanian leaders and foreign diplomats as the premiere educational institution in Albania, until King Ahmet Zog issued a decree to close the school and all Albanian private schools in 1933.

This book is a reprint of Christo Dako's history on the 100th anniversary of its publication and the Paris Peace

---

[21] Kyrias-Dako, *My Life*, 225.

Conference. Albanians consider it the 100th anniversary of their national salvation, a time to reflect and remember why they are among the most pro-American peoples on earth, and why they sometimes quip: "We Albanians are more pro-American than Americans."

Albania may or may not have been the master key to the Near East, but few can refute that it was—and still is—a crucial component of regional peace and stability, and that the Albanians are a liberty-loving people who still warrant the world's attention and respect.

ALBANIA

The Master Key to the Near East

By

CHRISTO A. DAKO

*President and Representative of the
Albanian National Party*

WITH NUMEROUS ILLUSTRATIONS AND MAPS

PREFACE BY
PROF. RICHARD GOTTHEIL
OF COLUMBIA UNIVERSITY

Boston, Massachusetts
E. L. GRIMES COMPANY
1919

To

Honorable and Mrs. Charles R. Crane

This Book is Dedicated

With Respect and Gratitude

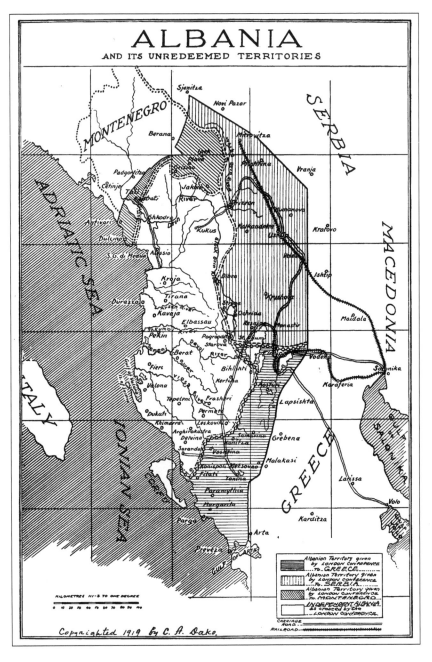

Sketch map of Albania showing the contrast between the ethnographic and political boundary drawn by the London Conference (1912–1913).

Introduction

ONE would be playing the part of a hostile friend if one suggested that the many and various questions touching sovereignty in Europe were all destined to be settled, and that finally, at the Conference that has been sitting in Paris during the last five months. Some of them are too intricate to make their unraveling possible in years, let alone months. Others will need the softening and the chastening hand of time so to mold them that they lend themselves to a solution that will be, in a measure, on all fours with the profession of our political faith.

Some few of the problems, however, appear to be so plain as regards the base upon which they rest as to point their solution as a matter of public duty. One of these is the so-called problem dealing with the Albanian people. Much speculation has been indulged in as to what in reality does and should constitute that which we designate a nation. Some authors have written glibly about racial affinities as being the origin from which the conglomerate comes; others have thought of language; and still others have mentioned religion as being the link that binds. With every circumstance of learning, these various theories have been boosted up, only to find themselves face to face with some facts into which they refuse to fit. If a definition must be had, it must be broad and long enough to fit the most varied cases; and it has been very properly said by a writer on the subject that, when brought down to a final analysis, it is the popular will that constitutes nationality.

Now if this were applied to the Albanians, he would be a hardy debater who would deny what that popular will is. How far back soever one pursues the history of this doughty people one finds it characterized by two passions—a passion for its language and an equal passion for its ancient customs. That its language fits in with difficulty into any one of the families into which modern scholars have classified the tongues spoken today, is no reason for its disqualification. That these customs are not always the ones to which we are used is no cause for their discontinuance. This language and these customs form the basis for their separated existence as a people which is as dear to the Albanians as is the breath of life. They have lived for this separate existence; they have died for it. Few people—and they are at most a handful—have fought either so resolutely or so successfully against the overwhelming odds that are always threatening to absorb them. Pushed up against the Adriatic, their sole place of flight being their own mountains, they have been invaded by Goths, Huns, Serbs, Bulgars, and Normans; until in 1478 they became the unwilling part of the Turkish Empire. But even in that all-absorbing chaos they still preserved their separateness. It did not need even a Scanderberg or an Ali of Janina to win their over-lords to a sense of the real relationship that existed between themselves and those whom they wished to treat as underlings. The Porte was always wise enough to know with whom it had to deal and the only manner in which the deal could be carried out..

Unfortunately, that which the Porte knew, others—supposedly more advanced in their reading of history—did not know, and do not seem to know today. Slavs, Montenegrins, and Serbs are pressing down from the North and East; Greeks are moving up from the South and East; and that which ought to have resulted in an Albania covering the territory occupied for these many hundreds of years by Albanians, is threatened with such diminution as to make the resultant country quite inappropriate and insufficient for the proper development of the Albanian people. On June 17, 1878, the three hundred delegates assembled at Prizren laid it down that Albanian land was that territory comprised within the four Turkish Vilayets of Scutari, Kossova, Monastir, and Janina; and that is the Albania that history and common sense demand.

Word, however, comes to us from across the sea that scant ceremony and less consideration are to be given to such elemental facts and demands as are these. It is all but incredible that to Italy also there is being granted foothold in the Balkans by turning over to her the harbor-city of Avlona. We have seen with ill-concealed surprise the act perpetrated by her on June 3, 1917, when she published a proclamation that practically assumed her power over Albania; and this despite the Pact of London of 1913 to which she had subscribed. The many friends that Italy has are pained to think of her as attempting to close the Adriatic Sea by such means as these. And one has only to read the history of the Albanians as told by Mr. Dako in the following pages to know that they will defend their soil to the long last, before they will bear the burden as heavy and as shameful as is that of contempt. It is with a feeling of sincere regret that the student of history watches these happenings and sees the tender illusions that he dared to hold a few months ago replaced by the harsh realities of the present. If the treatment that seems to be accorded to the Albanian is a true foretaste of the international morality of the future, one is lead to ask oneself in what manner the latter days are to differ from the former. One hesitates to stop to inquire why that which was wrong for Italy to do in regard to Fiume and the Jugo-Slavs is right to do with respect to Avlona and the Albanians; for it certainly cannot be because the Jugo-Slavs are many and the Albanians few.

Mr. Dako tells his story about his people with the knowledge of a student and with the feeling of a patriot. He writes with boldness and fearlessness, as is proper. He has passed through much of that which he relates; and for that reason, that which he says is of exceptional value. In the course of his work he has to touch upon various matters that are still the subject of discussion among students, and of discord among scholars. One need not always have to agree with him upon the positions he has taken; but one can always appreciate the breadth of his view and his sincere attempt to treat with justice and equity the opinions of his opponents.

RICHARD GOTTHEIL.

Columbia University, N. Y.
May 5, 1919.

Contents

CHAPTER I

The Unknown Country and Its People.

The ethnographic boundary of the country as compared with the boundary drawn by the London Conference. The population of Albania. Colonies abroad. Other races living in Albania. Physical geography of Albania. The language of the Albanians and their religious beliefs. The origin of the Albanians and their history in brief. Racial characteristics, customs, occupations and amusements.
Pages 1-37.

CHAPTER II

The Stumbling Block of the Turks.

The Turkish advance checked by Scanderberg. Albania nominally becoming a Turkish province. The Albanians, under the leadership of their chieftains, Ali Pasha Tepeleni and the Boushattis, fighting the Turks. Attempts to introduce the Turkish political system into Albania. Education and Greek propaganda in Albania, during the Turkish regime.
Pages 38-54.

CHAPTER III

Albania Defying the Congress of Berlin.

The critical condition of the European Provinces of the Turkish Empire. Russian intervention. The Russo-Turkish War. The Treaty of San-Stefano. The Albanian National League. Europe intervenes in favor of Turkey. The Congress of Berlin. The Greek Claims at the Congress of Berlin. Provisions of the Treaty of Berlin regarding Serbia. Provisions of the Treaty of Berlin regarding Bulgaria. Provisions of the Treaty of Berlin regarding Montenegro and Greece. Albania defying the Berlin Congress. The Balkan states disappointed with the results of the Berlin Congress, resume their work of propaganda in Macedonia and Albania. The work of the Bulgarian Macedo-Adrinopolitan Committee. The Greek action. The Serbians, the Bulgarians and the Greeks fighting among themselves to get the upper hand in Macedonia and Albania. An amusing comparison

vi ALBANIA — THE MASTER

of their statistics. Europe's intervention for new reforms in Turkey. The "Reval Program." The Movement of the Young Turks. Sultan Abdul Hamid grants Constitutional government. The real policy of the Young Turks to ottomanize all nationalities of the Empire.
The Albanians revolt and give a deadly stroke to Turkey. The real cause of the Balkan War.
Pages 55-79.

CHAPTER IV
The Mighty Power of the Spelling Book.

The splendid natural inclination of the Albanians. Their movement for national education. The first books in the Albanian language. The Greek Church and Turkey's persecutions against the pioneers of the Albanian educational movement. The headquarters of the educational movement moved from Constantinople to Roumania. Branches founded in Italy, Egypt, Russia, Bulgaria. "The Beacon Light." The Congress of Monastir. The Albanian Women's Society, "The Morning Star." The Orthodox League. The Congress of Elbassan. The Albanian newspapers and periodicals. Hon. and Mrs. Charles R. Crane and their generous help for the enlightenment and uplift of the Albanian nation. The Young Turks alarmed by the rapid progress of the Albanians take drastic measures to check it. The result of their foolish policy.
Pages 80-94.

CHAPTER V
Albania the Cause of the Balkan War.

Montenegrin military operations in Albania. Albania proclaims her independence, checking the policy of the Balkan allies for her partition. Europe's intervention in favor of the Albanians. Montenegro defies the Great Powers. The crisis. Montenegro forced to evacuate Scutari. Scutari occupied by an international contingent. Admiral Burney's proclamation to the Albanians. The joint festival of the representatives of the Great Powers and of the Albanians.

Serbian military operations in Albania. The European crisis becoming threatening. Serbia yields to the European pressure.

Greek military operations in Albania. Greek fleet bombarding Vallona. European intervention. The entrance of the Greek

KEY TO THE NEAR EAST

army in Kortcha described by an eye witness. Greek troops advancing from the south, after the capture of Janina. Pages 95-116.

CHAPTER VI

The European Importance of the Albanian Question.

The story of the proclamation of the independence of Albania related by the father of the country. The European crisis, avoided by Gladstone's formula, "The Balkans for the Balkan Peoples." The London Ambassadorial conference, in its second sitting, December 20, 1914, recognizes the independence of Albania. The principle of nationality. The Strength of the National Consciousness of the Albanian nation. England, Italy, Austria and Germany reject the claims of the Balkan allies on Albania. The silent attitude of Greece. Serbia's answer. Montenegro's protest against the attitude of the Powers. The appeal to Russia. The geographical and political importance of Albania. Albania, the Master Key to the Near East.
Pages 117-133.

CHAPTER VII

Albania and the Great Powers.

The policy of Great Britain regarding Albania. Her unselfish Balkan policy. England endeavors for the erection of a strong independent Albania, 1880. Lord Beaconsfield's objections regarding the French proposal in favor of Greece. Sir Edward Grey defending the rights of Albania. The British Balkan policy as stated by Sir Edward Grey.

Italian policy regarding Albania. The Albanians under the leadership of Scanderberg cross the Adriatic to help the Italians. The origin of the Albanian immigration in Italy. The Albanians fighting for the national unity and political independence of Italy. The Italian Balkan policy as formulated by Crispi. The imperialistic policy of Italy. Italy's claims on Vallona and Albania. The Albanians protest against Italy's unjust claims. The solemn decisions of the London Conference, a "scrap of paper" for Italy. The secret treaty of Italy for the partition of Albania. The present policy of Italy manifested by Baron Sonnino at the Supreme War Council of Paris, in flat contradiction with the principle of nationality.

The policy of France regarding Albania during the time of Ali

Pasha of Tepeleni. The great French scholar Pouqueville accredited diplomatic representative in Albania. The Mirdites under the moral protection of France. Mr. Waddington supporting the Greek claims at the Congress of Berlin to the expense of Albania. The reasons for this change of policy of the French Republic. Greece not a sincere friend of France. Albania hopes to have the support of France at the Paris Conference.

Austria's Balkan policy. Its origin and purpose. Austrian propaganda in Albania. Austria opposes the British proposal for the erection of a strong independent Albania. Austria takes the initiative in supporting the national claims of the Albanians. The world amazed by this sudden change, rightly expresses distrust of Austria's motives.

The Russian policy regarding Albania. Her fervent wish to get an open window to the Adriatic. The History of the Russian Balkan policy outlined. Prince Gortchakof reshaping the Russian policy on the basis of the principle of nationality. England, Germany and Austria oppose Russia's policy. The Russian Satellites in the Balkans, and their claims bringing Europe to the verge of a European war.
Pages 134-158.

CHAPTER VIII
Albania and the Balkan States.

The Greek policy in the Balkans. Count J. Capodistrias, the author of the imperialistic policy of Greece. Dr. A. C. Dandolo revises and enlarges Capodistrias' program. Greek methods employed for the achievement of their "Great Idea."

The Balkan policy of Roumania. The Wallachians and their movement of emancipation. Apostol Margarit supported by the Roumanian Government and by the Albanians. Roumania abandons the Wallachians, who are incorporated in Greece, against their wish.

Serbia, Montenegro and Bulgaria working in the Balkans as Russia's satellites. Their ambitions for dividing Albania.
Pages 159-166.

CHAPTER IX
Europe Struggling to Save Her Checker Board.

The London Ambassadorial Conference assembled to draw the

KEY TO THE NEAR EAST

boundaries of Albania. The projects proposed by the Balkan Allies and their respective arguments in support of their claims. Boundary proposed by Italy and Austria. Boundary proposed by the Albanian Provisional Government. Arguments advanced against the claims of the Balkan Allies and in support of the boundary proposed by the Provisional Government of Albania. Europe struggles to save her checker board. The unjust decisions of the London Conference. Threatening results of their selfish policy.
Pages 167-189.

CHAPTER X
Europe Begins to Play Her Tragedy in Albania.

European intrigues for the dissolution of the newly born state. The work of the provisional Government as related by its President. Albania during the regime of *Mbret William*. The Essad and the Greek disguised movement against the Albanian Government supported by some of the European Powers. Albania, the first scene of the European tragedy.
Pages 190-196.

CHAPTER XI
Future Prospects.

The vital questions upon which depends the national existence of Albania: The question of its boundaries, and that of her status. Albania capable to govern herself. History's testimony. The Albanian question comparatively a simple problem to solve. The problems which must receive the immediate attention of the Albanian Government: The administrative machinery; the improvement of agriculture; the creation of a national industry; the development of its commerce; the building of roads; the money system; the public revenue; the elimination of all foreign schools of propaganda, and the establishment of a national educational system for the whole country.
Pages 197-205.

CHAPTER XII
Reminiscences.

Introduction. First active associations of the author with the Albanian National Movement and his acquaintance with its pioneers. The author's interest in the educational movement of Albania. His preparation. A student of Oberlin College. Political events force him to interrupt his studies and return to Albania. The condition of the country on his return. Persecutions of the Young Turks. Jeanne d'Arc of Albania murdered by the Young Turks. The protest of the author. Impressions in Europe. His arrest and trial by the court martial. His release and marriage with Miss Sevasti Kyrias. The honeymoon trip to Bucharest. Protests addressed to the European Powers against the cruelties of the Young Turks. His return to Albania. Honorable Charles R. Crane visits Albania accompanied by the author. The author arrested at Scutari. Mr. Crane's protest releases him. Mr. Crane visits the Albanian refugees at Podgoritza. His gift for relief. Mr. Crane's statement regarding conditions of the country, as a result of which Tourgout Pasha, the General Commander of the Turkish troops resigns. Mr. Crane's interest and generous help for the uplift and enlightenment of the Albanian people. The author returns to America to complete his education, and after a year returns again to Albania. Activities in America. The story of the trip. Miss Paraskevi Kyrias in Kortcha during the Greek occupation describing condition of the inhabitants. Kortcha evacuated by the Greeks, the author returns to his native town and is plunged into a busy round of government duties. The first Greek disguised attack. The author in danger of being hanged. The second attack. The people of the district fleeing before the invader for their lives. The author and the staff of the Kyrias school saved by the intervention of the British Consul. Pages 206-228.

LIST OF APPENDICES

Pages

1. The Albanian Language, by Prof. Holger Pederson.. 229-231
2. An Interesting Debate, by M. G. Mihatelides and the author 232-238
3. An Official Russian Statement regarding the Ethnography of the district of Scutari 238-241
4. Albania's Rights, Hopes and Aspirations, as stated by the Albanian National Party...................... 241-248
5. The Development of Schools in the Turkish Emport and an Ideal System of Education for Albania, by Miss P. D. Kyrias 248-266

LIST OF PLATES

Facing Page

Sketch map of Albania showing the contrast between the ethnographic and political boundary fixed by the London Conference .... Frontispiece

View of Arghirokastra..................................... 4

The bridge over the Voiossa, at Permeti.................... 6

The gorges of Klisura..................................... 8

View of Klisura... 10

The Southern Albanian Costume............................. 30

The Northern Albanian Costume............................. 32

Albanians dancing the Pyrrhic............................. 36

Scanderberg, the Hero of Albania.......................... 40

Waso Pasha, prominent figure in the movement of the Albanian National League 56

Sketch map of the Balkans showing the conflicting aspirations of the Balkan nations............................ 75

John Vreto, prominent member of the Albanian Society *Bashkimi*, founded in Constantinople in 1878............ 78

Constantine Christoforidihi, the translator of the Bible...... 78

Gerasim D. Kyrias, the founder of the first Albānian Girls' School 80

George D. Kyrias.. 80

Mrs. Christo A. Dako, the brave principal of the first Albanian Girls' School.................................... 84

A group, representing the members of the Monastir Congress 86

A group, representing the Committee of the Alphabet...... 88

The Band of Freedom..................................... 90

Honorable Charles R. Crane.............................. 92

Mrs. Charles R. Crane................................... 92

Miss Paraskevi D. Kyrias, the President of the Albanian Women's Society, the Morning Star.................... 94

The flags of the five Powers on the citadel of Scutari....... 102

Ismail Kemal Bey Vlora, the Father of the Independence of Albania 118

Vallona, the place where the independence of Albania was proclaimed, November 28, 1912....................... 120

The port of Vallona, or the Gibraltar of the Adriatic........ 124

Sketch map of Albania showing the various proposed boundaries and the boundary fixed by the London Conference of 1913... 168

Ethnographic map of the district of Kortcha.............. 192

Greek regulars captured at Kortcha April 6, 1914, after the failure of the Greek disguised attack on the coveted city 194

Sketch map of Southern Albania showing villages burned by the Greeks during the disguised attack, summer of 1914 196

ALBANIA
The Master Key to the Near East
I.

THE UNKNOWN COUNTRY AND ITS PEOPLE

ALTHOUGH Albania holds the most important geographical position on the Adriatic; although it is the master key to the Near East; although it has been the scene of many celebrated exploits in ancient as well as in recent times; although only thirty-nine miles from Italy, yet, it is, probably, the least known country in Europe. The opposition of the Turkish authorities, its mountainous character and lack of roads rendered it almost inaccessible to the foreign traveller, and many of its geographical problems still wait to be solved.

The boundaries of the state of Albania as drawn by the London Conference (1912-1913), under the threat of Tsarist Russia, go a little further up the Boiana than the former frontier, and strike inland along a stream just below Korica, where they divide the district of Anamalit, and reach Scutari lake just west of Zogai. The line then crosses the lake to the inlets of Kastrati and Hoti, and runs northeast to the previous frontier, between Montenegro and Turkey (leaving the Hoti and Gruda tribes in Montenegro and Kastrati, Shkreli and Klementi in Albania); then, makes a bend to the south and includes Gusinje and Plava in Montenegro; then, bends south-east, leaving out Ipek, Jakova and Prizren (all of which are almost entirely inhabited by Albanians), and from a point a few miles west of Prizren, runs due south, leaving Dibra to Serbia, and then follows the Drin to the stream Pishkupstina, whence it keeps to the hill-tops on the west until it strikes lake Ochrida at Lin, near the monastery of San Nicolo. In the south the boundary starts from a point on the Ochrida lake between Pogradetz and St. Naum and strikes towards the southern extremity of the Prespa lake, then follows the eastern boundary of the Kortcha district passing not far from Kastoria, thence almost in straight line goes as far as Leskoviki. Another almost straight line directed from north-east to south-west ends at Cape Stylos. This boundary includes Kolonia, Permeti and Arghirokastro, with all its valley in Albania, while Konitza and the district of Pindus are in Greece.

Thus, the arbitrary and unjust decision of the London Conference left to the state of Albania only an area of 11,317 sq. miles and a population of about 1,000,000 people, while in fact the country is three times as large, having an area of about 30,000 sq. miles. Roughly speaking the region inhabited by the Albanians, or the *sons of the Mountain Eagle,* as they call themselves, is marked out by a line drawn from the Montenegrin frontier (before the Balkan War) at Berana to Mitrovitza and the Serbian frontier near Vrania; thence to Uskup, Perlepe, Monastir, Florina, Kastoria, Metzovo and the Gulf of Arta.

The Albanian nation until the middle ages was a larger nation[1] and occupied all the countries which form the Balkan Peninsula, on the right side of the Danube.[2]

---

[1] The Albanians of today are the descendants of the ancient Illyrians, part of whom were slavonized and therefore are considered as Slavs. **Wirchow.**

[2] Up to the period of the migration of the Barbarians, the whole Eastern part of the Balkan Peninsula, as far as the Danube, was held by the Albanians. But they were then pushed back, and Albania was entirely occupied by Serbians and Bulgarians. **Elisée Reclus. The Earth and its Inhabitants.** Vol. 1, pp. 118-119.

The Albanians of today are the descendants of the population which inhabited, before the arrival of the Greeks, the soil of the lands extending from the Adriatic Sea up to Halys. . . . **Louis Benloew, La Grèce avant les Grecs.**

But in the sixth and seventh centuries, when the Serbian and Bulgarian invasions took place, the Albanians were driven westward to the coast of the Adriatic and Ionian Seas.

No census of them has ever been taken, and different authors give different estimates regarding the population of Albania. So *Schaferik* estimated the Albanians living in Albania at about 1,800,000. Sir *Edwin Pears,* in his interesting chapter on this people, gives the probable figure of a million and a half; Mr. *Charles H. Woods* at between 1,100,000 and 1,250,000; the *Encyclopaedia of Missions* (1904) gives it at about 2,000,000. The difficulty for the foreign traveller rises from the mixed character of the population; from the fact that some writers consider part of "The Moslem" Albanians as Turks, and most of "The Orthodox" Albanians as Greeks. Persons who know the country well estimate the population of Albania at from two and a half million to three million.[1]

These figures, however, are far from including all the members of the widely scattered race; for besides the Albanians inhabiting Albania, there are 800,000 Albanians living in Southern Italy; 900,000 in Greece; 80,000-100,000 in the United States of America (not counting those who

---

[1] In his article in a number of "The Orient," Mr. Christo A. Dako gave the number of Albanians living in Albania as from 2,500,000 to 3,000,000. The editorial accompanying this article quoted various other estimates of this population, ranging from 2,000,000 to 1,000,000. We have just received from Mr. Dako a detailed statement in support of the figures he gives, based on the number of Albanian deputies in the last Parliament. According to article 65 of the Ottoman Constitution, the number of deputies is fixed on the basis of one deputy to each 50,000 of the male Ottoman population. On this basis, the twenty-six Albanian deputies would indicate a population of at least 1,300,000 males or a total of 2,600,000. This is exclusive of the Mirdita and Malisori tribes, who had no deputies. These Catholic Albanians are estimated by Mr. René Pinon to have over 130,000 population. This makes the figures given by Mr. Brailsford, Mr. Woods and Sir Edwin Pears seem like an underestimate.—The **Orient**, February 14, 1912, page 7.

emigrated from Italy but only those who come from Albania proper); 25,000-30,000 in Roumania, 40,000-50,000 in Turkey, and several thousand in Egypt, Bulgaria, Russia, and Austro-Hungary.

The Albanians who live now in Italy emigrated there after the Turks conquered Albania; but they kept their own language and social customs and their own form of Christianity with this exception, that instead of the Greek Patriarch of Constantinople they recognize the Pope as their religious head; and this in order to be free to use in their religious services their beloved mother tongue.

The Albanian population of the Greek kingdom occupy the whole of Attica, Megaris and the greater part of Boeotia. In the islands they possess the southern part of the island of Eubœa, and about one-third of Andros, while the whole of the island of Salamis, Poras, Hydra and Spetzia are exclusively peopled by a pure Albanian race, as well as a part of Aegina and the small Island of Anghistri in its vicinity. In the Peloponnesus, they compose the bulk of the population in Argolis, Corinthia, and Sicyonia; and they occupy considerable districts in Arcadia, Laconia, Messina and Elis. Throughout all this great extent of territory they preserve to the present day their own mother tongue, their manners, their simple social habits and their rude system of agriculture.

During the half century immediately preceding the conquest of Morea by the Turks, the Albanian population of Greece, more than once assumed a prominent part in public affairs, and at one time they even conceived the project of expelling the Greeks themselves from Morea.[1]

The migrations of Albanians to Egypt, Roumania, Bulgaria, Russia, America, etc., are of more recent date.

---
[1] Cf. Geo. Finlay, History of Greece.

View of Arghirokastra

Of the other races living in Albania, the Serbians and Bulgarians are the most numerous, possibly numbering 150,000. There is a Bulgarian colony in the neighborhood of Dibra and Ochrida. Farther south, Mount Zygos and the Pindus range are inhabited by Wallachians, who number about 100,000. In the extreme south, there are Greek settlements, which do not number more than 60,000.

Albania is a mountainous country in the full sense of the word, nevertheless it does not lack fertile valleys. It has at least ten chains of mountains, of which six are in the Southern Albania and four in the middle and northern part of the country. These chains run from north-west to south-east, with the exception of those which limit the *feud* of the Dibras and the Ochrida lake, and also with the exception of the Shar, which is situated south of another *feud* which extends from north-east to south-west. The highest peaks are *Liubotrn,* near *Kalkandelen,* 8858 ft.; *Skulsen,* 7533 ft.; *Babavreka,* 7306 ft. All these are in Northern Albania. In Central Albania the principal summit is *Tomori,* 7916 ft., overhanging the town of Berat.

The rivers generally flow from east to west. On account of the rapidity of their descent only two are navigable, *Boiana* and *Arta;* and, these only in their lower portions. The principal rivers of Albania are: The *Moraka* and *Paskola,* which unite their streams and pass through the lake of Scutari, into the Adriatic; assuming between the lake and the sea the name of *Boiana.* The general direction of the Moraka is south; the Paskola runs to the south-west and the distance from the source of the Moraka to the mouth of the Boiana, following the winding of the stream and including the length of the lake Scutari is more than 100 miles. Two streams, the *White* and the *Black-Drin,* proceeding from the mountains on the frontier, and flowing south, meet and run westwards into the Adriatic. The windings of their stream, measured from either source, render its course equal to about 150 to 160 miles, and make it the chief river of Northern Albania. Farther to the South, we meet with the *Shkumbi* (ancient Genesus); the *Baratina* (ancient Apsus); the *Voiossa* (ancient Aous), which rises in the northern part of the Pindus range and flows first above 75 miles in a northwestern direction; then, west by south for about 12 miles, between two high and steep mountains, which approach very near each other, forming the celebrated pass, anciently called *Fances Antigonenses,* and now, the pass of Voiossa. Leaving the pass at the village of Klisura, the river recovers its northwestern direction, which it retains till it reaches the sea, 16 miles north of *Cape Linguetta.* At the northern entrance of the pass it is joined by a considerable stream called *Drino.* The total length of the Voiossa is about 130 miles. The river *Kalamas,* the ancient Thyamis, falls into the sea, opposite Corfu; and farther to the South we have the ancient *Acheron,* now the *Garla,* or the river of Suli, and the *Arta,* ancient Aracthus, which falls into the Gulf of Arta.

The principal lakes of Albania are the *lake of Scutari,* which is about 16 miles in length from north-west to southeast and from 3-5 miles in breadth. It contains several small islands. The lake lies in the high land of Albania and is surrounded by offsets of the chain of Mount Scardus. *Ochrida lake* is about 18 miles long and 8 miles across in the widest part. It is in the valley watered by the Black Drin, which flows through the lake. It abounds with fish of excellent quality. The *Prespa lake,* separated from Ochrida by the Galinitza mountains, and is supposed to be connected with it by a subterranean channel. The *lake of Malik,* south-east of Ochrida, drained by the river of Devol.

The Bridge over Voiossa at Permeti.

KEY TO THE NEAR EAST

Butrinto, near the sea coast, opposite Corfu. Farther south is the *lake of Janina*, which in its greatest length measures 14 miles, from north-west to south-east; the greatest breadth is about 5 miles. It is bounded on the north-east by the Mitzikeli mountains (a branch of Pindus) which rise with very steep ascent to the height of 2500 feet, above the lake; on the south-east by a rocky mountain of moderate height crowned with the extensive ruins of ancient *Dodona*. On the south-west side of the lake is the plain of Janina, and beyond that a range of low vine-covered hills. Opposite the town of Janina is a small island, on which is a fishing village, containing, in Ali Pasha's time, about 200 houses. On this island were several convents, frequently used as state prisons. Ali Pasha, who had a house in it, kept a herd of red deer. The lake abounds with fish; among which are pike, perch, carp, tench and eels.

The climate of Albania, in the lower portion is about as warm as that of Italy; but draughts and sudden and violent north winds, render it less agreeable. In the part which lies south of Lat. 40°, the climate is colder than in Greece. The spring sets in, in the middle of March; in July and August the oppressive heat often dries up the streams and rivers and withers the plants and grass. September is the time of vintage, and the rains of December are succeeded by frost in January, which, however, seldom last long. The country is generally healthy.

The chief towns of Albania are Scutari, with a population of 32,000; Prizren 30,000; Janina 22,000; Jakova 12,000; Dibra 15,000; Prishtina 11,000; Ipek 15,000; Berat 15,000; Ochrida 11,000; Tirana 12,000; Kortcha 22,000; Monastir 60,000; Uskup 32,000; Veles 19,700; Kalkandelen 17,200; Prilep 24,000; Krushova 9,350; Resna 4,450; Florina 9824; Struga 4570; Kastoria 6190; Arghirokastra 11,000;

Elbassan 8,000; Metzova 7,500; Preveza 6,500; Vallona 6,000; Durazzo 5,000; Parga 5,000; Butrinto 2,000; Kroia 5,000.

For many years the Albanian language has been a difficult but interesting puzzle for the philologist.[1] Many prominent scholars have tried to solve this perplexing problem, but not having in hand sufficient monuments were unable to give a definite solution regarding its origin. In spite of this, some of the scholars were convinced that the Albanian language is the most ancient language of Europe, the mother of the Greek and the Latin, and that the solution of the problem of the Albanian will be of great service and will revolutionize a great many ethnographic and linguistic theories.[2] To avoid this revolution, which, they fully realized, would be to their disadvantage; to keep the Albanian people in ignorance, and to hinder the growth of their political independence, the Turkish Government, the prelates of the Greek Church, and the religious teachers of the Mohammedan bodies alike opposed, even with violence, every effort to transform the Albanian into a written language.

Notwithstanding this opposition and persecution, towards 1600 the Albanian Roman Catholic clergy began to transform the Albanian into a written language, publishing not only religious pamphlets, but also dictionaries and text books. In 1820 the British and Foreign Bible Society published the first edition of the New Testament in the Albanian language. A second edition followed in 1858; and, a third one was issued in 1879. Meanwhile, to promote the critical study of the Albanian language, care was taken by several Eu-

---
[1] At the end of this volume the reader will find an interesting article on the Albanian language written by a European Scholar.
[2] See O. Muller.

The Gorges of Klissura.

ropean scholars to commit to writing such historical ballads, tales, proverbs, etc. as have been handed down to the present time. Amongst these may be mentioned *Leake, Hahn, Mikloshich, Gustav Meyer* and *August Dozon.*

Comparatively within a few years there was enough written literature to enable the specialists to speculate with more accuracy on this subject.

Malte-Brun found that one-third of the Albanian vocabulary is of Pelgasgic origin; another third belongs to the languages of Central and Western Europe, and the rest belongs *probably* to the ancient dialects of Thrace and Asia Minor.

Gustav Meyer, one of the greatest workers on the problem of the Albanian language, classifies it among the Indo-Germanic languages and says that it descends from the ancient language of the Illyrians, and has *no kinship with the Greek;* for the sounds of *gh, dh, bh,* which are aspirated sounds in the Indo-Germanic, became also aspirated in Greek; but remained mild in Albanian. *V* and *j* have not disappeared from the Albanian, as from the Greek. The Indo-Germanic *a* has remained *a* in the Albanian language, but it had become *o* in Greek.

Carl Pauli is not of the same opinion. He thinks that the ancient language of the Illyrians was spoken by the Venetians, who inhabited part of Italy. The Albanians are, as far as their language is concerned, heirs of the Thracian trunk.

Herman Hirt arrives at the same conclusion, but through a different route. He says that the Indo-Germanic languages have separated into two groups, the Western and the Eastern, or the *Kentum* and the *Satem.* As the Venetians inhabiting Illyria spoke a *Kentum* language and since the Albanians used a *Satem* language, the latter did not speak the Illyrian idiom, but the Thracian.

Dr. Hahn[1] and *Edward Schneider,* who have made special study in Albania say, that the Albanian language is nothing else but the language of the ancient Pelasgians.

Prof. Max Muller, speaking about the Albanian language says, "This language is clearly a member of the Aryan family; and it is sufficiently distinct from Greek or any other recognized language. It has been traced back to one of the neighboring races of the Greeks, the Illyrians; and, is supposed to be the only surviving representative of the various so-called barbarous tongues, which surrounded and interpenetrated the dialects of Greece."[2]

It is true that the Albanian is not yet a fully developed language, but it has all the necessary elements to attain the highest development a language can reach. *Edward Schneider,* in his book *Une Race Oubliée,* gives 800 word-roots of the Albanian language. *G. De Rada,* an Albanian poet, philologist and collector of national folklore, calls our attention to the fact that in seven printed pages he has found 1796 consonants against 1446 vowels, among which 624 were e-s; 372 i-s; 224 a-s; 141 u-s; 128 o-s.

All this, together with the frequency of the use of the consonants *r* and *t* give to the language a special feature which makes it to be easily heard.

There are in the Albanian language six declensions, each with a definite and indefinite form. The Genetive, Dative and Ablative are usually represented by a single termination. The neuter gender is absent. There are four conjugations. The passive formation, now wanting in most of the Indo-European languages, has been retained in the Al-

---

[1] **Dr. Hahn** found an Alphabet of 52 letters, some interesting ancient Phoenician and Cretan forms, in partial use at Elbassan and Tirana.
[2] See **Prof. Max Muller's Lectures on the Science of Languages.**

View of Klisura.

banian, thus: *dua*, I love; *duem*, I am loved. The Infinitive is not found; but it is replaced with the Subjunctive with a particle. The two auxiliary verbs are, *kam, I have;* and, *jam, I am.*

An interesting and characteristic feature of the Albanian language is the definite article which is attached to the end of the word, e. g. *bari, shepherd; bari-u, the shepherd. Lesh, wool, leshi, the wool.* Another remarkable feature of the Albanian language is the *peculiar tense* which is called *i-papandehurë, the unexpected tense, imprévu, aprosdhoiktos,* e. g. *kam, I have, paskam, unexpectedly I find that I have.*

We stated above that some of the scholars saw from the very beginning that the solution of the origin of the Albanian will revolutionize many ethnographic and linguistic theories. As an illustration to this statement, we will mention briefly the following. Until lately, generally all text books on history presented *the Macedonians and Epirotes* as two tribes of the Greek people; but now we see scholars like *Baker, Clark, Vogüé,* etc., saying that *neither* the Macedonians, nor the Epirotes were Greeks, but the forefathers of the Albanians. Until lately, it was believed that the mythology, taught in schools as "The Greek mythology," was of Hellenic conception. The Albanian furnishes enough material to prove that this is not so; but of this we shall speak again in connection with the religious beliefs of the Albanians.

The Christian propaganda reached the Albanian coast as early as the first century.[1]

In the year 1054, when the Oriental schism took place, Albania being a part of the Eastern Empire, remained with the church of Constantinople, which refused to preach the Gospel in the language of the people; so when the Turks

---

[1] Cf. St. Paul's Epistle to Romans 1:14 and 15:19.

came to Europe, the Albanians were Christians in name *only*. Adding to this reason, the ignorance of the Greek clergy, and the *love of wearing a sword*, symbolizing *power*, which is one of the greatest characteristics of the Albanian people, we will understand easily why the majority of the Albanians took the Mohammedan pledge. Another reason why the Albanians embraced Islam was because this pledge gave special political rights for their country. Two-thirds of the Albanians are Moslems and the rest are Christians; those living in Southern Albania belonging to the Greek church and those inhabiting Northern Albania being Roman Catholics.[1]

The Moslem Albanians are again divided into two sets, the *Bektashis* and the *Softas*. The majority of the Moslem Tosks are Bektashis. The Bektashis are a monastic order and their priests are called *dervishes*, who unlike the regular Mohammedan clergy, are celibates and entirely devoted to the religious life. They are grouped around their monasteries with a *baba* (father) as their head. One of the most important monasteries is that of Kalkandelen.

The Bektashi doctrine is a secret discipline which is only fully revealed to its members. Its theology is pantheistic and as such, it is intolerant to all formalism. It hates all barriers which divide souls from one another and from God. It finds the way to union with God in a universal love and general tolerance. On its mystical side it teaches that the believer should endeavor even in this life, to overcome the barriers of individuality and merge himself in ecstasy with God.

---

[1] The Albanians began to become Catholics as early as 1250, when the episcopate of Northern Albania asked the Pope to accept the Bishop and his flock as members of the Roman Catholic Church. When Scanderbeg abjured the Mohammedan faith, for political reasons, he embraced the Roman Catholic faith and many noble Albanian families followed his example.

This teaching about a *Common Spiritual Substance* is somehow reconciled with the belief in the transmigration of souls. The human soul wanders through different animals before it attains union with God.

The ethics of the Bektashis attempts to substitute the external morality of precepts and commandments with some principles of universal charity and brotherhood. One of their truisms is that a man should follow the inward light indifferent of public opinion. Their teaching on morals was thus defined by the father of Kalkandelen Monastry, "It is evil to be full, when other men are empty. It is evil to boast one's own righteousness and to deny the good in others."

Mr. *H. N. Brailsford,* writing about the Bektashis of Albania, says, "To me the type of the good Bektashi is the *sheikh* (father) of the *Teke* in Prizren. Gentle, dignified, and courteous, he spends an innocent old age in a retired garden of red roses and old-fashioned stocks. To visit him was to step into an atmosphere of simplicity and peace. "Something we caught about the community of souls, before the time came for us to leave him laden with his roses that seemed to carry with them the rarer fragrance of his gentleness and piety."

Notwithstanding the co-existence of these creeds in Albania, the old Pelasgic faith still maintains its hold upon the people. So much so, that, the most solemn oath that can be taken, is not by the invocation of *Christ,* or *Mohammed,* but by the *stone.* Thus, when a question of boundaries arises between two clans, the elders of the two contentious parties having been chosen to *adjudicate* and having been sworn on *the stone* with befitting solemnity, proceed to examine and give their testimony. In Northern Albania, it is of common occurrence for two peasants to affirm the truth of their allegations, *për këtë peshë, by this weight;* taking in their hands the first *stone* they find. In Southern Albania, *për të rëndit e këtij guri, by the weight of this stone.* They also affirm, *për këtë qiell edhe për këtë dhe, by heavens and earth; për këtë zjar edhe për këtë ujë, by this fire and water; për këtë mal edhe për këtë fushë, by this mountain and plain; për këtë djellë edhe për këtë hënë, by this sun and moon,*[1] etc., etc. In other words, the Albanians swear by the *heavens, earth* and *elements* as personifications of the *Divine Essence.*

The origin of this old religious belief in *Heaven* and *Earth,* was considered in the classical epoch of Greece as *barbarian.* "From what parents the gods are derived or whether they were in existence from all time, and what they are like in shape, the Greeks do not know till this day when I write these lines," says *Herodotus.*

This historian, and after him Plato, declares that the Greeks have borrowed their deities from the Pelasgians. This fact of which history speaks, can be easily proved by considering the names of these gods. Indeed,

Zeus comes from *Zaa, Zëë,* which in Albanian means *voice.* The modern forms *Zaan Zoon, Zoot* all mean *God.* We can still hear in Albanian such phrases as this, *"Zee, lirona nga i ligu." "Voice, deliver us from the evil one."*

Metis, intelligence. Ment in Albanian, signifies *intelligence,* or *thought.* By dropping the *n* and adding the suffix, the Greeks made *Metis,* the origin of the Latin mens-mentis. *Mentor,* the faithful friend of *Ulysses,* means in Albanian *the wise, the thoughtful.*

Zeus combined with *Metis* produced *Athena.* The Greek

---

[1] The worship of the moon in itself is enough proof to show that the Albanians are a prehistoric race. **Lunaar** in Albanian means **July,** for it was during this month that the Albanians in ancient times celebrated the feasts of the Moon.

language so far has not been able to give us any satisfactory derivation for the word *Athena*, while in Albanian it is evident. *Thanë* and *thënë* signify *to say*. *E-thana* and *E-thëna*, is *the Fate*, or *the Word*. *The Word* or *The Logos* of the Pelasgians proceeded from *Zeus, the Force* and *Metis, the Intelligence*. In Albania, we will say *"Këjo është e-thëna jote," "This is your fate."*

Nemesis, the goddess of vengeance, comes from the Albanian word *nëmë*, which means *malediction*, or that which attracts evil. In Albania, when people get angry, they frequently use the phrase, *"Të martë nëma, May the evil one take you.*

Chaos, signifying *empty, shapeless* or *devourer*, is derived from the Pelasgic or Albanian words, *ha, has, I eat;* and *has-haos, eater*, or *devourer;* or the word *haap-haapsi, open, void*. *Chaos* begot *Erebus*, the root of which is *erh, erhem, erheni* or *erhesi, sombre, dark, obscurity*. In Albanian, *u erh* means *it grew dark, erhet, it is getting dark; erheni, a dark place*. *Erebus* is the abode of *eternal darkness*.

Gea, is *the Earth*. *G*, in the Dorian dialect becomes *dh, dha, erdha;* in Albanian, it becomes *dhe, earth*.

Uranos. In Albanian *vran-vrant, i-vranjtur*, means *cloudy*. Adding the Greek suffix, we have *i-vran-os, vranos*, which is the Albanian word for the region of the clouds.

Gea, combined with *Uranos, Heaven* and *Earth*, begot *Rhea* and *Chronos*.

Rhea, which in Albanian means *cloud* is derived by metathesis from the Albanian *ere, wind*. *Chronos*, in Albanian is *kohe* and *k* and *r* are interchangeable. So *kohë* would become *rohë, kohë, the time*. The addition of the Greek suffix gives *rohnos, Chronos*. *Rhea* is born of *Zeus* or of the Pelasgic *Zaa, Zee, voice*. *Rhea, the cloud,* could not be impregnated but by the lightning giving out a *sound* or *voice*. Thus *thunder* and *lightning* are *the Zaa* or *Zëë* of the Pelasgians and it may be remembered that the oracles of *Dodona* were given by a *voice* and that *Zëë* was *the* God of the Pelgasians, etc.

It is now evident, I think, that the mythology taught in schools generally as *"Greek Mythology,"* is *not* of Greek origin, but of Pelasgic or Albanian conception.

Ptolemy is the earliest writer, who makes mention of the Albanians;[1] but in fact *the Shkiptars,* the *Sons of the Mountain Eagle,* as they call themselves, are the most ancient existing race in Europe, the autochthonous inhabitants of the Balkan Peninsula, which they have ruled for thousands of years before the *Barbarians* ever crossed the Danube. They are descendants of the ancient *Macedonians, Illyrians* and *Epirotes,* who are the offsprings of the *Pelasgians.* These Pelasgians were the first people, who came into Europe. They occupied the land known today under the general name of the Balkan Peninsula, and divided themselves into several tribes. Some times these clans were each independently governed by a council of elders; sometimes, several of them coalesced into little kingdoms of greater or less extent. So, about 759 B. C. under *Karanus,* some of the Pelasgian tribes united and formed the *Macedonian kingdom,* which later on,

---

[1] The name of **Albanoi, Albanians**, was first given in the eleventh century, by the Greeks of the Lower Empire to the tribe inhabiting **Albassan** (Elbassan), and surroundings; but later, it was extended to all those who spoke the same language or dialects of the same language; and, the country itself, inhabited by these Albanians, that of **Albania**, from which the word **Albania**, has been adopted by the Italians, and through them by the rest of Europe. But the names of **Albania** and **Albanians**, are **not** known in our country even today. We call ourselves **Shkipetare**, and the country in which we live **Shkiperia**, and these names date from the time of **Pyrrhus**, king of the Epirotes, our ancestors.

KEY TO THE NEAR EAST

under *Philip* and his son *Alexander the Great*,[1] became one of the greatest empires of the ancient world; it made considerable progress in civilization, and it exerted no little influence in the affairs of Europe, Asia, and Africa.

A second series of Pelasgian tribes, which were inhabiting the south-west of Macedonia, under *Achilleus,* united themselves into another kingdom called *Epirus,* which under *Pyrrhus,*[2] a man of eminent ability, became quite illustrious. After he had defeated the Greeks and his kindred, the Macedonians, he crossed the Adriatic and grappled not unsuccessfully with the rising power of Rome, and so won for himself an honorable place among the great commanders of the ancient world.

A third series of Pelasgian tribes, inhabiting the northwest of Macedonia, about 1200 B. C., under *Illyrianus,* united themselves and formed the kingdom of *Illyria* or *Illyricum,* which from the times of the *Queen Teuta,* became a dangerous little state for the peace of the Roman Empire. She stretched a chain across the river Boiana, where two hills shut in the stream, above the village of Rechi, and levied a toll on all ships going up and down. The rings to which she fastened the chains are still to be seen in the rocks. Moreover, she raised an army, built a little fleet, and with a war-

---

[1] Let it be known that **Philip** and his son **Alexander the Great,** as well as all **the Macedonians** were not Greeks; but the forefathers of the Albanians. The Greek writers: **Demosthenes, Aristotle, Plutarch, Herodotus,** etc., themselves testify to our statement. See at the end of the volume an interesting debate on this subject.

[2] **Plutarch,** in his life of Pyrrhus tells us that the distinguished king of **Epirus** fought against the Greeks and his kindred, the Macedonians, with such great bravery that it attracted the admiration of his troops who compared him to an eagle. Pyrrhus answered that they were right to call him so; but, that they must not forget that they were his arrows, which he used while soaring. From this time on the inhabitants of Epirus and later all the people of Albania called themselves **Shkipetare,** or the Sons of the eagle; from **Shkiponje, eagle.** Cf. **Wassa Effendi: La Vérité sur les Albanais et l'Albanie.**

like spirit, characteristic of the Albanians, she set out to capture the island of Issa (Lissa) which was in alliance with the Romans. The Roman republic sent a mission to Teuta to ask for explanations; but she slew one of the envoys and sent the other back to inform the Roman senate of her policy, and at the same time attacked Durazzo and Corfu. The Romans thereupon turned their armies to the Illyrian coast and made short work of Teuta. She was driven from all the places she had occupied; even from her capital, Scutari; and was forced to accept an ignominious peace. But this peace did not last long. *Demetrius Pharos,* who succeeded Teuta, as ruler of the country, endeavored to unite the Albanian States in an alliance, but failed. And again the lands of the Illyrian Albanians fell under the power of the Romans, who contented themselves with exercising a protectorate over the realm of the young King *Perseus.* The three Albanian states, *Illyria, Epirus* and *Macedonia* rose against the Roman Empire under *Philip the Fifth* of Macedonia, when Hannibal seemed in a fair way to crush the Roman power. As soon as the Carthaginian danger had been disposed of, the Roman senate once more turned its attention to the lands of the Adriatic, this time fully determined to get rid once for all of these troublesome states. They sent *Paulus Emilianus* at the head of a powerful army, who defeated and subdued the Illyrians (168 B. C.) and then pounced upon the Epirotes who helped the Illyrians to resist the Roman power, wreaked terrible vengeance upon them; and reduced a hundred and fifty thousand of the people to slavery. At the same time (168 B. C.) Illyria, Epirus and Macedonia became provinces of the Roman Empire. The inhabitants took to their mountains, and so the Roman conquest wrought very little change in the social condition of the Albanians. They retained their language their na-

KEY TO THE NEAR EAST 19

tional manners and usages, and remained a distinct and peculiar people.

After the death of *Theodosius the Great,* in 395 A. D. the Roman Empire was divided between his two sons Honorius and Arcadius. The latter took *the Eastern Empire,* the other took *the Western.* Albania was part of the Eastern Empire and was under the Illyrian Prefecture. At this time Albania was divided into three sections, viz: *High Albania,* which extended from the Zetes and Moracia valleys to the Shkumbi river, and was known under the name of *Praevalis; Central Albania,* which extended from the Shkumbi to the Voiossa river, and was called *New Epirus;* and *Southern Albania,* which extended from the Voiossa to the Gulf of Arta and was called *Ancient Epirus.*

In the fifth century, *the Goths* became complete masters of the greater part of Albania, particularly the northern portion, where we afterwards find some of their descendants settled in quiet possession of a part of the country. We find one of them named *Sidismund,* in alliance with Theodoric the Great, when in his campaign against the Romans of the Lower Empire he entered Macedonia, and the Macedonians procured for him, by stratagem, the city of *Dyrrhachium.*

About the same time, another tribe of strangers, who proved to be the most numerous, and the most formidable of any to the Byzantine Emperors, began to make its appearance in the same part of the country. *The Bulgarians* continued their incursions into the European provinces of the Empire, during the seventh, eighth and ninth centuries. About the year 870 Ochrida was the residence of a King of Bulgaria, and the see of an Archbishop, whose spiritual authority extended to *Kanina,* and *Jeriko.* In the tenth century, the same race was settled at Nicopolis, which comprehended all *old Epirus*. It appears that about this time, all the more accessible parts of Epirus were occupied by strangers of Slavonian origin. Until the last periods of the Lower Empire, the Kings of Bulgaria and Serbia continued to make occasional conquests and settlements in Greece, and even in Morea. They have to this day left traces of their long residences, by the numerous names of places of Slavic derivation to be found in every part of the country. It was in these ages of Bulgarian hegemony, that the Albanians, the remains of the *Illyrian, Macedonian* and *Epirotic* clans became finally included within the boundaries which they have held ever since. Nearly a century after the Emperor *Basil Second* had crushed the Bulgarians, the Albanians appear acting an important part in history. They formed a part of the army of *Nicephorus Basilacus*, when he marched against his sovereign *Nicephorus Botaniates*, and was defeated and made prisoner by *Alexius Comnenus* in 1079. The four nations, viz., *Franks, Bulgarians, Greeks* and *Albanians*, of which the army of Basilacus was composed, are here distinguished by their languages and were all collected in the country about *Dyrrhachium*.

The Franks had been invited from Italy by the *Bishop of Deabolis* (the part of Albania now called Devol); and they were a part of the same Normans, who soon afterwards gave so much trouble to the Greek Emperors. Under *Robert Guiscard*, and his son *Bohemond*, they succeeded in taking *Dyrrhachium, Achris* and *Janina;* defeated the Greeks in several actions and occupied the country as far east as the river of Vardar.

In the reigns of *Andronicus, Comnenus* and *Isaac Angelo*, about the year 1185, we find the Norman Kings of Sicily with their troops occupying Thessaly, a great part of Macedonia including *Thessalonica,* and the fertile plain of the

Strymon, with its principal cities *Serres*, and *Amphipolis*. These monarchs, with their relatives, the Princes of Taranto, obtained permanent possessions on the Western coast of Greece. In these operations, as well as throughout the whole course of the Crusaders, during 150 years, the coast of Albania was the frequent resort of Franks; and Durazzo was very often their depot and place of retreat and safety.

When the Oriental Empire was dismembered in consequence of the conquest of Constantinople by the Franks in 1204, *Michael Angelos,* a bastard of the Comneni, founded a principality consisting of the ancient *Acarnania, Aetolia* and *Epirus,* and containing the towns of Janina, Arta, and Naupactus which with some short interruptions, continued to be a separate state under the name of the *Despotate of Epirus,* till it fell under the Turkish yoke in 1431. The despots of Epirus, or of Aetolia, or of the West, as they were variously called, were sometimes tributary to Constantinople; but more frequently independent of or in a state of hostility to the Empire. Some of them extended their boundaries at the expense of the Franks and Bulgarians, and one of them *Theordore,* is mentioned as having occupied Elbassan, which also is mentioned as having been again taken by the Bulgarians in 1230.

In 1257, *Albanon* or *Elbassan* was the chief town of a prefecture under the superior intendance of a Praetor, who was sent by *Theodore Lascaris,* the second, emperor of Nicae, to restore order in all these provinces. The Albanians, however, preferred the alliance of the *Despot;* and the Praetor, who was *George Acropolita,* the historian, was soon under the necessity of retiring.

Towards the end of the same century, the Albanians are found *"plundering" Dyrrhachium,* which had been ruined by an earthquake. They afterward rebuilt it. *Pachymer* calls them indifferently Albanians, or Illyrians, thus showing his conviction that they were a remnant of this ancient stock, a fact confirmed by the whole tenor of their history.

As we advance in the history of these countries, the Albanians arise in importance. They began about this time to establish their authority over the maritime plains of *New Epirus,* as we find that a short time before the death of Emperor *Michael Palæologus,* who died in 1282, they were in complete possession of Durazzo; in a state of declared independence of the Byzantine Emperors and in alliance with *Charles,* King of Sicily, who at that time possessed the Island of Corfu, and Kanina and a strong town situated on the site of the ancient *Bullis,* upon a height above Vallona. Berat was then in the hands of the Byzantine emperors, so that the dominion of the Albanians did not yet extend to the southern extremity of the plains.

Philip, Duke of Taranto, second son of Charles the Second, King of the Sicilies, who married the daughter of the Despot Nicephorus, and thus obtained a part of his territory, received also from his father, in the year 1294, the principality of Achaia, and all his other dominions in Greece; and, upon this occasion assumed, among other titles relative to these acquisitions, that of *Lord of Albania.* This titular dignity descended to his brother, and nephew, but it does not appear that it gave the Latin prince any more real authority over the mountaineers of Albania, than a similar title assumed in the middle of the fourteenth century by *Stephen Dushan,* King of Serbia, when he made himself master of the greater part of the country, north of Mount Aeta and proclaimed himself emperor of *Roumania, Slavonia,* and *Albania.* The power of the Serbians lasted no longer than the life of Stephen, and in none of these revolutions were the Albanians ever long prevented from forming alliances with the Franks, or despots of Epirus, or from seeking their fortunes in the service of those powers as their interest or inclinations prompted. The Albanians of Kolonia, Devol and the neighborhood of Ochrida are mentioned by *Cantacuzenus* as having joined the younger *Andronicus Palæologus,* against his grandfather in the year 1327; and the same historian speaks of twelve thousand Albanians of *Malakasi, Bui,* and *Mesaria,* (names still found in the country), as having made their submission to the younger Andronicus, then sole emperor; when, upon a subsequent occasion, he undertook an expedition into Thessaly against two rebel governors. These branches of the Albanian nation are noticed by Cantacuzenus precisely as we find them at the present day, namely an independent race, living in the vicinity of Thessaly addicted both to war and to a pastoral life, and under the necessity in the winter season, of seeking pasture for their flocks in the plains.

In 1338, the same emperor Andronicus Palæologus the Second, enraged at the repeated incursions of the natives of the Western side of Albania, who had very much distressed the Imperial fortresses of Berat, Kanina, Skrapari and Klisura, seized the favorable moment afforded by the death of the Despot John, and the minority of his son, Nicephorus, for the double purpose of reducing the Despotate and chastising the Albanians, and marched through Thessaly into Albania. He was assisted upon this occasion by a body of Turks from Asia Minor; and these auxiliaries were so formidable, as to penetrate into the very heart of the Albanian mountains and carry off an immense quantity of booty.

The Albanians became very formidable in the course of the 14th century and two of their chiefs, *Balzha* in the north, and *Shpata* in the South, made themselves particularly conspicuous. They are recorded as having possessed themselves of Durazzo, Berat, Kanina, Kastoria, Janina, Arta and Great part of Acarnania, Thessaly and Macedonia. One of the latter, named Charles Tocco, who was made despot by emperor *Manuel Palæologus*, about the year 1400, took Epirus and Acarnania from the Albanians. It was about this time that the Albanians first began to meet with a more formidable enemy than they had yet encountered, the Turks. In the year 1383, in an action near Berat, they were defeated by the troops of Sultan Murat the First, with the loss of their leader, the only surviving son of the above-mentioned Balzha. Some of their towns fell into the hand of the Turks; but their submission to the Ottoman Government was greatly delayed by the talents and valor of their hero *George Kastriota*, more commonly known under the name of *Scanderbeg* and of his father-in-law, *Arianiti Topia*. In 1478 Kroia, which the Venetians had occupied after Scanderbeg's death, surrendered to Mohammed II, and in 1479 Scutari, after a memorable defence, was reduced by blockade. Many of its Christian defenders emigrated to Dalmatia and Italy; others took refuge in the mountains. In 1502 the Turks captured Durazzo and in 1571 Antivari and Dulcigno, were the last fortresses of Albania to fall. Notwithstanding the abandonment of Christianity by a large section of the population, the authority of the sultans was never effectively established in Albania. The succeeding centuries present a record of interminable conflicts between the Albanians and the Turks and between the Albanians and Serbians, their traditional enemy. The decline of the Ottoman power, which began towards the end of the 17th century, was marked by increasing anarchy in the outlying portions of the empire. About 1760 a mountain chieftain *Mehmet of Bushat*, after obtaining the *pash-*

alek of Scutari from the Porte, succeeded in establishing an almost independent sovereignty in Upper Albania, which remained in his family for some generations. In southern Albania *Ali Pasha of Tepeleni*, an able man, subdued the neighboring pashas and chiefs, and exercised a practical independent sovereignty from the Adriatic to the Aegean. He introduced comparative civilization at Janina, his capital and maintained direct relations with foreign powers. Eventually he renounced his allegiance to the Sultan, but was overthrown by a Turkish army in 1822. Shortly afterwards the dynasty of Scutari came to an end with the surrender of *Mustapha Pasha*, the last of the house of Bushat, to the grand vizier *Reshid Pasha*, in 1831.

The opposition of the Albanians, Christian as well as Moslem, to the reforms introduced by the Sultan *Mahmud II* led to the devastation of the country and the expatriation of thousands of its inhabitants. During the next half century several local revolts occurred, but the most important took place after the Berlin Treaty (July 13, 1878), when the Moslem and Christian Albanians continued to resist the stipulated transferrence of Albanian territory to Austro-Hungary, Serbia, Montenegro and Greece and the *Albanian League* was formed by an assemblage of chiefs at Prizren. The movement was so successful that the restoration of *Plava, Gusinje* and *Janina* to Albania was sanctioned by the Powers. The Albanian leaders, soon after, displayed a spirit of independence, which proved embarrassing to Turkish diplomacy and caused alarm at Constantinople; their forces came into conflict with a Turkish army under *Dervish Pasha*, near Dulcigno (Nov. 1880), and eventually the League was suppressed. In the spring of 1903 serious disturbances took place in north-western Albania; but the Turks succeeded in pacifying the Albanians, partly by force and partly by concessions.

In 1908, the Young Turks succeeded in getting the upper hand in Turkey with the assistance of the Albanians. The Albanians' dream of Utopia seemed to be realized at last, when national equality and freedom of opinions were reluctantly granted. But alas! the Young Turks failed to keep their promises, and began to put in practice their shortsighted policy of forcibly ottomanizing the people of the empire.

This conduct resulted in the three great Albanian uprisings, which finally forced the Turkish Government to grant certain demands, and modify the stringency of their policy. Albania now was on equal standing with the other nationalities of the Ottoman Empire.

The Albanians as a nation, have always desired freedom, and when denied them, they have held it as a sacred duty "to sharpen the sword, and hold it ready for defense." They refused to submit to aggression, intrigue, or to be considered simply as an organization, which can be used as tools and instruments of domination and tyranny.

The Balkan States foresaw the gradual creation of a great Albania, in the union of Kossovo, Scutari, Janina and part of Monastir vilayets, with the help of Great Britain, as advised by *Lord E. Fitzmaurice,* the English Ambassador in Constantinople, and also by *Lord Goschen,* in 1880. To prevent a free and independent government in Albania, the Balkan States suddenly declared war against Turkey.

Soon after war was declared, Serbia occupied the Northern part of Albania, and Greece, most of the southern districts. The independence of Albania was proclaimed finally at Vallona, on November 28, 1912, and a provisional Government was then formed under the leadership of *Ismail Kemal*

KEY TO THE NEAR EAST 27

Bey. On December 20, 1912, the London Ambassadorial Conference agreed in principle for Albania's autonomy and roughly decided the frontiers of Albania. Subsequently the same Conference agreed that a European Prince be nominated to rule it, and Prince *William* of Wied having accepted the offer of the throne of Albania, arrived at Durazzo on March 7, 1914.

The Government of Albania, was vested in the hands of the *Mbret*, supported and advised by the International Commission of Control as agreed to by the Ambassadorial Conference on July, 1913. Unfortunately, distrust envy and rivalry between protective powers, the greed and the intrigues and attacks that came from Serbia and Greece, caused the death of thousands and thousands of innocent men, women and children, who perished victims of unscrupulous politicians and war lords.

Shortly after the outbreak of the European War, the *Mbret* left Albania Sept. 3, 1914, conferring the functions of Government upon the International Commission of Control, and issued a proclamation to the Albanian people, in which he stated the reasons of his departure, and acknowledged that the sovereign powers had been transferred to the International Commission of Control.

As a result of the war, the International Commission of Control separated and retired; but despite their departure, this International Commission of Control, instituted by the London Conference, is still the sovereign power in Albania, by virtue of the proclamation issued by *Mbret William.*

The sovereignty of Albania and the validity of the solemn decisions and declarations of the London Conference was attested by the Austrian proclamation, which reached this continent March 3, 1917, by the formal statement of *Baron*

Sonnino, speaking on behalf of the Entente Powers, October, 1915 when the solemn declaration was made by him, that Italy guaranteed the validity of the decisions of the London Conference, and the integrity and independence of Albania; and lastly, by the proclamation of *Colonel Descoin,* issued at Kortcha, December, 1916, on behalf of the Government of France.

Since the outbreak of the Great War, Albania has been successively invaded by the Serbians three times; by the Greeks twice; and by the Austrians. At present, the entire territory of Albania is occupied by Italian and French troops. All of these Powers have declared as we have already stated above, that such occupation is *purely of military* and *not political character and significance.*

The Albanians are the most beautiful race of the Balkan Peninsula. Physiologically considered they differ from the surrounding races in the formation of the cranium. The occipital region is flat colloguially; and they have no backs to their heads. Their faces are of a long oval shape with prominent cheek bones and a flat but raised forehead. The expression of their eyes, which are hazel and blue, but seldom black, is very lively. Their mouths are small and their teeth of a good color and well formed. Their noses are for the most part high and straight, with thin but open nostrils. Their eye brows are arched.

The color of the Albanians, when they are young is a pure white with a tinge of vermillion on their cheeks, but labor and exposure to heat and cold, give a dusky hue to the skin of their bodies, though their faces mostly preserve a clearness of complexion. The Albanians are generally of middle stature, about five feet, six inches in height. They are muscular and straight; but not large and they are particularly small round the loins without corpulency which is attributed to their active life, and also to the tight girdle they wear round their waists.

The Albanian dress is well adapted to the life of the mountaineers, extremely elegant; but often very costly. The Southern Albanians wear the usual white kilt or petticoat, known as the *fustanelle*,[1] which the Greeks have taken for the uniform of the king's guard, with embroidered gaiters and *opingas*. The dress of the Northern Albanians is different. It consists of a short close fitting red, blue or black jacket and long close fitting crimson *trews*, which reach from the waist to the ankle. A broad leather belt and a well filled bandolier complete their attire. The dress of the woman is fanciful, and varies in different districts. In some they wear a kind of white woolen helmet and the younger women a skull-cap composed of pieces of gold and silver coin, with their hair falling in long braids, also strung with money.

The Albanians have always been of a warlike character. They were the soldiers of *Pyrrhus,* one of the most formidable opponents whom the Romans encountered; they were the soldiers of *Alexander the Great,* who conquered the whole known world of his day.

Under their more recent hero *Scanderbeg,* they arrested the tide of Turkish conquest. They take the field without baggage or tents and are far more active than any of the Balkan soldiery. They begin the profession of arms as children, and stick to it till they become decrepit. They are equally capable of using the sword and the gun; the latter weapon, when slung across their right shoulders, they carry

---

[1] Until the Greek revolution, when Albanian valor made the **fustanella** (kilt) fashionable in Greece, **the kilt** was a common Romaic term of contempt applied impartially to Albanians. This is the origin of what every Greek now imagines to be his traditional national dress.

without any apparent effort, running up their hills with great ease and agility. Nor are their arms for show. For about 500 years they were in rebellion against the Porte. They justly pride themselves in their proved reputation as the best soldiers of the Balkans.[1]

Loyalty to his word, *besa-besën*, is his greatest virtue. Indeed the honor of the Albanians is such that if they have entertained you in their homes, or if you succeed in winning their confidence and attaching them to your person, or if once they have given you a promise, you may be absolutely sure that nothing will be too great a sacrifice for them to make in order that the promise may be fulfilled. No impartial foreign traveller has ever been brought into intimacy with the Albanians without acquiring a lasting respect and liking for their many high qualities.

> Fierce are Albania's children, yet they lack
> Not virtues; were those virtues more mature
> Where is the foe that ever saw their back?
> Who can so well the toils of war endure?
> Their native fastnesses not more secure;
> Than they in doubtful time of troublous need.
> Their wrath, how deadly! but their friendship sure.
> When gratitude or valor bids them bleed,
> Unshaken, rushing on where'er their chief may lead.[2]

---

[1] The republic of Venice, the Kings of France, the Dukes of Milan, and several other Italian Princes long had Albanian troops in their service. The Albanian cavalry seems to have been first employed in the west by Charles VII of France in his wars against the English. The office of **Captain General** of the Albanian Cavalry, created in 1449 was an important one, as it first included the command of all foreign cavalry in the French service. They always wore the national dress. At first they were equipped as lancers, but subsequently as carbineers. During the war against Napoleon, there were some Albanian regiments among the English auxiliary troops. Probably the last Albanian regiment in a foreign service was the **Royal Macedonian** of the Kings of Naples, which survived far into the last century.

[2] Cf. Lord Byron, Childe Harold.

The Albanian National Costume

The Albanians are extremely sensitive, and the feeling they have of their vast antiquity gives them personal dignity and great national pride. They are never cowardly, never mean. They are not only an Ayran people, but they are European in their national instincts. Even the Moslems among them are monogamists. They never marry outside their own race and their own rank. Their sense of family life is European and not Turkish. The Albanians treat women with great consideration, consult them willingly in their affairs, both public and private and accord them a position in the family equal to their own. And well do they merit the respect of their husbands and brothers, for often have they proved themselves to be fit companions for men, unmindful of fatigue, danger and even death in the cause of liberty. When the armies of the Sultan menaced the privileges of which the people of Albania had always been proud, it was the women who were the first to give the alarm and to excite the men to resist to death; themselves following to aid in the combat. Restraining the tears natural to their sex, they would carry the bodies of their loved ones among the combatants in order to excite them to avenge their deaths; and the same women refused to receive back into their homes the husbands and sons who had for a moment turned their backs upon the enemy. Albanian women too, are often entrusted with negotiations for truce or peace.

Such is the respect with which Albanians regard their women that they may traverse the camps of belligerents with greater safety than men. The terms of treaties of peace, too, are often discussed by the women belonging to the hostile parties. They carry arms and are more unapproachable than men. Such being the character of the Albanian woman, it is not surprising that they have played a considerable part in the history of their country.

It is the fashion among journalists to talk of the lawless Albanians; but there is perhaps no other people in Europe so much under the tyranny of Law. For all their habits, customs and laws the people, and especially those of Northern Albania, as a rule have but one explanation, it is in the *canon of Lek*. The law is said to be laid down by Lek Dukaghini. His fame among the Albanians equals that of Scanderbeg. He must have been of insistent individuality to have so influenced the people that *Lek* said *so*. He obtained far more obedience than the ten commandments. The teaching of Christianity and of Islam, *the Sheriat* and the church law, all have to yield to the canon of Lek. He comes from the ruling family of Dukaghin in the 15th century.

This unwritten law, is administered among the *Malesori* by a Council of Elders. A full council must consist of the *Bairaktars,* (banner-bearers), four leaders and 12 elders, especially chosen for their knowledge of law, and 12 heads of houses. The council meets near the church or the mosque in the open air.

All cases are brought before the banner-bearer, and it is he who decides the number of conjurors before whom the accused may swear his innocence and who are willing to swear to it with him. The plaintiff has the right to nominate them. All meet before the council. The accused and plaintiff are heard. Should the conjurors agree that the accused is innocent, the elders acquit him. Should all conjurors, but one, agree to his innocence, that one can be dismissed; but two must replace him. The plaintiff if not satisfied, has the right to demand more conjurors up to a fixed number according to the crime. Twenty-four may be demanded for murder; and from two to ten for stealing, according to the value of the thing stolen. If the verdict be

DR. MUCHO QULLI.
In National Costume of Northern Albania.

"*guilty*," the elders decide the punishment. The canon of Lek has but two punishments, *fine* and *burning of property.* Neither death nor imprisonment can be inflicted. Prison, there is none. Death would start but a new feud, and Lek's object appears to have been to check it. If the accused be found innocent, the whole party goes into the church. The candles are lighted on the altar, and in the presence of the priest the accused, first swears his innocence on the gospel.

The Albanian obeys the law; but what he resents to the utmost is not the administration of law, but the attempt to force on him laws to which he has never assented.

The most important custom in Northern Albania, and especially in the district of Dukaghini, is blood vengeance or the *vendeta,* which is indeed the old idea of purification by blood. What profit is life to a man if his honor be not clean? To cleanse his honor no price is too great. Blood can be wiped out only with blood. A blow also demands blood; so do the insulting words, abduction of a girl, adultery, etc. Blood vengeance, slaying a man according to the laws of honor must not be confounded with murder. Murder starts a blood feud. In blood vengeance, the rules of the custom are strictly observed. A man never is shot for vengeance, when he is with a woman, nor when with a child, nor when he is met in company, nor when "*besa*," oath of peace has been given. The two parties may swear such an oath if they choose, for business purposes, and especially when the country is in danger. When the avenger has slain his victim, he first reaches a place of safety; and, then proclaims that he has done the deed. He wishes all to know his honor is clean. Any house to which *the ghaksur* flies for shelter is bound to give him food and protection, even if he happens, by chance, to fly in the house of his victim. He is a guest and as such sacred.

It is very rare that a woman is killed; no Albanian would do it. It is considered very mean. To kill a married woman entails two bloods: blood with her husband's and with her own family.[1]

The hospitality of the Albanians is proverbial. The personality of the guest is sacred to the host. The custom in the province of Dukaghini is very strict when a friend is killed, whom a Malesori (Mountaineer) defends. There is never any forgiveness for this act. A man from Dukaghini forgives such an act practised against his father, brother or son, but he never forgives anyone for taking the life of his friend. He that kills a friend of someone never dares to appear before his companions; and he, is greatly disgraced, who does not defend his friend. It has happened that for a friend, a brother has killed his brother.

Friends are of two kinds, *introduced* and *natural,* that is those to whom we are naturally attached. The *introduced* friend is he who, through other friends comes and asks the protection from several persons that they may not let him suffer. Then those who receive him feel it is their duty to defend him from all harm. It may happen that such a friend is killed by someone. Then the defenders, together with the relatives of the victim, seek his blood. Besides these, all that did not approve of this deed accompany the rest and set the house of the guilty one on fire, cut all the trees and vines, pull down the walls of the fields, and desolate the

---

[1] The Ghiak or blood revenge, is a sacred duty to the names of the deceased. Of this we find many instances in classical history or historic myth. Polyxena was sacrificed to appease the manes of Achilles. **Placat Achilles mactata Polyxena Manes.** Iphigenia was condemned to death to appease the contrary winds. The mythical history of Greece terms with similar cases. Now, as the Greeks did not sacrifice human beings otherwise than punitively, it is fair to infer that these persons were not Greeks but Pelasgians, and as this practice of atoning sacrifice continues in Albania in the form of the Ghiak it follows that the modern Albanians are descendants of the Pelasgians.

earth that no seed may grow there. The land left belongs to the friends and relatives of the victim, which is not to be ploughed before the terms of peace come from the authority.

If any of the friends of the victim kills a friend or relative of the guilty, he will not suffer at all, because the murder is counted as a recompense for the one killed before. If the people of the victim wish to make peace with the guilty one they can never do it without the consent of the defenders.

But much more serious and critical is the matter when a natural friend of a Malesori is murdered. Great is the responsibility and disgrace of the one who does the act. Such a friend is killed either when there is blood to be paid, or if he is a coward or weak. Well, when it thus happens the Malesori, whose friend is killed takes all the males of the house and his friends, and goes on the mountains trying to take the life of the guilty.

Another interesting custom of hospitality is the following: Usually a little boy or girl with a jug of water and a loaf of bread sit at the roadside to help any wearied traveller, who might by chance pass by. *"Zotni,* Sir, Will you partake of my humble meal and a draught of water? This is all I can offer to my fellow brother, and I offer it heartily." When a traveller is overtaken by the night, he tries to get to the nearest village possible. He is welcome to any house he may happen to knock. He knocks and the answer comes from inside, "Who is it?" "A guest; can you give me a shelter for the night?" "You are the guest of God. He sent you, and you are welcome to our shelter. We are poor, bread and salt and our hearts is all we can offer; but you are welcome to stay as long as you wish." Poor though he be, a choice lamb is selected and killed for the guest and other friends are invited to entertain him. When he departs, they fill his bag with the best piece of meat and bread.

The Albanians have a great inclination for mechanical arts; besides being noted as the best architects, joiners, bridge-builders and sculptors of the Balkan peninsula. The gold embroidery on the velvet jackets and ladies' coats is extremely artistic. The apparel both for men and women is worked on native looms, and nothing surpasses the fine silk gauze. They are also skillful in silver handwork.

Agriculture in Albania is primitive and backward. Yet with an improved system it would not only suffice for its people, but for an increased population leaving a good margin for exportation. The Albanian is, however, rather a shepherd and herdsman, than an agriculturist; and he raises a large number of cattle, horses, sheep, and goats.

Dancing is one of their common amusements. The musical instrument in general use among the Albanians is a kind of guitar or lute, called *tamboura,* with three strings, a long neck and a small round base. They strike the chords not with the hand, but with a piece of quill half an inch long. Though primitive it is sufficient as an accompaniment to their songs and makes time.

There are in practice in Albania, many dances but the most important are the handkerchief dances and the *Pyrrhic.* The handkerchief dance, holds the hands of the party (usually a dozen in number) locked in each other behind their backs; or every man has a handkerchief in his hand, which is held by the next to him. The first is a slow dance. The dancing party stands in a semi-circle and their musicians in the middle accompanying with their music the dancing movements of the party, which are the bending and unbending of the two ends of the semi-circle, with some very slow footing, and now and then a hop.

In the other handkerchief dance, the movements are vio-

Albanians dancing the Pyrrhic.

lent. It is upon the leader of the string that the principal movements revolve, and every member in the party takes the leadership by turns. He begins at first opening the ring and footing quietly from side to side then he hops quickly forward dragging the whole string after him in a circle and then twirls around, dropping frequently on his knee, and rebounding from the ground with a shout. The next man takes the lead and takes the party through the same evolutions, but endeavors to exceed his predecessor in the quickness and violence of his measures.

The Pyrrhic, is one of the most ancient dances of the world, executed by men in arms. This famous dance is still practised by the Albanians at their great national festivals.

II

THE STUMBLING BLOCK OF THE TURKS.

IN 1431 the Turks made a further advance into Albania with the capture of Janina, whose fortresses were most valiantly defended by Albanians and not by Greeks as it is commonly supposed. This is according to the Ottoman history of this epoch, which says that after the siege of Janina three thousand heads of Albanians, *inhabitants* of Janina were used to make a pyramid of trophy. Soon after, the Albanian chiefs combined against the invader under a single leader, the celebrated *George Kastriota,* who fought thirteen campaigns in a period of 22 years, (1444-1466).

The narrative of *Scanderbeg's* life and deeds is a veritable romance of chivalry. His father, *John Kastriota,* who was the hereditary ruling prince of the most important Albanian district of this time, had his residence in *Kroia.* Hard pressed by *Bayazid I,* about the year 1403, he was compelled to submit to the Turks, to pay tribute and to surrender his four sons as hostages, with this understanding that after John Kastriota's death, Turkey would send his oldest son to rule over Albania. George, the future Scanderbeg, was at that time but eight years of age. His sprightliness, manly bearing and extraordinary abilities soon attracted the attention of the Sultan, who caused him to be circumcised, received him into the imperial household and educated him for the military service. He was henceforth known by the name of *Iskender bey,* or *Lord Alexander,* and under this name was destined to become one of the most renowned champions of the Christian faith. He very soon became famous for his military exploits and was made commander of a body of five thousand Turkish cavalry.

As soon as John Kastriota died, Mourad II, caused the three older sons to be put out of the way and privily seized the Albanian principality. Mourat thought that Scanderbeg was bound securely to himself, but he was greatly deceived; for as soon as the young Albanian prince heard about the sad fate of his three older brothers, his heart was filled with bitter exasperation and a thirst for revenge; and he only waited an opportunity. This opportunity soon came. In the confusion which followed the defeat suffered by the Turkish armies in the Hungarian war near Belgrade, Scanderbeg who had the general command of the Turkish troops, seized the secretary of state and compelled him to sign an order to the Ottoman governor of Kroia, requiring him to surrender the city and fortress to himself; and then Scanderbeg put the secretary of the Sultan to death, that his flight might not be immediately known. The Turkish garrison obeyed the imperial order and Scanderbeg was master of Albania.

He at once abjured the Mohammedan religion and proclaimed himself the avenger of his family and the champion of the Christian faith.[1] The Albanians, who were at this time all Christians, flocked to his standard and at the head of his forces, by his valor, energy and great qualities as a military leader, Scanderbeg withstood for twenty-three years the mightiest efforts of the Turks. Every year Mourad II and Mohammed II, the greatest Sultans Turkey had ever had, sent against Scanderbeg their ablest generals at the head of from 60,000 to 200,000 men; and some times the Sultans themselves went against Scanderbeg, but all of them met only defeat and destruction; until at last full of years and honours, the Albanian hero breathed his last, surround-

---

[1] See Longfellow, **Tales of a Wayside Inn.**

ed by his loyal generals (1468), bequeathing his kingdom and his youthful son to the friendly guardianship of the Venetians.[1]

The last great struggle of the Albanians against the Turks was the siege of Shkdora,[2] a place marked by the hand of nature for the capital of *Illyria,* and still preserving its ancient name unaltered. This defence confers as much honor upon the Albanians as the exploits of Scanderbeg. It lasted a year, and is one of the most curious sieges recorded in history, from the gallantry of the besieged, the disparity of power in the two parties, and the immense calibre of the

---

[1] The following is the story of the last moments of Scanderbeg, as given by an Albanian ballad. When he departed for the battle, on the road that he pursued he encountered Death, the ill omened messenger of melancholy fortune. "My name is Death: return back, O Scanderbeg, for thy life approacheth its end!" He hears him and beholds him: he draws his sword and Death remains unmoved.

"Phantom of air, dreaded only by cowards, whence knowest thou that I must die? Can thy icy heart foretell my death? or is the book of heavens' destiny open into thee?"

"Yesterday in heaven were opened before me the books of destiny and cold and black like a veil it descended on thy head, and then passed on and fell on others also!"

Scanderbeg smote his hands together, and his heart gave vent to a sigh. "Ah! woe is me! I shall live no more!" He turns to contemplate the times that must come after him; he beholds his son fatherless, and his kingdom filled with tears. He assembles his warriors and says to them:

"My trusty warriors, the Turk will conquer all your country, and you will become his slaves. Dukaghin, bring hither my son, my lovely boy, that I may give him my commands. Unprotected flower, flower of my love, take with thee thy mother and prepare three of thy finest galleys. If the Turk know it, he will come and lay hands on thee, and will insult thy mother. Descend to the shore; there grows a cypress dark and sad. Fasten the horse to that cypress and unfold my standard upon my horse to the sea breeze and from my standard hang my sword. On its edge is the blood of the Turks, and death sleepeth there. The arms of the dreaded champion say, will remain dumb beneath the dark tree. When the north wind blows furiously, the horse will neigh, the flag will wave in the wind, the sword will ring again. The Turk will hear it and trembling, pale and sad, will retreat, thinking on Death." (**Revue des Deux Mondes,** vol. 53, p. 404.)

[2] The history of the siege of Shkodra is related by a native and eyewitness, **Marinus Barletius,** who published the account in Latin at Venice, in the year 1504.

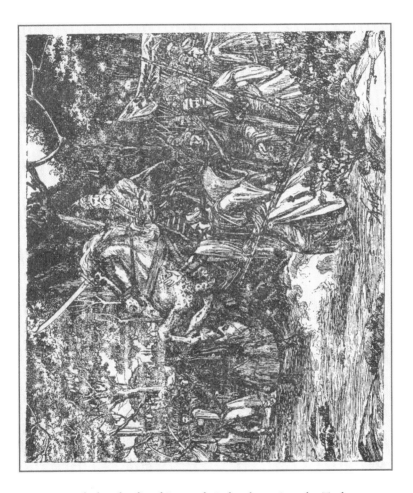

Scanderbeg leading his people in battle against the Turks.

Turkish artillery in that early period of the art; some of the stone shot thrown against the walls having weighed 1300 lbs. After resisting the utmost efforts of Mahomet II in person, the place was upon the point of yielding to famine, when the Venetians, by one of the articles of their treaty with the Porte in 1478, saved the *Shkodrans* from the disgrace of submission, by taken upon themselves to stipulate that the place should be yielded to the Turks, and that the inhabitants should obtain a refuge in the Venetian states.

From this period it is true that Albania was forced to acknowledge a certain amount of nominal Turkish domination; but she never consented to renounce entirely her sovereignty, never consented to give up her national aspirations, her submission being only temporary and apparent. This is evident by the subsequent expeditions undertaken by the Sultans against Albania with doubtful success, and from the many revolutions which followed one after another, at very short intervals, with the purpose of regaining her complete freedom; but the European Powers for selfish motives refused more than once to recognize her independence.

At the beginning of the eighteenth century an Albanian chieftain, *Mehmet Bushati*, seized the city and massacred his rivals. He was so powerful that the Porte was obliged to acknowledge him as the hereditary Governor not only of *Shkodra*, but also of Alessio, Tirana, Elbassan and Dukaghini. *Kara Mahmoud*, his son became entirely an independent prince. He twice invaded Montenegro, burned Cettigne, and a little later defeated the Ottoman troops at *Kossovopolie;* but in 1796 he was defeated and slain in Montenegro. His descendants continued to rule northern Albania.

While the Boushattis were defying the Sultan in Northern Albania, *Ali Pasha of Janina,* whom Byron visited, when in that part of the world, and whom he has described in *Childe Harold* was meditating a rebellion. This rebellion was rendered the more probable by the excessive court paid to Ali in his Pashalik by England and France. When the Venetian Republic was destroyed by the Treaty of *Campo Formio,* in 1797, the territories which that State possessed on the coast of Albania, were made over to France; but in the constant changes of those troublous days they fell into a condition of anarchy, and Ali Pasha acquired an ascendancy in them. By successive addition to the sphere of his power, he had come to be the ruler of Albania, Epirus, Thessaly and the whole of Continental Greece. The Porte considering the services rendered by him to the Empire in the latter part of the eighteenth century, extended to him a confirmation of the authority which he had assumed at Janina. For many years he continued to improve his dominions, of which, owing to the distracted condition of the Ottoman Empire, he was almost the independent sovereign. That he aimed to get formal recognition for the complete Independence of his country is certain. The Government of the Sultan was well aware of this, but for a long while hesitated to attack him. His power was great; his valour and ability had, on several occasions, done good service to the Porte; and it was feared that, if provoked, he would be a formidable opponent to the Empire. But Ali's attitude became unendurable; and, it was resolved to take measures of repression. Ali, was in many respects a wise and successful governor, and a distinguished diplomat. But he was now growing old, and it seemed unlikely that he could display the same vigour of resistance that might have been expected at an earlier time. He was excommunicated at the beginning of 1820, and all the Pashas, commanders in the European Provinces of the Empire were ordered to march against him. The struggle was long and difficult, but at last the fortunes of Ali proved to be on the wane. His armies being at length worsted by the Turks, he surrendered on the first of February, 1822, under a promise that his life and property should be spared. But the lieutenants of the Sultan broke faith and Ali was sentenced to death and executed on the 5th of February, and his head was sent to Constantinople, where it was displayed at the *Seraglio gates*.

The contest between Ali Pasha and the Sultan offers an unprecedented opportunity for rousing the whole of Greece to action. After a few years of struggle, being assisted by a number of Albanian heroes, *Miaulis, Djavela, Botchari, Bubulina,* etc. the Greeks secured the independence of their country.

After the Greek war of Independence four powerful Albanian chiefs, *Mustapha,* the last hereditary Pasha of Scutari, *Veli Bey of Janina, Silehdar Poda,* and *Arslan bey* agreed to make common cause against the Turks. *Reshid Pasha,* the Grand Vizier determined to crush this movement, and commenced by an act of meanest treachery. He proclaimed a general amnesty and invited all the Albanians Beys to a peaceful conference and a grand banquet to be held at Monastir. About five hundred Albanian leaders appeared headed by Veli and Arslan, and were received with every attention of courtesy. When they appeared in gala costumes in the parade ground, where the banquet was to be held, they were suddenly surrounded by Ottoman troops and massacred to a man. Though Arslan succeeded in breaking through the Turkish lines, he was pursued and slain a few miles outside the town.

After this massacre it only remained to crush Silehdar in the South and Mustapha in the North. The former, who had made himself master of Janina, was easily disposed of, and all southern Albania was brought into subjection. Mustapha Pasha was less easy to deal with; but was finally conquered. After being severely defeated in Perlepe, he was besieged in Scutari and compelled to surrender. When the Turks acquired possession of new land they tried to establish their own system of administration by creating a local feudal system of what were called *Timar Ziamets* and *Beyleks*, which were grants of property carrying with them the obligation of providing a military force for the service of the state in case of need. A Timar contained from three to five hundred acres of land, and the owner, who was called a *Spahi* or Cavalier, was bound to supply a mounted cavalry-soldier for every three thousand aspers of his revenue. The Ziamets and the Beyleks were still larger grants of land. These fiefs were hereditary in the male line; and when a certain number of grants had been grouped together, the district was placed under an officer who bore the title of Sandjak bey. A bey is equivalent to a lieutenant colonel in the army; but the title is hereditary. Sandjak means a standard or flag, to which was generally attached the command of five thousand horses. To each Sandjak bey was given a horse's tail, as a distinctive mark of command; for with the Turks, who were originally a nomadic people, the horse was a symbol of power. The whole system of government was based on the idea of feudal tenure; the tenure of land on the condition of giving military service, and helping in the work of protection and government. With respect to political administration, the chief functions were entrusted to the Vizier. In the next degree, power was given to the *Kadiaskers*, who were two in number, one for Europe, and one for Asia. Their duties were legal; and under them were the *Khodja*, or tutors of the royal princes, the *Muftis* or expounders of the sacred law, and after the capture of Constantinople, the judge of that city. When these officers assembled in council, they formed the *Divan*. This deliberative body was attended by a chief secretary, the *Reis Effendi*, who frequently became an officer of great power and importance. The Grand Vizier sat at the head of the *Divan*, in the absence of the Sultan; but the Sultan himself was often present, and of course on those occasions he himself presided. The term Pasha, which means, "the Shah's foot," was originally given to Turkish subjects who had distinguished themselves in any way, though it is now generally associated with military command. A Pasha of three tails was one to whom had been presented three horses' tails as a token of exceptional power.

The territorial possessions of the conquering Ottomans were divided into: *church lands,* lands set apart for private property, and *domain lands.* The domain lands contributed to the support of the Sultan, and to the expenses of the state; and it was from these that the great feudal lords received the price of their military service. After a time, the demand for soldiers became so extreme, owing to the continual extension of the Empire, that a system of slavery was introduced, by which a fifth of the conquered races passed into a state of servitude to the victors. *Orchan,* the son and successor of *Othman,* began by taking annually a thousand Christian children, ranging from twelve to fourteen years of age, who were educated in the Mohammedan faith, and so trained that in after years they might be fitted for military, civil, or ecclesiastical employment.

The Turks are the most conservative people in the world, but the ruling Sultan Selim III, saw clearly that the old methods, which had been sufficient to give the most brilliant triumph to Turkey in the Middle Ages, were altogether inadequate to withstand the forces of Europe at the close of the 18th century. The nations of Christendom had been advancing for many generations, the Turks had been falling back, and the disproportion of resources was now alarmingly manifested. Various endeavors have been made to break down the barriers for the formation of an homogeneous Ottoman nation. The most earnest and important of these attempts were made under Abdul Medjid (1839-1861), who was supported by able and courageous Ministers and who were resolved to persevere in those schemes of regeneration which Mahmud had begun, but had very imperfectly carried out. On the 3rd of November, 1839, a *Hatti-Sherif*, solemnly issued at *Gulhané*, ratified and confirmed the civil reforms of the late sovereign, and added some others. By this measure, the Sultan guaranteed to all his subjects, without regard to rank or religion, security for person and property and promised to introduce a regular and impartial system of taxation, public administration of justice, the right of free transmission of property, an amelioration of the system of the conscription, and other improvements.

The great territorial divisions corresponding to different conquered nationalities were maintained till the latter part of the eighteenth century. Thus they officially called *Bulgaristan*, the land of the Bulgarians, *Arnaoutlek*, that of the Albanians, etc. But in 1861 by *"the law of the vilayets"* the immediate possessions of the Sultan were divided into vilayets (provinces), which were again subdivided into *sanjaks* or *mutesarifliks* (arrondissements), these into *kazas* (cantons) and the *kazas* into *nahies* (parishes or communes).[1] These were administered respectively by a *Vali* or governor-general, nominated by the Sultan, the *kaimakams*, *mutassarifs*,

---

[1] In 1865 Albania was divided into three vilayets, Janina, Monastir and Kossova. The northern part of the country was divided between the vilayets of Kossova, Monastir and Nish. Cf. **F. Gibert, Les Pays d'Albanie et leurs Histoire,** page 273.

defterdars and other administrators of the minor divisions. All these officials unite in their own persons the judicial and executive functions, under the *law of the Vilayets*, which purported to confer on the provinces large measure of self-government, in which both Musulmans and non-Musulmans should take part. In reality, however, it had the effect of centralizing the whole power of the country more absolutely than ever in the Sultan's hands, since the *Valis* were wholly in his undisputed power, which the ex-officio officials, members of the local councils secured a perpetual Turkish majority. Under such a system, and the legal protection enjoyed through it by the Ottoman functionaries against evil consequences of their own misdeeds, corruption was ripe throughout the empire.[1]

The Albanians realizing that these "reforms" were aiming to deprive them of their privileges, opposed them openly from the very beginning and the Turks found it difficult in carrying them out in Albania; but, in the middle of the nineteenth century a great army was sent against them, which devastated the country and expatriated a great number of its inhabitants.[2] After this the Porte abolished the hereditary native Pashalek and appointed Turkish Pashas to the

---

[1] In the middle of the fifteenth century, the Turks were in the main a virtuous race. The era of their depravity dates from their appearance in South Eastern Europe. In the Byzantine Empire of the middle ages, morals had fallen to the lowest point of degradation. The Greeks of those days were feeble, cowardly, cunning and dissolute, and they dragged down the Turks. The enormous corruption of the Turkish Empire in later times, the degradation of society in the chief cities of the Sultan, are due, not to anything naturally inherent in the Turkish race, but to the base example of the Greeks. The profligacy of the official world and of the upper classes, has eaten deeply into the political and social body of Turkey.

[2] About 25,000 Albanians were expatriated to Roumania. A record of their sojourn in Thrace survives in the names of **Arnaout Planina**, borne by one of the Rhodope ridges, by **Arnaout-keuy**, a suburban place of Constantinople, etc.

office throughout Albania. During the next half century several revolts occurred; but no organized movement of a strictly political character took place until the time of the San-Stefano and Berlin treaties of 1878.

The state of education in Turkey until 1846 was theological. The schools were attached to the mosques, and the whole system of instruction was managed by the priests whose conception of a school was a place where boys squatted upon the ground and recited the Koran by heart. But in that year an approach was made towards a system of secular education. In 1869 an Imperial *Iradé* promulgated an organic law of public instruction, which divided the schools of the Empire into two catagories, viz., public schools, which are placed exclusively under the control of the Government, and private schools, which are inspected by the Government, but depend on private enterprise, and are carried on for propaganda or business purposes. Almost all the nationalities had their private schools except the Albanians, who were not allowed to educate themselves in their own language.

The school under the supervision of the Patriarchate, of the "Greek Church"[1] engaged special privileges, which privileges were granted by *Mahomet II,* soon after he conquered and made Constantinople the capital of his Empire, when he issued a decree recognizing the Patriarch Gennadius and his successors not only as the spiritual head, but also as the civil chief of the Greek communities *(roum-milleti),* which embraced beside the Greeks by race, the Roumanians, the

---

[1] The title "**Greek Church**" is hardly an appropriate one. A community embracing several other nations, which rightly refuse to be known as Greeks, and in which, out of the sixty-six millions of its members, 59 million are **Slavonians**, and pray in the slavonic tongue; several millions are **Roumanians** and pray in the vernacular, etc., cannot properly be called Greek.

Serbians, the Bulgarians and the Albanians, which at this time were all Christians. This decree has put the *Orthodox Church* entirely under the control of the Greeks, who always exploited it as a political expression of their *"great idea,"* the restoration of the Byzantine Empire. They used it to fire the fanaticism of the Greeks—whose national consciousness was dead,—to promote the spirit of revolt against the Turks, to strengthen the movement for liberty and to assimilate the other Balkan nations, which were under its spiritual jurisdiction. Thus the "Greek Church" became a more serious obstacle to the national progress of all the other Balkan nationalities, a more dreadful tyrant, than the Turk himself.

The Government of the "Greek Church" is Episcopal with orders of Patriarch, bishops, priests, deacons, sub-deacons, etc. In the Turkish Empire it was divided into four metropolitan sees: Constantinople, Alexandria, Antioch and Jerusalem. Each of these is presided over by a Patriarch. All have equal rights, but special honor is conceded to the Patriarch of Constantinople. The latter presides over the *"Grand Synod,"* which is made up of the Bishops of the surrounding provinces. It is theirs to elect or rather nominate the Patriarchs. The full election waits upon the approval and confirmation of His Majesty the Sultan. He recognizes the Patriarch of Constantinople as the responsible head of the church and the medium of communication between the sovereign and the Greek people.

The spiritual courts in the east have permanently acquired jurisdiction in the matrimonial causes of baptized persons. The Patriarch of Constantinople was enabled to exercise an extensive criminal jurisdiction over the members of his church. He had his own court at *the Phanar,* and his own prison.

Long ago the chiefs of the Greeks like those of the Latin chiefs established regulations which they calculated to preserve at once its unity and the supremacy of themselves and their successors. They insisted on the ritual being in the Greek language, even amongst nations which understood not a word of Greek. They also outdid the Roman Pontiff, in ordaining that the upper clergy should invariably be of the Greek race and tongue. They recognized indeed, that purely Greek clergymen would be very useless as parish priests amongst Slavonian, Roumanian or Albanians, for the people would not have heeded a priest not speaking their tongue. A line of separation was drawn between the upper and lower clergy. The latter as parish priests, were confined to their humble task, and allowed to marry and mingle with the population.

When natives, they were recruited from the most ignorant class of people; persons who could not get an inspiration from the Holy Scripture for the uplift of their flock, persons even who could not read and understand the Bible. Many a time out of their ignorance the priests have performed the liturgy for a funeral when the occasion required a Te Deum, and vice-versa!

The bishoprics, abbacies, and all lucrative and authoritative positions, were reserved for the Greek clergy, who were brought up in convents, especially in those of Mount Athos, whence they issued to become bishops and archimandrits in Albania and elsewhere. In order that this foreign race of clergy might not be isolated in the countries where they were sent, convents were founded there of Greek monks, which became centers of Greek propaganda.

In 1856, after the Crimean war Sultan *Abdul Medjid*, issued an Imperial Decree granting to his Christian subjects equal rights with the Mohammedans and proclaiming liberty of conscience for all. This was a great event for all the nationalities of the Empire, for it granted them the right to throw off the oppression of the Greek Church. Two years later, while the Supreme Council of the Greek Patriarchate was in session, a petition was presented from the Bulgarian and Roumanian delegates demanding that bishops of their respective nationalities should be appointed for their dioceses, or such as have the language of the people and could conduct religious services in the vernacular; that the dioceses should have the right to recommend those whom they wished consecrated as bishops, and the Greek language should not be imposed upon the people in their churches and in their schools. All these demands were scornfully rejected by the Council saying that they were incompatible with the tenets of the Church, which recognizes no racial distinctions.

The question of using the Bible in translations which would be understood by the people was discussed again by the Greek clergy and by the entire Greek press in 1870, when the Bulgarians applied again to the Greek Patriarch to let them have their religious services in their own language. The Greek Church refused to grant this request, and when the Bulgarians put their language in their Churches, they were declared schismatics. The same question came up again in 1901, when the discussion was followed in Athens by a general student riot; and the "definitive" answer to this question was that the original text should remain the palladium of the *"Greek Orthodoxy,"* so long as a Greek people exists; that a translation of it, *even into modern Greek,* would be an unnecessary profanation; that the possession of the Testaments in ancient Greek is one of the special glories of the Churches of Constantinople and Athens and the other Hellenic Sees of the East; that, if a translation into modern Greek were sanctioned, the Greek division of the Eastern

Church would lose her quasi-premacy and Russia would come into undisputed supremacy; finally that the translation would be injurious to Hellenic national aspirations! This question came up for the fourth time in the spring of 1911 and the Greeks "settled" it by introducing an article into their new constitution. According to this article, "the text of the Holy Scripture" is maintained unchanged; the rendering thereof in *another linguistic form* without the previous sanction of the Greek Church in Constantinople is absolutely prohibited. In this article the words "the text of the Holy Scriptures" includes the *Septuagint* version of the Old Testament in ancient Greek. Before the new constitution was voted the new Testament only in modern Greek was prohibited, and that only by an administrative order. Now the *whole* Bible in any other linguistic form except ancient Greek is absolutely prohibited by an article of the 20th century Greek Constitution! The responsibilty for the prohibition appears to rest on the Patriarchate of Constantinople, but the introduction of the word *"also"* prevents even the Patriarchate of Constantinople from overruling the wishes of the Synod in Athens.

After the declaration of the Bulgarian schism, the Greek Patriarchate extended and fostered the measure of persecution against all its members. Even outside the realm of the church the Patriarchate inaugurated a policy of persecution against all those working or favoring any educational movement, which would help to enlighten the people through their vernacular. Particularly, the Patriarchate, hand in hand with the Turkish Government, made very active efforts to suppress the Albanian language altogether. Many persons have been excommunicated, imprisoned, exiled and even killed for posessing books or papers in the Albanian tongue. Needless to say that sermons in the Albanian language were

Vallona, the place where the Independence of Albania was proclaimed, November 28, 1912.

strictly prohibited under danger of excommunication or death.

At the same time strict orders were given to all schools of the Christian communities, throughout Albania to comply with their policy. A work published in Germany under the title *Macedonian Sketches* (Mittheilungen aus Macedonien), gives some interesting information on the establishment of teachers' schools and seminaries in Macedonia and Albania, after the model of German schools of this class. The founder of these institutions was *Dr. Demetrios Maroulis,* who after finishing his education in the German universities, was for some time director of the Greek Gymnasium at Salonica, and subsequently (1870) of that of Seres. Enthusiasm to strengthen the Hellenic propaganda in Macedonia and Albania induced Dr. Maroulis to resign his presidency and to devote himself entirely to this cause; and being assisted by the Patriarchate and by the Greek Government succeeded in establishing several male and female training schools for teachers of propaganda. Here the young Albanians were taught that they were Greeks; that they must speak Greek and that their mother tongue was only a nursery dialect for children or a barbarous *patois* for Turks.

Thus the churches and the schools under the jurisdiction of Patriarchate, instead of being centers of teaching and propagating the Christian doctrine of brotherhood among the people, became centers of persecution and propaganda, whose aim was to denationalize all the non-Hellenic nations. A few instances to illustrate the practice of this policy will not be out of place here. In 1904, the Greek church condemned to death and murdered two Albanians, *Rev. Christo H. Negovani* and *Rev. Vasil Negovani,* both priests of the Greek church. Their sin being the preaching of the Gospel in their mother tongue to their flock! In 1906 *Spiro Kosturi* of Kortcha, a prominent Albanian merchant, was secretly sentenced and murdered simply because he asked that the religious service of the marriage of his brother be performed in Albanian. *Rev. G. M. Tsilka* an Albanian preacher and teacher, on March 30th, 1907, was arrested and put in jail because one of his friends sent to him from Bucharest a letter written in his mother tongue! He was released in 1908, three days before the proclamation of the Turkish Constitution by the local revolutionary Committee because they needed his advice and assistance.

III.

ALBANIA DEFYING THE CONGRESS OF BERLIN.

I N the latter part of the autumn of 1876, the state of things in European Turkey, was such as to engage the most serious attention of every government of Europe. After a few months of diplomatic interventions the hope was given up that the Turkish authorities would remedy the anarchy and terrorism which filled the northern provinces. Meanwhile the sympathy of the Russian people in behalf of their Slavonian kindred, who were suffering from the Turkish misrule, had been roused to the highest pitch of intensity and so the government of Petrograd was forced to declare war upon Turkey on the 24th of April, 1877. On the 22nd of June the Russian troops crossed the Danube, and on the tenth of December the Turkish forces were completely defeated, at Plevna; and, about a month later, on the 20th of January, the grand *Duke Nicholas* of Russia entered Adrianople; and on the 3rd of March the treaty of San-Stefano was signed, which treaty contained the germ of the Balkan war.

This treaty of San-Stefano, however, was signed while the Russian armies were lying encamped at the gates of Constantinople, unresisted and unresistable, holding the Turkish government secure in their grasp. In other words this treaty was the dictation of a relentless power to a crushed and helpless state. The most important provisions of the San-Stefano treaty which are of interest to us are as follows: Montenegro became about three times as large as before, acquiring seven towns together with their beautiful little valleys, and also two seaports on the Adriatic, with the important valley which lies north of Scutari. Serbia gained four Albanian districts. By these two provisions Russia wanted to bring Montenegro into close continguity with Serbia, thus facilitating the eventual union of the Serbian race and by so doing to close the path of Austria towards the Aegean Sea.

But the most important article of the San-Stefano treaty is that which constituted the new principality of Bulgaria, which included almost all that was left of European Turkey, extending from the Danube to the Aegean Sea, and from the Black Sea to the Center of Albania. As soon as the provisions of the San-Stefano treaty were known, two important factors interfered in this matter, and more than half of the territory given by this treaty to the Slavic States was saved to Turkey. The first of these factors was England; the second was the Albanian National League.

Indeed, hardly had the Russian armies taken their position before Constantinople when they found themselves confronted by a British fleet, while the English government put forth its peremptory demand that the Russians should still hold themselves bound by the treaty of 1856 and submit the treaty of San-Stefano to a Congress of the European Powers. It seemed at first that this demand could not be considered; but wise and peaceful counsels at last prevailed and Russia yielded to the voice of Europe, and on the 14th of June, 1878, the Congress opened at Berlin.

On the other hand, the Albanians were made desperate by the provisions of the treaty of San-Stefano, by which more than half of their country was given to the Balkan states. Under the leadership of *Abdul Bey Frasheri, Hodo Bey* of Scutari *Waso Pasha* and *Prenk Bib Doda* of *Mirdita* formed a national league known as the League of Prizren, with the purpose of fighting to the last to preserve the integrity of their country. On the 17th of June, 1878, three

WASO PASHA OF SCUTARI

KEY TO THE NEAR EAST

hundred delegates were gathered from all over Albania at Prizren. The program of the National League was written by Waso Pasha. It was affirmed here that no portion of Albanian territory should be annexed to any other nation; that the *vilayets* of Scutari, Kossovo, Janina and Monastir should be formed into a single province, the administration of which should be given to a capable and honest governor, familiar with the country and the character and wants of the populace; that all branches of the administration should be confided to officials acquainted with the Albanian language; that the communal counsels, those of the *Sandjaks,* and the General counsel of the province should be elected by universal suffrage irrespective of race or religion; that the affairs of the country should be managed by its own councils; that Albanian should be the official language of the administration and of the tribunals, that a national militia of 200 battalions should be formed in which all those capable of bearing arms, should be enrolled without distinction of class or creed; that the League shall use all the power at its command to secure autonomy for Albania,[1] that it shall act for this object at the Courts of Europe as well as at the Congress of Berlin. These resolutions supported by the signatures of the Albanian delegates were presented to the Congress of Berlin, which had opened a few days before. But *Bismarck,* with his brutal disregard of facts which did not suit him, told the Albanian delegates that "There is no Albanian Nationality."

---

[1] **E. F. Knight,** who was visiting the country at that time writing of the movement of the Albanian League says, "The League has waxed too strong for the government who could not crush it now were it desirous of doing so. The Leaguesmen, feeling their strength, have extended their program. Defence of their native land against foreign invasion is now not their only cry, but autonomy and the shaking off of the Turkish yoke are boldly discussed in the Bazars of the garrisoned towns. To resist the advances of Austria on the North and Greece on the South are the avowed objects of the League."

Let us now leave for a moment the Albanian National League and consider briefly that part of the work of the Berlin Congress as it is of interest to us.

In the ninth sitting of the Congress held on the 29th of June 1878, the order of the day had relation in the first place to article fifteen of the treaty of *San-Stefano*, which referred to the Island of Crete, and the provinces bordering on the kingdom of Greece. The representatives of the Hellenic government were invited to make to the High Assembly the communication which they desired. As an exposition of the views of his government, *Mr. Delyannis,* Minister for foreign affairs, read a long communication, declaring that nothing more was sought than the annexation of Crete and the provinces bordering on the kingdom of Greece. The following is a summary of his communication:

The natives of the Greek provinces of the Ottoman Empire are counted by thousands; a great number occupy high positions in all branches of the administration, in the navy, and in the army; others not less numerous are distinguished by their commercial and industrial activity. The echo which the news of an Hellenic insurrection in Turkey produces in their hearts is too powerful not to move them. Some it drives to cross the frontiers to join the combatants; others, to empty their purses for the common cause. This excitement is rapidly communicated to all the inhabitants of the country although not natives of the fighting provinces; and the whole population of the kingdom which cannot forget what it owes to the former struggles of these disinherited brethren, nor remain impassive in view of their efforts for deliverance, rushes to join their ranks in order to assist them in reconquering their liberty; . . . Even if the government had the power of opposing a barrier to the national current, all these efforts would be without effect, by reason of the extent and conformation of the frontier line of the kingdom, which an army of a hundred thousand men would not be sufficient to guard, so as to be able to prevent the clandestine departure of volunteers. The situation created for the Hellenic Government by these insurrectional movements is not less diffi-

KEY TO THE NEAR EAST

cult and untenable from a financial point of view. The budget of the kingdom has often experienced, and is even now experiencing the influence of like events. However great and striking may be the difference between the budgets of public revenues, drawn up in 1829 by the president of Greece, and that of last year 1877, it is none the less true that the pecuniary assistance granted each time to refugees from the insurgent provinces and to the repatriated combatants, and the armaments caused by this abnormal situation, and by the somewhat strained relations with a neighboring state which have always resulted therefrom, have often swallowed up several millions, increased the public debt, and appropriated in fruitless outlay, the greater part of the public revenues which, if employed in the material development of the country would have greatly increased its resources and well being.

Mr. Rangabé presented some supplementary considerations and dwelt especially on the progress which had taken place in Greece since the proclamation of independence, as well as under difficulties which the smallness of the territory, the absence of natural frontiers and the permanent agitations of neighboring populations of the same race had perpetually opposed to the prosperity and development of the Hellenic kingdom. After a few words from Prince Bismarck, who promised that the Greek memorandum should be printed, distributed, and that the Congress would examine it with attention, Messrs. Delyannis and Rangabé retired.

At the 13th meeting of the Congress the boundaries of Greece formed the chief subject of consideration. On the fifth of July 1878, article fifteen of the treaty of San Stefano was passed under review. After delivering an address calling attention to the serious evils which resulted from the incomplete formation of the Hellenic kingdom Mr. Waddington, in common with the First Plenipotentiary of Italy, submitted a resolution by which their Congress invited the sublime Porte to arrange with Greece for a rectification of frontiers in *Thessaly* and *Epirus,* and expressed an opinion that this rectification should follow the valley of the *Salambria* (The ancient Peneus) on the side of the Aegean Sea, and that of the *Kalama* on the side of the Ionian Sea. It was also proposed that to facilitate the success of the negotiations the powers should offer to mediate between the two parties. To these suggestions, Turkey, not unnaturally, objected; for she was about to lose much territory and could hardly be expected to contemplate with satisfaction the loss of more. The opinion of Congress, however, was in favor of the French proposal and *Lord Beaconsfield* supported it in a speech. He characterized the frontier traced in 1831, as insufficient and imperfect and observed that in the eyes of every competent statesman this frontier was a danger and a disaster as well for Turkey as for Greece. He looked upon the boundary proposed by the first Plenipotentiary of France, however, *as open to discussion;* but harmony being above all things desirable he would withdraw his objections in presence of unanimous vote of the other powers. The proposal of the Italian and French Plenipotentiaries having been submitted to the suffrages of the High Assembly, *Karatheodori Pasha* declared that he had no instructions from his government as to any rectification of the Greek frontier. He accordingly reserved the opinion of the Sublime Porte upon this point, but all the other powers agreed in accepting the proposition.

The Ottoman Plenipotentiaries as above stated declared at Berlin Congress that the Porte reserved to itself the right of explaining to the powers what they regarded as the real condition of affairs concerning Greece; and in accordance with this reservation a Turkish circular was issued on the 8th of August. The substance of which is as follows:[1]

---

[1] This circular was called for by a note from the Greek government dated July 17th, requesting the Porte to nominate commissioners in com-

The Turkish government conceived it had a right to affirm that the abstention of Greece from any direct act of hostility towards Turkey was due not merely to regard for the counsels and promises of certain European powers, but more especially to the constant defeat of all its measures for getting itself guaranteed against the results of such an enterprise. Yet it was now demanded by Greece that *Epirus, Thessaly*, and the Island of Crete should be annexed to the kingdom; and this requirement was justified by arguments which the Turkish Government entirely repudiated. Such a demand contradicted all the principles of political right and rested on entirely erroneous historical data. . . .

It was alleged by the Greeks that the provinces of *Epirus* and *Thessaly* had for many years been plunged into a state of suffering, discontent, and effervescence. In opposition to this statement the Turkish Government affirmed that from 1829, when the Feudal system was abolished, to 1853, the provinces in question had lived in perfect tranquility excepting only for a brief period in 1845 when the Moslem population of lower Albania arose in rebellion—a rebellion which was soon quelled. In 1853, said the Turkish dispatch, *Epirus* and *Thessaly* were invaded by two Greek army corps which laid the country waste and perpetrated on the property and persons of the Christians themselves, whom they pretended they had come to deliver, such excesses as compelled France and England to occupy the *Piraeus* in order to put an end to them. Again after fifteen years of quiet, these two provinces were troubled afresh with hostile attempts publicly prepared under the eyes of the Hellenic Government. Bands of volunteers crossed from Greece to *Thessaly* and *Epirus*, carrying into those countries fire and sword, obliging the inhabitants, as the Imperial government is prepared to prove, to rise against their lawful rulers; but finally failed before the wisdom and loyalty of all the people. It was, in view of these failures, that the government of his Hellenic Majesty, discour-

---

mon with the Hellenic Cabinet to settle the question of the boundaries. Turkey made no direct answer to this note, but the circular of August 8th was apparently intended as an indirect reply. At the outset it was remarked that the cabinet of Athens had endeavored to prove that it was owing to the counsels and assurances of some of the great powers that it had abstained during a long period of time from any act of agression against the estates of the Sultan, hoping in this way to show that the powers would have thus paralyzed the action of Greece, were now its debtors and loyally bound to support the Hellenic claims.

aged by the inflexible refusal of Russia to give Greece a share in the fruit of her victories, and feeling that opportunities slipping away caused its army to invade Ottoman territory without rupture of diplomatic relations and in full peace, in order to secure what Mr. Delyannis called the objects of the National Aspirations. It was contended by Safvet Pasha, the Turkish foreign minister, that the inhabitants of *Epirus* and *Thessaly* had always lived in peace under the Ottoman authorities; that they had never taken up arms to assert supposititious claims; that they had some times endured, but never invoked, the intervention of a neighboring country, and that if rendered secure from the enterprises set on foot by that neighbor, they would continue to live happily and prosperously under the laws of the Ottoman Empire. Greece had contended that by giving *Epirus* and *Thessaly* to her, Europe would close forever the era of struggles and conflicts between that kingdom and the Turkish Empire and would thus consolidate its work of peace. But Mr. Delyannis, the Greek minister of foreign affairs, and the chief representative of his country at the Congress, had taken pains to deprive this argument of all credibility and force by letting it be understood at the very outset of his communication to the High Assembly, that the true and only wishes of the Hellenic Government were and always had been to unite under the same sway all countries inhabited by Greeks.

It was therefore evident that even if her present demands were allowed, similar claims would speedily be made in respect of other provinces. Such, concluded Safvet Pash, are the chief facts and conditions which impose on the Sublime Porte the duty of appealing to Europe itself from the opinion expressed in the Congress concerning the granting to Greece of some additional territory.

The Sultan and his government were convinced that the Great Power would modify their first opinion, and would urge on the cabinet of Athens counsels of rectitude and prudence, calculated to turn it from an enterprise equally unjust and impolitic.

The arguments contained in this Turkish dispatch were warmly upheld by some influential parties in England, saying that if Greece had joined in the late war, as Serbia and

KEY TO THE NEAR EAST 63

Roumania had done, and had obtained definite successes, the demand for a rectification of the frontier would have been reasonable. But a country which has taken no part in the war has no grounds to come forward at the close and say, "I must have this or that province in satisfaction of what I believe to be my rights." The Greek argument that Greece was entitled to receive something on account of her generosity in abstaining from a junction with the enemies of Turkey was absurd. She had every disposition to join in the crusade, and that she abstained was due not so much to the discussion of England as to the fear of consequences, if the issue should be against her and if Russia (as was highly probable) should decline to support her cause. The demand for *Thessaly, Epirus* and *Crete,* was a request that Turkey, without being under any military compulsion so far as Greece was concerned should make that power a present of three large and valuable provinces without getting anything in return. If the same requisition had been made of any other Power in the world, its absurdity would have been universally acknowledged, but for many years past it has been the custom to make Turkey an exception to all rules and to deal with her on assumptions which in the West of Europe would be condemned as at once dishonest and ridiculous.

Greece, however, was not disposed to give up her cause without making an effort to obtain success. On the 7th of September, the Hellenic Government, sent a circular note to the six Powers, soliciting their mediation, in order that the provisions of the treaty of Berlin might be carried into effect. The Grand Vizier had told the Greek Government that the Porte could not act upon the invitation of Greece before receiving from the Powers an answer to its recent despatch. "This evasive reply," said the Greek circular, "is calculated to prejudice any understanding between the two Governments as regards the execution of the decision formed by the Congress, and tends to drive the Hellenic Government into a vicious circle, by placing insurmountable difficulties in its path. In the presence of this attitude of the Porte, the Greek Government considers that the time has arrived for addressing itself to the Powers who have the right of mediation." The appeal did not meet with a very warm reception at the time. England was disinclined to take any immediate action, and the other Powers were apparently not willing to move without the concurrence of the British Government. The proposed cession to Greece sanctioned by the Congress included the greater part of *Thessaly* and *Epirus,* though not the whole of these provinces; but the demands of Greece went farther; their demands seemed to have a faculty of endless growth.

The question, after going to sleep for a while, was revived in the later autumn, when the French Cabinet made proposals for joint action on the part of the six Powers, with a view to obtaining from the Porte a recognition of the principle that the Greek frontiers ought to be rectified. The suggestions contained in this circular were accepted by Italy, Germany and Russia, and urgent representations were made by France and Italy, combined, to induce the Porte to yield. In response to these solicitations the Turkish Ministry evinced some willingness to grant a slight rectification of the Turko-Greek frontier; but the Greek demands underwent no abatement, and even exceeded what had been sanctioned by the Congress, for the Government of Athens required the district of Janina, the capital of southern Albania, which was north of the line traced out by the assembled Powers.

After a time on the 15th of November 1878, the Porte was privately warned by one of the Ambassadors that it was

KEY TO THE NEAR EAST

about to receive a reminder in the form of identical notes from all the Powers simultaneously. Under the stress of this intimation, the Turkish Government appointed delegates for discussing the question of the Greek frontier; but being really disinclined for action, Turkey entered on a series of pretext and delays.

Finally the Greco-Turkish commission for the delimitation of the frontier met in 1879, first at Preveza, and subsequently at Constantinople; but the conferences were without any result. The Turkish commissioners declined the boundary suggested at Berlin, saying that the territory is inhabited entirely by Albanians and strengthening their argument by calling attention to the Albanian National League, which had assumed a menacing attitude. Greece then invoked the arbitration of the Powers and the settlement of the question was undertaken by a conference of ambassadors at Berlin (1880). The line approved by the conference was practically that suggested by the Congress; but Turkey again refused to accept for the reason already mentioned above. The Greek army was mobilized; but at this time nothing could be gained by an appeal to arms, as the Powers were not prepared to apply coercion to Turkey. Finally the demarcation was entrusted in July 1881, by a convention, to a commission representing the six Powers and the two interested parties. The line drawn ran westwards, from a point between the mouth of the *Peneus* and *Platamona*, the course of the river Arta to its mouth. An area of 13,395 square kilometres, with a population of 300,000 souls was thus added to the kingdom of Greece; while the city of Janina, Metzova and about half of the Southern Albania was saved to our country, which was due to the patriotic movement of the Albanian National League.

Serbia was recognized as a free and independent state, by

the treaty of Berlin and her boundaries received certain modifications from those outlined in the San-Stefano treaty, that is, all the territory given to her by the San-Stefano treaty except the Novi-Bazar section, which was restored to Turkey.

Bulgaria, the province lying north of the Balkans and extending west to the new boundary of Servia, was constituted by the Berlin Treaty a semi-independent principality, on the same footing formerly occupied by Serbia.

The so-called "Central Bulgaria," the district south of the Balkans, of which Philipopolis is the capital, was constituted an autonomous province subject to the Sultan under the name of *Eastern Roumalia*. Thus the Berlin Treaty reduced the territory of Bulgaria to about one-half of what was accorded to her in the San-Stefano Treaty.

The Treaty of Berlin recognized Montenegro as free and independent, and besides this gave to it the towns of *Nikshitch, Shpuzh, Podgoritza, Plava, Gusinje* and the seaport of *Antivari;* but restored to Turkey half of the territory of the *Novi-Bazar* district, and *Dulcigno* with the valley north of Scutari. The resistance of the Albanian National League to annexation of the territories above mentioned led to long negotiations.

To quell the Albanian agitation, the Sultan sent *Mehmet Ali* as extraordinary Commissioner. On the 6th of September 1878, he arrived at Jakova, where he found the greatest excitement prevailing among the inhabitants. He was violently upbraided with having come to hand over the country to the Serbians. The agitation went on increasing and the house selected by Mehmet Ali for a lodging was set on fire by the Albanians of Jakova and Ipek. This done, there arose between the incendiaries and Mehmet Ali's escort a regular fight in the course of which twenty of the latter's men fell. Towards evening the struggle spread and resulted in the death of the Marshal's adjutant and several officers, and the house in which they had taken refuge was fired. Mehmet Ali succeeded in escaping from the burning building and concealing himself near by; but his hiding place was soon discovered and he too was put to death.

In April, a proclamation was issued by the leaders of the Albanian League, declaring that Europe had created a principality for the Bulgarians, had delivered *Bosnia* and *Herzegovina* to Austria, had endowed Serbia and Montenegro with increased territory and independence, and had given Roumalia autonomy; but Albania had received nothing. The Albanians, it added, must claim the right to create a state for themselves. The paper was signed by *Ali Pasha* and other influential representatives of the Albanians. A conference was held at Scutari, May 29, when the party which was adverse to offensive action and willing to await the decision of the Powers, proved to be predominant, and it was decided to address another memorandum to the consular corps. At the same time the representatives of the Albanian League sent a dispatch to Mr. Gladstone congratulating him on his appointment as First Minister of the Crown, and invoking "the exalted protection of the English nation for the cause of their territorial integrity and the preservation of their rights, to which they had devoted their efforts and their life."

Later the Albanian League sent a message to the conference at Berlin, saying that its members would never consent to the dismemberment of their country, or to an exchange by which they might be subjected to foreign rule.

The Italian diplomat, *Mr. Corti,* suggested a compromise

which was agreed to by a conference of the Powers at Constantinople (April 18, 1880). According to the *"Corti Compromise"* Plava and *Gusinje* were to be restored to Turkey while the Montenegro frontier was extended so as to include the *Hoti* and the greater part of the *Klementi* clans. These were Catholics, and Mr. Corti thought that they would be glad to be a part of the Montenegrin kingdom. The suggestion was accepted by the Powers, but was received by the Albanians with indignation, and bodies of men were promptly stationed at points commanding those places to prevent their occupation. At the same time necessary preparations were made to formally ask the Powers to recognize the independence of their country.

The Porte resolved to take severe measures against the Albanians and the suppression of the Albanian League was ordered in December. Agitation again broke out in northern Albania near the end of that month, when the men liable to military service refused to obey the conscription regulations, and the order to call out the reserves remained without effect. Turkish functionaries at Prizren, Uskup and Ipek were dismissed and replaced by Albanians, and the League issued a summons calling the male population to arms. The year ended with the authority of the Porte seriously compromised. The proceedings of the conference at Berlin, and the action of the Powers with reference to it, were watched by the Porte, with strict attention, and an evident disposition to make the most of every defect in form or substance of its decisions, and to take advantage of any sign that might appear of disagreement or of interruption to the European concert. The conference adopted a note to be presented by the Powers as a collective one, describing the territory that should be allotted to Montenegro, defining the line which should be followed as to the boundary of Greece, so as to give it a large part of *Thessaly* and *Epirus*, etc. This note was presented to the Porte, July 15th, 1880, by *Count Hatzfeld*, the German Ambassador. Great excitement had prevailed on the subject among the Turkish population of Constantinople and in court circles, but things had begun to calm down, and the disposition of the Sultan and his Ministers was more conciliatory than when the conference first met. Still, the communication was far from being pleasant, and many of its demands were extremely disagreeable. The Porte replied that it objected to ceding Janina, Metzovo and Larissa to Greece, as well for strategical reasons as on the ground of nationality; but was willing to make concession to the Hellenic kingdom; and it hoped that the Powers would not deny its right to take part in the uttermost of the Greek frontier, as it had done in those of Serbia and Montenegro, and that they would authorize the representatives at Constantinople to treat with it concerning these and other questions. A second collective note was addressed to the Porte, declining to reopen the discussion, and insisting upon the resolutions of the conference, but expressing the willingness of the Powers to receive the proposals of the Porte as to the manner in which the territory should be evacuated and handed over. Before a reply to this note was received, the Powers had instituted a grand naval demonstration in the waters of the Adriatic under *Admiral Seymour* to enforce the surrender of *Dulcigno* to Montenegro. On the 17th of September the Porte addressed a note to its representatives abroad, explaining what it had done to overcome the objections of the Albanians to the ceding of territory and to secure the execution of the demands of the Powers, and complaining of their urgency and uncompromising attitude. On the 4th of October the Turkish Government presented a note to the Ambassadors, undertaking to induce the local population of

Dulcigno to consent to the cession to Montenegro, but disavowing all complications that might arise from the failure of the attempt; declaring it impossible to give to Greece the territory designated by the conference, and suggesting another boundary which it would establish within a hundred days, promising certain reforms. The Powers presented their ultimatum on the next day, and on the 11th of November the Porte made a positive agreement to deliver Dulcigno to Montenegro. Evidently the Sultan was glad now to be asked by the Powers to send troops against the Albanian National League, which was working not only to defend the integrity, but also to obtain formal recognition for the Independence of Albania. After many battles between the troops of the Albanian National League and the Turkish troops the Albanians were defeated on the 22nd of November and on the 25th Montenegro obtained possession of Dulcigno. The last battle between the Albanians and the Turkish troops was fought at *Koshara,* a village near Prizren, where four thousand Albanians were defeated by thirty thousand Turks, the leaders of the movement were arrested and sent to exile.

The movement of the Albanian National League has laid the corner stone for the Independence of Albania. It made it clear to all the Powers that they were wrong in their decisions and later, after thousands of lives had been wasted, they were forced to recede from the position they had taken in ignorance, and acknowledge that both Scutari and Janina, the former coveted by Montenegro, the latter by Greece, were Albanian territories as well as Monastir and Kossovo.[1]

---

[1] The Independence of Abania, though not expressly recognized, had been tacitly admitted by diplomacy over and over again, as by Russia for instance, in the partition planned at San-Stefano; and by England in dropping the cession of **Epirus** to Greece proposed at Berlin. (**Nationalism and the War in the Near East, by a Diplomatist,** p. 343.)

The Treaty of Berlin was of course made the subject of animated debates in all Houses of Parliament of the Great Powers. The discussion in the House of Lords took place on July 18th when a numerous assemblage crowded to hear the Premier's explanation. In laying on the table of the House the Protocols of the Congress of Berlin, *Lord Beaconsfield* delivered an address, in which he minutely reviewed all the features of the Treaty.

With respect to Greece, Lord Beaconsfield said that the Porte had exhibited every disposition to treat the Hellenes in a liberal manner; but the views entertained at Athens were such as Turkey could not be expected to favor. The Greeks evidently desired Constantinople for their capital, and although the Congress recommended Turkey to grant a considerable accession of territory to the little kingdom, the Plenipotentiaries did not find on the part of its representatives the response, which they desired. The minds of those representatives were in another quarter, said Lord Beaconsfield, and it was impossible to meet the *extravagant demands made by Greece, demands which were not in any way within the scope of the Congress, or the area of its duty.*

At first, England supported Greece, but seeing that the Hellenic Government had formulated demands with a peculiar faculty of endless growth withdrew her valuable assistance. On the other hand the British Government, realizing the justice of the Albanian claims, strove to create a strong Independent Albania, including within her boundaries *Kossova, Scutari, Janina* and the greater part of *Monastir* vilayet. *Lord Goschen* and *Lord E. Fitzmaurice,* both foreseeing the importance of the Albanian question worked hard for this end. Had they succeeded, many recent complications and much bloodshed and misery would have been prevented. But unfortunately the Powers could not come to an agreement, so they contented themselves merely with a recommendation for certain administrative reforms for the Turkish Provinces, which were never put into practice.

The Balkan states were very much disappointed with the provisions of the Treaty of Berlin, but none of them gave up the idea of gaining sometime in the future what they thought belonged to them.

With this hope in their hearts they started new schools of propaganda throughout Macedonia and in Albania; and, at the same time, the Greek and Bulgarian churches were doing their part of the work for the realization of the ideal of their respective nations. The Bulgarians worked thus peacefully until 1893, when a number of secret revolutionary societies were set on foot in Macedonia, and in 1896 simliar bodies were organized as legal corporations in Bulgaria. The fall of *Stambouloff* in that year and the reconciliation of Bulgaria with Russia encouraged the revolutionaries in the belief that Russia would take steps to revive the provisions of the San-Stefano Treaty. In 1895 the *"Supreme Macedo-Adrianopolitan Committee"* was formed at Sofia and forthwith dispatched armed bands into northern Macedonia, the town of *Melnik* was occupied for a short time by the revolutionaries under the famous *Boris Sarafoff*, but the enterprise ended in failure.

Meanwhile the "Centralist," or local Macedonian societies, were welded by two remarkable men, *Damian Grueff* and *Cotze Delcheff*, into a formidable power known as the *"Internal Organization,"* which was founded in 1893 and which maintained its own police, held its own tribunals, assessed and collected contributions and otherwise exercised an *imperium in imperio* throughout the country.

It is said that this Internal Organization aimed at the attainment of Macedonian autonomy and at first endeavored

KEY TO THE NEAR EAST

to enlist the sympathies of the Greeks and Serbians for the programme of "Macedonia for the Macedonians," but this was only to throw ashes in the eyes of their adversaries. The principle of autonomy was suspected at Athens and Belgrade, as calculated to insure Bulgarian predominance and to delay or preclude the ultimate partition of the country. At Athens especially the progress of the Bulgarian movement was viewed with much alarm; it was feared that Macedonia would be lost to Hellenism, and in 1896 *"the National Board"* sent numerous bands into the southern districts of the country. The Board aimed at bringing about a war between Greece and Turkey and the outbreak of trouble in Crete enabled it to accomplish its purpose. During the Greco-Turkish war Macedonia remained quiet, Bulgaria and Serbia refraining from interference under the pressure from Austria, Russia and the other great Powers. The reverses of the Greeks were to the advantage of the Bulgarian movement.

Contemporaneously with a series of Russo-Bulgarian celebrations in the *Shipka* pass in September 1902, an effort was made by *Colonel Yankoff* to provoke a rising in the Monastir vilayet. In November a number of bands entered the *Razlog* district under the personal direction of *General Zoncheff*. These movements ended in failure because they did not have the support of the population.

The state of the country became now such as to necessitate the intervention of the Powers, and the Austrian and Russian governments, which had acted in concert since April, 1897, drew up an elaborate scheme of reforms. The Porte, as usual endeavored to forestall foreign interference by producing a project of its own, which was promulgated in November, 1902, and *Hilmi Pasha* was appointed Inspector General of the Rumelian vilayets and charged with its application. The two Powers, however, persevered in their intention and on the 21st of February, 1903, they presented to the Porte an identical memorandum proposing a series of reforms in the administration, police and finance, including the employment of *"foreign specialists"* for the reorganization of the *gendarmerie*.

Meanwhile the Bulgarians, who did not wish the application of reforms, because the reforms if applied would have cleared up things and would have shown that the Bulgarians were not the only people of "Macedonia," made rapid preparation for an insurrection. At the end of April a number of dynamite outrages took place at Salonica. On the 2nd of August a general insurrection broke out in Monastir vilayet, followed by sporadic revolts in other districts. The insurgents achieved some temporary success and occupied the towns of *Krushevo, Klisura* and *Neveska,* but by the end of September their resistance was overcome.

The Austrian and the Russian governments then drew up a further series of reforms known as the *"Murzsteg programme"* (Oct. 9, 1903), to which the Porte assented in principle, though many difficulties were raised over details. Two officials, an Austrian and Russian, called *"Civil agents"* and charged with the supervision of the local authorities in the application of reforms, were placed by the side of the inspector-general, while the reorganization of the *gendarmerie* was entrusted to a foreign general in the Turkish service, aided by a certain number of officers from the armies of the great Powers. The latter task was entrusted to the Italian general *De Giorgio* (April, 1904). The reforms proved a failure mainly because they did not do justice to the Albanian element and because of the deplorable financial situation.

In 1905 the Powers agreed upon the establishment of a financial commission in which the representatives of Great

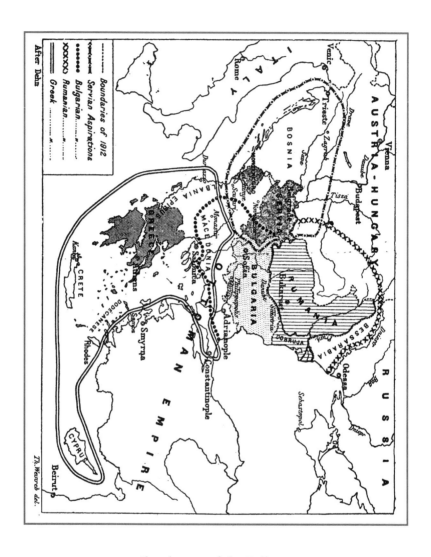

Sketch map of the Balkans.
Showing the conflicting aspirations of the Balkan nations.

KEY TO THE NEAR EAST 75

Britain, France, Germany and Italy could sit as colleagues of the *civil agents*. The Porte offered an obstinate resistance to the project and only yielded (December 5) when the fleets of the Powers appeared near the *Dardanelles*. Some improvement was now effected in the financial administration. But soon the Greeks interfered by dispatching numerous bands largely composed of Cretans into the southern districts, the Serbians displayed renewed activity in the north while the Bulgarians offered a dogged resistance to all their foes, everyone doing their best to prove to Europe that Macedonia at the same time was theirs.

In support of their claims the Bulgarians, the Greeks and the Serbians, besides their bands, their schools and their churches drew up statistics regarding the population of Macedonia, a comparison of which is very amusing.

	Gobchevitch Serb.	Kantcheff Bulg.	Nicolaides Greek.
Turks	231,400	489,664	576,000
Bulg.	51,600	1,184,036	454,700
Serb.	2,048,320	700	
Greeks	201,140	222,152	656,300
Alb.	165,620	124,211	None
Wlacks	74,465	77,267	41,200
Various	101,875	147,224	91,700
Total	2,880,420	2,248,224	1,820,500

The Austro-Russian Entente came to an end in the beginning of 1908; and owing to the Austrian project of connecting the Bosnian and Macedonian railway systems, Great Britain and Russia now took the foremost place in the demand for reforms. After a meeting between *King Edward VII* and *Emperor Nicholas II* at *Reval,* in the early summer of 1908, an Anglo-Russian scheme, known as the *"Reval pro-*

gramme" was announced. The project aimed at more effective European supervision and dealt especially with the administration of justice.

The "Reval programme" scared the young Turks and they decided to make an effort to overthrow the despotic rule of the Sultan Hamid, and so save Turkey. The Albanians were invited to join them against Hamid; they were promised full educational and religious freedom, and were told that the new regime would build roads, that it would erect schools and hospitals throughout Albania.

The *rôle* played by the Albanians in this movement for the reformation of Turkey was of utmost importance. A brief statement of facts as they occurred will clearly show this.

I quote two of the first dispatches, which brought to the world the news of this revolution. One said, *"One hundred thousand Albanians are for constitution."* Another said, *"The true reason for his (Sultan's) concern is first of all, the revolt of the Albanians upon whose loyalty he blindly relied, and to which he sacrificed so much."*

On the other hand, every one who followed the events knows that the uprising began at *Resna. Niazi Bey,* who was an Albanian, the commander of the Resna garrison, left the town, together with his soldiers, after he had taken away everything of value for the movement. Soon after this, the general commander of the third army corps, *Semshi Pasha,* being informed of Niazi's step sent a battalion for the suppression of the uprising. It must be remembered also that the third army corps was mainly Albanian with regard to officers as well as men. The battalion, after marching several hours, returned to Monastir reporting that they could not find the rebels. It was not difficult for a general like Semshi Pasha to guess that there was an understanding between *"his"* battalion and the rebels, and that the uprising of Resna would be followed by others. He went at once to the telegraph office to inform the Sultan, and to ask him for new orders and assistance, for he could no longer trust his soldiers. At this time the officers condemned Semshi Pasha, and the death sentence was immediately executed at the door of the telegraph office. *Marshal Osman Pasha,* commander in the vilayet of Monastir, was abducted during the night and carried off to Ochrida, in Albania, where he was a prisoner of Niazi Bey. As soon as the Sultan heard of these events, he appointed *Osman Pasha* to succeed Semshi Pasha, ordering him to call all the rebels together and to tell them that the Sultan did not wish to punish them, but instead that he would promote all those who would obey his orders. It is clear enough that the Sultan did not yield at once, for he thought at first that it was but a movement of the young Turk party, and of these he had little fear. He tried to repress the rebellion by using the Albanian forces. It was at this time when the Sultan and his *Camerilla* were intending to use the Albanian and to put down the uprising of the young Turk party as they thought it was the case,— that they received the famous telegram from these one hundred thousand Albanians, saying "We demand a constitution." It was then that the Sultan yielded. Albania was taken as the scene for the beginning of the revolution because the leaders were residents of Albania, and because they could blindly trust the Albanians, now that their *"besa-besen,"* or word of honor, was given.

The beginning of the new *regime* was a very happy one. The Constitution was proclaimed throughout the Empire with great joy, the Young Turkish party promising to solve all difficulties and pacify all hatreds by substituting justice for arbitrary rule, and freedom for despotism. First and foremost, it proclaimed complete equality between the different nationalities inhabiting Turkey.

The Albanian leaders instead of waiting to be helped, preferred to help themselves, and thus at once were actively engaged in the noble work of enlightening the nation. During the first ten months of the Constitutional Government, four national congresses were held; sixty-six national clubs were founded, thirty-four day schools and twenty-four night schools were opened, fifteen literary societies, three musical societies were formed, four printing presses established and eleven newspapers issued. After five centuries of struggle, the people began to breathe free and to endow themselves with the blessings of education.

But it was merely a dream, which lasted only a moment! The Young Turks, whose real programme was the othomanization of the non-Turkish nationalities of the Empire, and *not liberty, fraternity* and *equality,* could not stand this rapid progress of the Albanians, and determined to stop it. A beginning was made in 1909, when they tried to close the clubs by violating the article of the Constitution, which proclaimed the liberty of associations. The Albanians protested declaring that they would defend their rights with the force of arms. A powerful army under the command of *Djavid Pasha* was sent to disarm the Albanians of the district of *Luma;* but only the low-lands were occupied, while the distinguished Albanian patriot and chieftain, *Issa Boletini* (whom foreign money could not purchase; whom foreign decorations could not subdue; whom foreign guns could not scare), fought most valiantly on the highland borders. In April, of the following year, 15,000 Albanians **gathered** at Prishtina, delivered an ultimatum to the Committee, the main complaints being against service in Asia, against their policy of stopping the private educational movement of the country, destruction of the towers and the census. In other words the Albanians were fighting for their lives, their liber-

CONSTANTINE CHRISTOPHORIDHI.
The translator of the Bible

JOHN VRETO

ties and their land. As a reply the Committee of *"Union and Progress,"* sent another force of 50,000 men, regulars and irregulars, under *Torgut Pasha* which invaded the mountains of Northern Albania. There was severe fighting in the neighbourhood of Tuzi; fearful devastation and unspeakable atrocities being committed especially upon old men, women and children. The Albanian mountaineers were driven across the border in thousands, thus forcing them to take refuge with their old enemies, the Montenegrins. In the spring of 1911 the *Malesori* returned from Montenegro and soon the revolution became general. The Young Turks were obliged to grant the demands of the *Malesori*, which amounted to a practical recognition of the Independence of Albania. But the Turks broke faith again, and again in 1912 the Albanians revolted. In summer the revolt bore fruit which exceeded all expectations. The cabinet resigned, the chamber was dissolved, the executive committee of "Union and Progress" threatened with complete defeat, was compelled to grant the Albanians all they asked. Thus the campaign of Torgut Pasha proved after all to be the war of liberation of the Albanian people. This show of weakness on the part of Turkey encouraged the Balkan States the more so that the Young Turks by their foolish policy, lost now the sympathy and the invaluable support of the Albanians. Under the auspices of Tsarist Russia the Balkan League was formed and war against Turkey was declared hastily, to oppose the plan of a *"great Albania,"* covering the *vilayets* of Scutari, Kossovo, Monastir and Janina dividing it among themselves. This was the real cause of the Balkan war, and not as it was then announced so loudly— the disinterested wish of the Balkan Allies to liberate Macedonia and Albania.

IV.

THE MIGHTY POWER OF THE SPELLING BOOK.

N ancient times the Albanians have enjoyed a considerable amount of civilization. *Dr. Hahn* in his monumental work on Albania *(Albanische Studien),*[1] tells us that the Pelagians—this is the ancient name of the Albanians—were the distinguished architects of the Balkan Peninsula, and he ascribes to them all of the most ancient monuments of architecture and pottery, etc., found in Greece and the rest of the Balkan lands. He further says that they were writing their language in the *Phoenician Alphabet.* Later, the Greeks borrowed from the Albanians this alphabet as well as many of their conceptions of myths, rules of reason, etc., and began to speculate[2] on them.

Endowed with such splendid natural inclination for civilization and learning the Albanians would have developed a literature of their own, but events which have been arising continuously from the fact that Albania is the key to the Near East, have forced them to spend almost all their time in war. For official business the Albanians, as all other nations used the Greek language till the Middle Ages, when they began to write in Latin.

As soon as 1626, A. D. the Albanians began to write their own language. In that year a learned Albanian, *Bogdanus,*

---

[1] **Albanische Studien**, is a vast storehouse of facts of every conceivable description; archæology and philology predominating. Everything is there treated from the earliest origin of the people in the old prehistoric period down to their modern descendants, the Albanians.

[2] No man is more dependent on the opinion of others, or on obtaining from abroad the raw material of culture for the industry of his intellect than the Greek. Cf. **Nationalism and War in the Near East, by a Diplomatist.**

GEORGE D. KYRIAS.
Editor of the Bashkimie Kombit.

GERASIM D. KYRIAS.
The Founder of the first Albanian Girls' School.

KEY TO THE NEAR EAST

archbishop of Uskup, published in Venice, *"Imitatio Christi,"* in Albanian, using the Latin Alphabet. Later, a teacher *Theodore of Elbassan,* who was the first pioneer to attempt a scholarly study of his language in his *Lexicon Tetraglossan,* Latin, Greek, Wallachian and Albanian claimed for the Albanian language a place among the languages of Europe. He employed the old Alphabet[1] used by his ancestors, the Pelasgians. Theodore's life ambition was to establish an Albanian press in its native town, and accordingly he worked and saved and finally was able to give an order to the Wallachian printers of Moschopolis,[2] for a supply of Albanian types. The order was duly executed, and the Albanian pioneer, excited with joy seeing his patriotic dream to approach its realization, went in person to Moschopolis to take and escort the types to Elbassan. Theodore's concern regarding their safety was so great that it made the Wallachian muleteers believe that the heavy boxes contained money, and taking counsel among themselves they murdered him.

Fifty years later, another Albanian, *Naoum Vekilarxhi,* published a few little booklets using another Alphabet. These booklets were widely spread all over southern Albania and aroused a great deal of anxiety amongst the high clergy

---

[1] Evidently there arose some difficulty among the followers of archbishop Bogdanus and those of the teacher Theodore, as to what was the alphabet best fitted for the Albanian language. LE JOURNAL DE SCUTARI of January 1872, published a notice saying that a congress was going to meet to discuss and resolve this difficulty. But from the publications which were issued after this date, it is clear that the proposed Congress failed to accomplish its mission.

[2] Moschopolis became a nest of culture when the learned Wallachians of Constantinople found a refuge in it after the capture of the city by the Turks 1453. It had in its great days a population of 60,000. It boasted of a famous school, a public library, and a printing press. Its inhabitants rendered it opulent by trading with Germany. Ali Pasha ruined Moschopolis, but its inhabitants escaped with their lives. Half of them settled in Pisoderi; the other half fled as far north as Prizsen. Among the treasures of the Wallachian colony in Prizsen there is still a little store of books, which were issued in Moschopolis.

of the Greek church. Vekilarxhi, being taken ill, entrusted himself to the Greek hospital of Constantinople, where he was poisoned by the order of the Patriarch. His Holiness thought that by the untimely deaths of its leaders, the Albanian movement of education and emancipation from the yoke of the Greek church could be checked while in its infancy. Meanwhile the Albanian Catholic clergy of Northern Albania, and especially *the Jesuits* published a number of books, mostly legends of Saints. A religious periodical was also published by them in Shkodra.

Political events were moving fast now and the instinctive diplomatic sense taught the Albanians that they needed a wider educational movement to support their claim for national independence. Thus in 1877 while the Porte's attention was absorbed by the Russo-Turkish war, the learned Albanians called a Congress in Constantinople and elaborated a phonetical Alphabet mainly Latin, for the Albanian language and founded the first Albanian society, *Bashkimi* (The Union), whose aim was to publish books and periodicals in the Albanian language. The Congress and society numbered among its members, scholars with European reputation, such as *Waso-Pasha of Scutari*,[1] *Sami Bey Frasher*,[2] *John Vreto, Tahsim Philati*, etc. This Albanian educational society soon after it was founded published an Albanian spelling book and two periodicals, *Drita* (The Light), and *Dituria* (The Knowledge), all of which were widely circulated all over Albania, the people receiving them with the greatest of enthusiasm. The propaganda of the Albanian society was greatly strengthened by new editions of the Bible

---

[1] Waso Pasha of Scutari is the author of a celebrated book entitled "The Truth about Albania and the Albanians," translated into all European languages, and of the "Pelasgic origin of the Homeric poems."

[2] Sami Bey Frasher is the author of the Arabic-French dictionary and of a number of Albanian books.

in the new Alphabet by the British and Foreign Society under the supervision of the Albanian scholar, *Constantine Christoforidhi*, and circulated all over the country by her own native colporteurs. The work of the newly-born society "*Bashkimi*," and especially the little spelling book which was issued, aroused the passion both of the Turkish Government and of the Greek church and both institutions began to prosecute, boycott, excommunicate and imprison all those who could be caught making use of them. They looked upon that spelling book with terror, fearing it more than the bombs of the Bulgarian revolutionists.[1] The society removed its headquarters to Bucharest, where it established a printing press, and books and periodicals were issued regularly, amongst which the most important are a grammar, a poem, relating the life of the hero of Albania, Scanderbeg, Albania in the past, the present and in the future, etc., etc.

Albanian committees were formed by Albanians residing in Italy, Roumania, Egypt, Russia, Bulgaria and books and periodicals were published in Albanian to strengthen the Albanians in their fight for freedom; and large number of copies found their way into Albania, through the foreign mail, in spite of the Turkish opposition.

---

[1] Mr. **H. N. Brailsford**, in his interesting book, **Macedonis, its Races and their Future**, speaking on this subject says, "If the secret hearts of these two officials could be bared to the world, it would deserve to rank among the rarest curiosities of officialdom. They have one master passion, the **Bishop** and the **Pasha**, and when they have finished praying for each other's destruction in their daily secret devotions, I suspect that a fervent little clause in Greek and in Turkish is addressed in much the same phraseology to **Allah** and the **Trinity**. And that is a prayer for the destruction of a spelling book. They look upon that spelling book as much as the Jews regarded the torches of **Prometheus**. The end of the Turkish Empire is somehow predestined in the cabalistic symbols of its alphabet and its little reading lessons in words of one syllable are like to be more fatal to the Greek church than all tractates of the heretics. I saw it once and turned its pages with timid care, as one might handle a torpedo. It was locked in a glass case in the sacred precincts of the Kyrias Girls' School of Kortcha, where it sheltered safely on foreign soil, under the shadows of treaties and capitulations."

In 1884, however, a change took place. A number of prominent Albanians were invited by the Sultan to assist him in the State Affairs. Through the influence of these high Albanian officials the Albanian Society of Bucharest succeeded in opening a secondary school for boys in Kortcha. A few years later in the Fall of 1891, a girls' school was opened through the influence of the same Albanian personages.

The following year a number of other Albanian schools were opened in the district of Kolonia and Pogradetz. All these schools were making capital progress in spite of the systematic persecution of the Greek clergy, which made the reading of anathema against them a regular part of their ritual. Failing to achieve their purpose by this method they denounced the Albanian teachers as traitors, conspiring against the Sultan, and in 1902 they were arrested, and all Albanian schools were closed.

The fear of the Turks and the jealousies of the Greek clergy have worked their will upon the Albanian educational movement. But the Albanians concentrated all their forces in the Kyrias Girls' School which enjoyed a certain amount of foreign protection, being supported mainly by contributions which came from America and England and which could not be disposed of so easily.

The story of this Albanian Girls' school reads like a romance. It is the story of a series of historical events with results of resplendent significance and value. As if a cloud of dust swept up from a desert, borne here and there by the wind was suddenly changed at a magician's word, changed into a strong, solid and beautiful column for the adornment and enlightenment of a nation.

Before this only Albanian Girls' School crowned the place where it stands, it existed in the mind of a noble soul, who

MRS. CHRISTO A. DAKO.
The Principal of the first Albanian Girls' School.

Blank in the original

believed in the need of such an institution for the regeneration of the Albanian people. The honor of being the first to entertain this noble idea belongs to the late Gerasim D. Kyrias. It was natural that the idea originated with him, for he was in a position to see the great advantages of education and the misfortune involved in the lack of it; and, to respond to the voice and dumb yearnings of the Albanian youth for knowledge, which gives power and light. So the first and only Albanian Girls' School was opened in the autumn of the year of 1891 in Kortcha, in the midst of great difficulties and obstacles under the direction of *Miss Sevasti Kyrias* (now Mrs. C. A. Dako), who had just graduated from the Constantinople College. It was like the seed which fell on the hardened path; but fortunately no bird came to devour the seed; but instead it took root in good soil and brought forth abundant fruit.

The idea of an Albanian Girls' School brought a real joy to the Albanians, but a curse to the clergy. It was not a healthy air for the Greek propaganda, so they started their persecutions, which went so far, that the founder was condemned by the ecclesiastical council of the Greek church to be murdered; but with the strength promised, he, as well, as his brave sister, determined to stand firmly saying, "We will fight it to the end." The criminal, in the person of a butcher, that was assigned to do this evil act, entered the house to commit the crime; but fortunately he was drunk and failed to fulfil his mission. Three months of constant watch around the school grounds was too strenuous a task for his nervous constitution. Being under the influence of liquor he could not control himself, but revealed in detail the net that was wrought and set for Mr. Kyrias. He was imprisoned, but soon was released for the clergy and Government worked hand in hand; and, the bakshish was too good to refuse.

Soon after, there came the great earthquakes, which terrorized the whole city of Kortcha. All the population was induced to abandon their homes and live in sheds built in open spaces. It lasted for about six months. Mr. Kyrias was taken ill, and this ended one of the noblest and most useful lives. The physicians, who pretented to be his friends, and in whom he had confidence were against him for they ventured to end his life before the time by poison. This great loss was felt not only by the leaders of our nation, but also by all the people, for one of their greatest leaders had fallen. The members of the Greek clergy, enemies though they were, could not but admit his greatness and there was but one thing which relieved them, that now there was no such man in all Albania to succeed him.

Mr. Kyrias died two years after the school was founded and thus the whole burden of the institution was thrown on the shoulders of his sister. The seed had taken root in good soil; but for its development money was required. Faith did not fail her. She worked hard, and never gave up hope. The school was supported by the personal friends of hers and of her brother; but can a growing and promising school be supported with $200. Her distress was great. She wrote letters asking help for this *only* Albanian school; but a deaf ear was turned to all her earnest pleadings. In the dark cloudy sky, however, there was glimmer of light to enliven her hope. Financial help came to her assistance; though small, still helped to carry on this great and promising work. *The Women's Board of Missions of the Interior* became interested and decided to help towards its support.

For many years the main supporters of the school were the *Bible Lands Aid Society*, the *Sunday school children of*

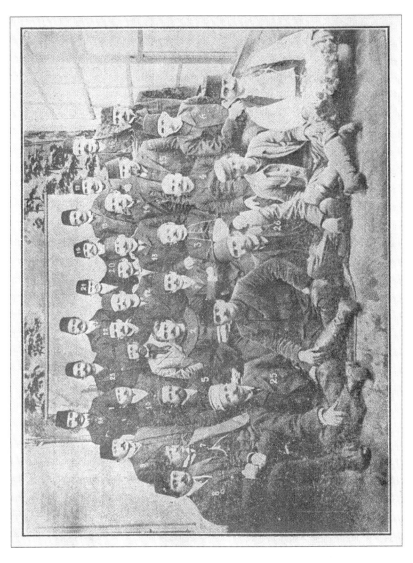

The Members of the Monastir Congress, 1908.

KEY TO THE NEAR EAST

Bebek, and the *Women's Board of Missions of the Interior.* The Albanian nation owes them a debt of gratitude for all their financial and moral support.

Another great difficulty Mrs. Dako had to contend with was lack of text books. Teachers can alone know the hardships of teaching; but how much more difficult must it be, when you have to prepare the text books, hectograph them, and prepare for the school room. She had very few books to start with, viz., a primer and a few readers. Had to work very hard; very often nights were turned into days; but is very happy for all that has been accomplished and quite proud that she had a good and full program for the school. All the text books were worked out by the circle of the teachers. A special word of gratitude must be said here on behalf of the Kyrias School for *Miss Fanka Efthim,* who worked faithfully for twenty years helping to prepare copies for the students. These text books are, so far, the only ones of this kind in Albania, which will be used for many years to come, not only in this school, but in the public schools of the country.

The steady growth of the school was so conspicuous that it aroused indignation and anxiety of both government and clergy. This little leaven enleavened "many measures" and was becoming a great danger to the clergy and the government.

The Sultan again changed his policy with a firm determination to crush once for all the nationalistic spirit of the Albanians, not only in the schools and churches, but also in private letters; but to make good the order he had to close the Kyrias School first, which legally could not be done, for it already had an *Iradé,* which was secured the first year the school was opened, and so tried to destroy it by intrigues, threats and persecutions against the principal, her staff and the parents of the pupils.[1]

The following is one of the interesting experiences of the principal of this school, which has become the cradle of the educational as well as of the national movement of Albania, as it was related to the author by her.

One day I was quite amused but not surprised to see the Commissioner, four policemen, some gendarmes and several *hamals* with sacks under their arms. As soon as I saw the party I understood the plot. When the Commissioner met me his face beamed at once, for he thought his mission was accomplished when he saw before him a small, insignificant person. He soon found out, however, that small people, as well, can display pluck and heroism, and this aroused his indignation. He came with the purpose of taking all our books and closing the school; but failed, and had to walk out with his party after a four hours' fight. After this we were very closely watched; policemen were constantly watching our streets and preventing our scholars admittance, while the priests went to their homes threatening their parents with excommunication and imprisonment. Some did not heed their threats, but many had to relent, for they said it is bad enough to fall into the hands of the Turkish Government, but worse to fall into the hands of the Greek clergy. During this time the number of scholars was reduced to 20. This was a great blow both to teachers and scholars, but especially to our Moslem friends and pupils. Fortunately, this did not last long, for the great zeal and yearning for an education in their vernacular strengthened their national sentiment

---

[1] Mr. H. N. Brailsford, as an eye-witness writing of these persecutions against the Kyrias School says, "It was given out that the father of any "Mohammedan" child attending the school would be sent immediately, and without trial into life-long exile. . . . With the Christians the Greek clergy knew how to deal. There were the usual amathemas, excommunications and boycotts, and in 1904 when I visited Kortcha, Miss Kyrias found her pupils reduced to about 20 boarders. Her teaching is carried on as though it were a furtive and shameful practice, and her school centre of high influence, model of order and sweetness and goodwill, would be more readily tolerated, if it were a nest of vice and crime. At any moment the chief of police may come clanking into the courtyard, and more than once the brave woman who works there alone and unprotected has stood in her doorway and dared him to execute his threat of confiscating her books."

The Members of the Alphabet Committee.

and they were ready to face whatever came. The cruel persecutions instead of injuring our work helped it to grow and its good Christian influence spread like a beaming light all over the country. "*The beacon light,*" as it is termed by our countrymen, proud of its high moral standing.

After the proclamation of the Constitution, the Albanian leaders resumed their noble work of enlightening the nation through the vernacular. In December, 1908, a Congress was called by the Albanian Club of Monastir to meet, discuss and solve the Alphabet question, which had become very complicated. The occasion was great, for it was the first Albanian Congress of the kind ever held. Learned Albanians, representing all classes of people, *Moslems, Catholics, Orthodox* and *Protestants,* came together like brothers. Patriotic speeches and literary addresses were delivered and were received by the public with the greatest of enthusiasm. Academic discussions were carried on as though they were life members of some European academy. The Congress resolved by unanimous vote to recommend to all Albanians to write their language hereafter only with the Latin Alphabet. And every patriotic Albanian feels proud of the fact that the nation as a body received the decision of the Monastir Congress as though it came from a body of prophets.[1]

Books and periodicals were printed in the new Alphabet

---

[1] The object of the Albanians in wishing to adopt the Latin, or national characters, and in objecting to the Arabic alphabet, is twofold: in the first place they are more easily learnt by the people, and in the second, they are more suitable for expressing the language. The Turks, on their part, have a deep rooted objection to the employment of the Latin characters in Albania, not only because this system of writing and reading will eventually tend to unite the tribes and districts by a literature which is common to all, but because it will make it possible for Albanian books to be printed in Europe. If, on the other hand, the Arabic characters, could be enforced, the Ottoman authorities fully realize that a much greater difficulty would be experienced in providing the means of educating and developing the mental capacities of the Albanian people. **H. Charles Woods, "The Danger Zone of Europe,"** p. 115.

and day and night-schools were opened all over the country. Several musical, literary and religious societies were organized, of which "The Band of Freedom, "The Morning Star," and "The Orthodox League," with headquarters in Kortcha, played the predominant rôle.

"The Morning Star" was the first women's society organized by *Miss P. D. Kyrias*, a younger sister of Mrs. Dako. One hundred women of the prominent Albanian families of Kortcha enrolled at once, and branches of the same were organized in all the important towns of Albania. Weekly meetings and lectures were held in the building of the Kyrias School.

"*Lidhja Orthodokse*" (The Orthodox League), was founded on the first of February, 1909, by several prominent Albanians, among whom the most important figure is the brave and distinguished fighter for liberty, *Mr. Mihal Grameno*, the editor of *Koha* (The Times), with branches in Elbassan, Berat, Durazzo, Janina, etc. The main object of "The Orthodox League" was to oblige the Patriarch to abandon his policy of trying to "hellenize" the Albanians, to accept the Albanian language as the language for the Liturgy in all the churches of Albania, and, instead of the Greek, as the language of education in all schools of the country. If these concessions were not grantel, the League intended to form with the two hundred thousand Orthodox Albanians an Independent Church, like that of the Bulgarians.

In August, 1909, another Congress was called to meet at Elbassan by the Albanian Club of Salonica. All the Albanian clubs sent delegates, the order of day being to reorganize the clubs, to foster the educational movement throughout the country and to found a *Normal School* to supply a sufficient number of educated young men to occupy the position of teachers, all of which were carried unani-

The Band of Freedom

mously. At the same time the Congress confirmed the decisions of the Monastir Congress held in 1909, appointed three committees, one with headquarters in Kortcha, *"Perparimi"* (The Progress), to raise funds and direct the day and night-schools throughout the country; another, with headquarters at Monastir, to reorganize and direct the national movement of the clubs; and the third one, to oversee and direct the work of the *Normal School,* which opened in the Fall of the same year, having in the first year an attendance of 143 students.

For months the Albanian educational movement was supported by a number of papers and reviews, amongst which the most important are: *"Lirija"* (The Freedom), and *"Dituria"* (The Knowledge), published at Salonica and edited by *Midhat Frasheri,* the president of the Congress held in Monastir in 1908; *"Bashkimi i Kombit"* (The Union of the Nation), published in Monastir by the *"Printing Literary Society"* and edited by *George D. Kyrias; "Kortcha," "Koha"* (The Times) and *"Lidhja Orthodokse,"* published in Kortcha, the former edited by *Sami Bey Poiani,* the latter two, by *Mr. Mihal Grameno; "Tomori,"* published in Elbassan, and edited by a staff of highly educated men, published by *Lef Nossi; "Drita,"* published in Monastir, edited by *Dr. Mutcho Qulli; "Besa"* and *Bashkimi,"* published in Scutari; and *"Zgjimi",* published at Janina; and by a number of others, published in America, Bucharest, Constantinople, Sofia, Egypt, Constantza, Bruxelles, London, Raguza, Italy, which were established long before the Proclamation of the Constitution. The Albanian cause, too, was greatly furthered by the Albanian clubs, the chief of which was at Monastir, and by the Albanian societies established in Roumania, Russia, Bulgaria, Egypt and America, etc.

In the spring of 1911 the Albanian educational movement made a greater step forward, through the generous help of the distinguished statesman and diplomat, *the Honorable Charles R. Crane,* of New York. During his trip of several weeks in Albania, Mr. Crane saw for himself the great suffering of the people, and with his keen insight perceived that the root of all this calamity was due to lack of education, and most magnanimously offered himself to help to enlighten and uplift this ancient and noble race, forgotten by Europe. He asked the author to select seven young Albanian boys and seven girls and send them to get an education, at his expense, in the American Colleges of Constantinople and become apostles for their nation.

Since 1912 the Albanians, forced by political events, have not been able to do much towards the education of their countrymen. Since that time the honor of leading the Albanian educational movement belongs to Mr. and Mrs. Crane. They have regularly continued to send every year a number of young men and women to the American Colleges of Constantinople. Besides they are doing a great deal for the enlightenment and uplift of the Albanians, who have come as refugees in the U. S. of America, where a number of men are educated in different institutions. The Albanian nation will be forever grateful to Mr. and Mrs. Crane, who will always be living monuments in the history of Albania.

The Young Turks were alarmed with this rapid progress of the Albanians, and since they could not check their movement by the administrative measures, as the Sultan Hamid tried to divide the Albanians by means of intrigues. They appealed to the religious sentiment of their faith, and represented to the "Moslem" Albanians that the employment of other than the Arabic characters was treason to their

HONORABLE CHARLES R. CRANE

MRS. CHARLES R. CRANE

prophet. This appeal was addressed to them by the head of Islam, the *Sheik-ul-Islam;* but the plea of utility and of service for the welfare of their nation, had a heavier weight with them than that of the Sheik-ul-Islam. The Young Turks, however, did not give up their determination to check the Albanian educational movement, in which they saw the dismemberment of the Turkish empire, and so they issued an Albanian periodical and books with the Arabic letters and widely circulated them in Albania, giving orders at the same time to the *hodjas* to exite the religious fanaticism of the Moslems against the Latin alphabet. Meanwhile they passed resolutions in the Parliament against the Latin Alphabet and gave orders to all public schools to teach the Albanian, not with the Latin, but with the Arabic characters. The Albanian students in Constantinople, Salonica, Monastir, Janina, Uskup, etc. deserted the schools rather than abnegate their Alphabet. This mean policy of intrigues of the chauvinist Young Turks led to serious disturbances. The Turkish authorities found it now easier to suit the leaders and when possible to arrest and imprison them. A very interesting and amusing case is the suit against Miss P. D. Kyrias, the energetic and daring President of the Women's Society, "The Morning Star." Two months after the society was founded, an entertainment was given by its members for the people of Kortcha. The drama *"Wilhelm Tell"* was played, national songs were sung, some of them composed by Miss Kyrias herself and short speeches were delivered. On the following day the President of this society, received a notice from the police authorities to appear before the court. On the assigned date Miss Kyrias accompanied by Rev. Tsilka and by the cavass went to court, where she was put in the criminal dock to be questioned. Finally she was sentenced to a fine. The purpose of the suit evidently was to intimidate her and so force her to resign rather than to be summoned to appear before the court, which generally speaking is considered to be a disgrace. But the daring President is an exceptionally brave little thing, and she came out of this affair strengthened with new energy and endowed with a firmer determination to do her own share for the enlightenment, uplift and emancipation of her people from the unbearable Turkish yoke. She kept steadily appealing to higher and higher courts, defying the Cadis with her daring but unchallenged answers, until she was acquitted.

To defend their Alphabet the Albanians organized and held great meetings in the open air, and resolutions of protests were sent to the Porte, Sultan and the representatives of the Great Powers, saying that the Albanian nation is firmly determined to stand for the Alphabet, defending it even with the force of arms and shedding the last drop of blood for it. The short-sighted Young Turks were unable to understand the warning and they continued their foolish policy. The discontent and disturbances spread all over Albania. Finally in the spring of 1912, the whole Albanian nation rose and gave such a stroke to the Turkish Empire that it brought its downfall.

MISS PARASKEVI D. KYRIAS.

V

ALBANIA, THE CAUSE OF THE BALKAN WAR

THE first of the Balkan States to declare war against Turkey was Montenegro. The first shot was fired on Oct. 9, 1912, the main objective being *Scutari*, the Capital of Northern Albania, a town inhabited exclusively by Albanians. They advanced towards *Chipchanik*, the first post on the road to Scutari, but they encountered serious resistance. After a fierce fight the Turkish frontier was crossed and the fortified position of Chipchanik, six miles away over the plain from Podgoritza, fell into Montenegrin hands, and in October 14, *Tuzi* was captured.

The road to Scutari was open now, and *General Martinovitch* advanced towards the most desperate fight in the campaign, which the Montenegrins hope to culminate in the capture of *Tarabosh,* and place Scutari at their mercy, as the capture of Chipchanik placed Tuzi at their feet.

Shiroka mountain was taken on the evening of October 24, after a desperate assault. On the morrow a spectator of the bombardment from Mount Mourikan saw the whole theatre of war spread out before him. Tarabosh stretches sheer and bare, rising bleakly to the sky, grey and enormous. Behind lies Scutari, the key to Albania. Only this fortress lies between the town and General Martinovitch's army.

On Sunday, October 27, at ten in the morning, the bombardment of the city began, and Scutari was subjected to a cross fire from the Montenegrin batteries on the northwest and south, and from those on the island of *Vranjina* in the Lake of Scutari, whence King Nicholas watched the action.

General Martinovitch, to cut off the supply of the fortress from the south, occupied *San-Giovanni di Medua* October

29, and joined the Serbians at Alessio, who advanced to cooperate with them and thus the blockade was completed.

Meanwhile a fresh factor was complicating the conflict. On November 28, the Albanians, the most ancient inhabitants of the Balkan Peninsula, under the leadership of Ismail Kemal began to assert their legitimate claims, asking Europe to preserve the integrity of their country and pleading for the recognition of the uncontested right to govern themselves. As an answer to this plea, the Conference of Ambassadors assembled at London recognized the independence of Albania, and considering the international importance of the country resolved to draw the boundaries itself. It further resolved that whatever the result of the attack on Scutari, the town was to be part of the new state of Albania; and informing the Montenegrin Government of the decision, asked the King Nicholas to suspend hostilities. Undeterred by this diplomatic warning, the Montenegrins continued to press forward the siege of Scutari; and Tarabosh was undergoing a terrible bombardment. The Montenegrin artillery on Mourikan poured a dense and continuous hail of shrapnel and shell up on the two summits of the mountain and upon the saddle which unites them. But in spite of the fire which invested them, the Albanians replied with much spirit and considerable accuracy.

The artillery duel was resumed on November 28. The Montenegrins brought up several battalions to strengthen the positions they held to the east of Scutari, and held a line running from *Dristi* on the North, through *Muselini* and *Rogani* to *Gajtani* on the south-east of the town. From their batteries at Gajtani they bombarded the Turkish positions to the south of the city, especially the detached hill 445 feet high, near *Bardanjolt,* which was looked upon as the key to the defences, which were the weakest on that side.

KEY TO THE NEAR EAST

On November 29 hostilities were suspended by orders from Cettigne on account of the negotiations for an armistice, which were in progress in Thrace.

The preparations for this bombardment had been very complete. The heavy guns from Mourikan were brought up to the advanced position of *Oblok,* and every available mountain including that of Shiroka, which directly commands Tarabosh, was occupied by Montenegrin artillery men. Between Maurikan and Oblok twenty-four battalions were concentrated, whilst other troops were stationed between *Zogai* on the lake and Mount Shiroka. Hand grenades were provided for the stormers.

The attack upon Scutari, was resumed on March 31 and the place was violently bombarded. In this attack the Montenegrin were aided by the Serbians. A demonstration was made on the River Kiri, but the real attack was upon the Turkish positions on the great Tarabosh.

On Monday, April 21, *Essad Pasha* sent a message to the Montenegrin officer commanding the siege operations and informed him of his intentions to surrender Scutari, on condition that Montenegro would let him march freely into the interior of Albania with the forty thousand troops under his command and with all his guns and that it would support him in his claim to the kingship of Albania. On receiving the news, King Nicholas convened the Privy Council, who sent *General Vukotitch* and Mr. *Plamenatz,* formerly Montenegrin Minister at Constantinople, to treat with Essad Pasha. The protocol of the capitulation of Scutari was signed about midnight. Subsequently Essad Pasha and the troops of the garrison, according to the agreement, marched out of the town with the honors of war.

Great was the demonstration at Cettigne when the news reached the capital; crowds rushed out into the streets firing revolvers and singing patriotic songs. The King, accompanied by the Princesses, appeared on the balcony of the Palace and made a speech amid thunders of applause.

But Europe received the news with anxiety. Never had the Great Powers seen themselves in such a position since the day when Belgium became, in 1830, an Independent state. The *Fremdenblatt*, uttered hopes that, "this brutal attack upon the authority of the Great Powers will have the effect of raising Europe from her lethargy, and bringing home to her a sense of the error hitherto committed. . . . In view of the tidings of victory from Cettigne, which are at the same time tidings of a European defeat, we cherish the certain expectation that Europe will now at last resolve to employ sharper methods in order to restore her damaged prestige and to break the resistance of Montenegro. In France, though the popular feeling was in favour of Montenegro, it was recognized that she could not hope to retain Scutari. To England the news came as an unexpected shock. The tidings were discussed at the Conference of Ambassadors sitting on April 23, but they came to no conclusion. Austro-Hungary intimated that if the Powers were unable to arrive at a speedy decision she might herself be obliged to take action to vindicate the authority of Europe. Soon Austria agreed to accept the aid of Italy instead of acting alone in coercing Montenegro. The concert of Europe was defied, Pan-Slav sentiment once more rose high in Russia.

Diplomacy was for the moment baffled by the apparition of Essad Pasha as king of Albania. King Nicholas was reported to have given his cordial assent to Essad's assumption of the regal dignity, and to have received his reward in the shape of a treaty by which the new sovereign ceded

KEY TO THE NEAR EAST

to him the whole of Albania north of the river Drin. Such was the scene of the long drawn drama.

The Ambassadors met, but they decided nothing. Fortunately for the peace of Europe, the Great Powers were not in a hurry. Italy professed herself willing to join Austria in the task of coercing Montenegro, on the other hand, the Queen of Italy had not forgotten that she was a daughter of the King of Montenegro. The wires flashed burning words of congratulation and rejoicing from the *Quirinal* to the *Konak* at Scutari. The Easter of the Eastern Church in 1913 fell a month later than that of the Western one. They found a welcome pretext for delay. Never were the precepts of the Church observed more rigidly, although the object was not only trivial but also a threat to plunge Europe into war.

Austria threatened separate intervention, and the Emperor held prolonged conferences with *Count Berchtold and Konrad von Hotzendorff,* the chief of the General staff. Austria indeed saw that the decision arrived at unanimously by the conference of Ambassadors in London in April 26, officially to notify King Nicholas that he must give up Scutari, could only be put into force by military coercion. But Russian opinion had to be considered, for it was evident that Austrian intervention would lead to a violent outburst of Pan-Slavist feeling. Moreover were war to break out between Austria and Montenegro the latter would undoubtedly be supported by the other Slav States in the Balkans, if not by Greece, and whilst the Serbian army was concentrating nearer its base, the Bulgarians were making use of the armistice to withdraw troops from the lines of *Tchataldja.* Russia would be supported by France, if not by England in her refusal to undertake a collective intervention of the Powers, and it looked as if the Dual Monarchy would swallow the affront. But in spite of this a collective note was prepared and presented to the Montenegrin Government; but the reply was deferred until after the Easter holidays. Russia was straining every nerve to preserve the peace. Her Ambassador at Vienna had informed the Austrian Government that Russia, considering that all means of putting pressure upon Montenegro had not been exhausted, begged Austria to refrain from taking any precipitate action, lest grave consequences should follow, adding at the same time that Russia felt herself bound to work for the removal of the Montenegrin troops. Germany urged Austria not to intervene unless jointly with Italy.

Though the situation was difficult and manacing, there were some elements of hope. Italian public opinion was turning against Montenegro owing to the discovery of King Nicholas' intrigues with Essad Pasha. In Russia the excitement was largely on the surface. The Powers were straining every nerve to keep together through the Ambassadorial Conference in London. Austria finally recognized that the military coercion of Montenegro would be a hard task, and consequently was disposed to wait for the decisions to be adopted in London.

The Montenegrin reply was handed to the Powers on May 1. They claimed that the delimitation of Albania should have been undertaken after the Balkan Allies had been consulted on the subject after the conclusion of peace with the Porte, and that any demand by the Powers for the evacuation of Albanian territory, before such a Peace had been signed, was a violation of neutrality. Moreover, Montenegro had occupied Scutari as the legitimate consequence of warlike operations, and her troops had been warmly welcomed by its inhabitants. They therefore reserved the right of deciding as to the evacuation of the town until the question of the definite delimitation of Albania came to be discussed between the Allies and the Great Powers in the course of the peace negotiations with the Ottoman Empire. That same evening the Russian Minister at Cettigne again urged the Montenegrins to evacuate Scutari immediately, and said they ran a risk of meeting their ruin, which meant that Austria Hungary would intervene alone. It was thought that in such a case Italy would intervene by herself in southern Albania, and that the excellent relations between the two Powers would not long survive the rivalry and friction which would ensure. In Russia it was clearly seen that in the interests of the new Albanian state, Albania should be jointly occupied by the Powers and that the occupation should continue until the new Government was in a position to assert authority. If Russia herself refrained from participating in the intervention of the Powers, whilst allowing France to do so, the Concert would be dissolved. Men felt that the peace of Europe lay in Russian hands. In spite of all these grave warnings sent to Cettigne, Montenegrin troops continued to gather upon the Austrian frontier towards *Cattaro*. But the influence of Russia prevailed in Montenegro. At the last moment King Nicholas yielded to the pressure of Europe. In a telegram to Sir Edward Grey, he placed the future of Scutari in the hands of the Powers. The telegram was read by Sir Edward Grey to the conference, which decided that a contingent from the international blockading fleet should take over the place from the Montenegrin authorities. On May 5, the decision of King Nicholas to leave the question of Scutari to the Powers was announced in the House of Commons by the Prime Minister and in the House of Lords by Lord Morley.

The news was everywhere hailed with joy. Many indeed, rejoiced that no pretext any longer existed for the joint intervention of Austria and Italy. Scutari was duly handed over by *General Becir*, the Montenegrin commander, to *Vice-Admiral Burney*, the commander of the international fleet on May 14. Early in the morning, May 15, the Montenegrin flag was handed down from the citadel and the flags of the five Powers were hoisted instead. A regular administration was organized by the International Commission to conduct the affairs of the place under the Presidency of Vice-Admiral Burney.

The state of the town was made known to the inhabitants by the following proclamation, printed in English and Albanian side by side:

In the name of the international fleet representing the Great Powers of Europe.

A PROCLAMATION.

On the withdrawal of the forces of His Majesty King Nicholas of Montenegro, the town of Scutari will be taken over and administered by a commission of officers of the international fleet representing the Great Powers of Europe until such time as autonomous government has been established in Albania.

All persons are hereby warned that they must obey the orders of the officers of the Commission under penalty of military law.

With regard to the Customs administration, it has been arranged that it shall be given into the charge of an official to be nominated by the Consular Body and appointed by the Commission, and that the proceeds of the dues, which will remain at 11 per cent. as under the Turkish Government, shall be handed over to the municipality. This body, which consists of some half dozen Moslem Albanians and a similar number of Christians, was called together this morning and was requested to resume its duties, which were interrupted in consequence of the occupation. The Commission having been informed that there are a large number of cases of disease in the town, a sanitary commission, consisting of Albanian, Austrian and Italian doctors, has been formed to report on the best course of action to be taken.

The Flags of the Five Powers on the citadel of Scutari

KEY TO THE NEAR EAST 103

Scutari settled down as a quiet country town, abandoned even by the Montenegrin sightseers, in their red and blue national costumes, who had thronged its streets during the first days of the occupation. One interesting event, however, was a visit paid on May 26 to Admiral Burney by 130 of the principal men of the five Malissori tribes the *Hoti, Gruda, Klementi, Shkrelli* and *Kastrati*. Their object was to petition him to use his influence to prevent the Hoti and Gruda tribes from being severed from the "Five Banner Group" and incorporated in Montenegro.

In this petition, to which twenty-two of the principal men of the five tribes set their mark, it is pointed out that by blood, language, and customs the tribes in question form a whole, and that in religion they differ from Montenegro. Their interests, further, are closely bound up with the province of Scutari, since they own lands in the district stretching from *Scutari* to *Kavaja*. Instead of any diminution there has been an increase of hostility between the Serbians and Albanians as a result of the war, at the beginning of which they fought with the Montenegrins until it was evident that the latter desired not the liberation but the conquest of Albania. Finally it is predicted that unless the five tribes are allowed to remain entirely Albanian, blood will continue to flow.

Vice-Admiral Burney in reply promised that the petition should be laid before the Ambassadorial Conference in London. The details of the tribesmen's reception by a British Admiral are worthy of record.

The tribesmen, who had come down from the mountains on the eastern side of the lake earlier in the day, leaving their arms at the outposts on the edge of the town, were received by the British Admiral, with whom were the other members of the International Commission, in the garden of his residence. Here the men, dressed in their picturesque costumes of rough white cloth braided with black and wearing white feses, stood round in a large circle, while the following speech was read to them in Albanian by the British Vice-Consul on behalf of Admiral Burney:

Chiefs of the Malissori tribes, I, on behalf of the International Commission, am very glad to welcome you, especially as I know that your presence here today is a token of your loyalty and good will to us who were sent by the Great Powers to inaugurate the first steps in the formation of an autonomous Albania. We sincerely hope that you will preserve absolute order and quietude among your tribesmen, for by so doing you will materially assist us in our task.

On the conclusion of the speeches, the Malissori, accompanied by the Admiral and members of the Commission, went to the barracks, where, to the strains of a ship's band, they sat down to dinner. The proceedings were brought to a close by the playing of the National Anthems of the five Powers, and shouts of Long live the Powers! Long live Albania! It was easy to see throughout the importance which the tribesmen attached to the visit and the pleasure which they felt at the friendly and hospitable way in which they were received. So anxious indeed were as many as possible to take part in the visit and to manifest their feelings of respect for the representatives of the Powers that the number of the deputation was more than double that originally arranged. As one of the men expressed it, it was the greatest day for the Mountains since the day when Christ was born.

Montenegro had fired the first shot in the Balkan war, but it was not long before the forces of the other Balkan states followed her into the field. The Serbians took the offensive, crossed the boundary at *Bujanovatz* and the first collision with the Turks took place on October 23, near

Kumanova, forcing them to retreat. On the 22nd of the same month the fourth Serbian army, which entered the *Sandjak* of *Novi-Bazar* occupied the important town of *Prizren.* After the occupation of Prizren the "northern army" was divided into two divisions. The first of which continuing its march towards *Ipek,* joined the Montenegrins at *Allesio,* on November 17; the other turned south and on the 24th joined the rest of the Serbian armies at Uskup.

From Alessio the Serbian troops hastened to advance on Durazzo forty miles to the south. Durazzo is the ancient *Dyrrachium,* which played so great a part in the civil wars between Caesar and Pompey. It is the usual port of transit from Brindisi, by which travellers reach the *Via Egnatia,* which is the shortest route to Salonica, Constantinople and the Near East.

On November 27, the Albanians lowered the Turkish flags at *Durazzo* and hoisted the Albanian flag on the Government buildings. The Turkish functionaires, who refused to recognize the new government were expelled.

On November 26, the Serbians had reached the village of *Milot,* only a few hours distant from Durazzo. A commission consisting of several notables, accompanied by the resident Consuls went over and met the Serbian troops; informed them of the change of government and asked them to suspend the military operations, since Albania was not in war with any of the Balkan states. The Serbians encamped close to the town. Reinforcements of seven infantry battalions and one cavalry regiment, numbering about seven thousand men were hurried down from Prizren which arrived after seven days.

While the fourth Army was pressing on to the Adriatic, the rest of the Serbian forces were busily engaged in driving the Turks from Macedonia. From Uskup the first Serbian army marched towards *Kupruli* and defeated the Turks at *Prilep,* November fourth. The second army gained another victory at *Kitchevo* and concentrated before Monastir, on November 15, whence they attached the sixth and the seventh corps of the Turkish army. On the 17th of the same month, the Serbian troops occupied the hills dominating Monastir. On the 18th they cut the route of retreat towards Ochrida, forcing a part of the Turkish forces, after a fierce fight, to surrender. The greater part of the Turkish army numbering 30-40 thousand men, after being defeated at *Banitza* by the Greek forces which advanced from *Kozhani,* fled towards *Kortcha.*

The *Morava* division of the second army corps advancing from Kitchevo, occupied Dibra on November 22, after a fierce fight. After the capitulation of Monastir, this same army advanced south and occupied without any resistance Resna, Ochrida and Elbassan, November 28. With the capture of these places the whole of Northern and Central Albania fell into the Serbian hands.

While hymns of victory were sounding at Belgrade, the representatives of the Triple Alliance were instructed to inform the Serbian Government that the Triple Alliance would consider the arrival of the Serbians on the Adriatic as contrary to its interests. Serbia, however, defied all warnings coming from the Triple Alliance, relying upon the eventual support of Russia.

The crisis became threatening when news reached Europe of the unspeakable atrocities committed by the Serbian troops upon the Albanians.[1] The Great Powers used their influence to induce Serbia to exercise moderation; but all was in vain.

---

[1] **Miss M. E. Durham,** speaking of the Serbian and Montenegrin atrocities in Albania, says, "At dinner at the hotel I, with the excep-

On November 25 a rumor that Austria had mobilized five army corps reached the European capitals. Germany used her influence to induce Austria to adopt a proposal to hold a European Conference to solve all pending questions in the Balkans. Formal proposals for an International Congress were made by England. Austria-Hungary, however, was greatly inclined to dissent from any proposal to invest an international Congress with power to adjudicate on matters deemed vital to the *Dual Monarchy,* such as the Independence of Albania and the annexation of Durazzo by Serbia. To support her diplomacy on the request addressed to Serbia to evacuate Durazzo and all other Albanian territory occupied by her troops, Austria massed large forces in Southern Hungary destined to act against Belgrade and Semendria, while her forces in Bosnia and Herzegovina were to advance against western Serbia. Besides, two army

---

tion of a Russian sister at the other end of the table, was the only woman among a pack of officers, officials, and Montenegrin doctors, and these discussed and joked over the hideous doings. I had hoped and believed that the Serbian army was more civilized. A report had come to me that an Albanian passing through Podgoritza had declared that, in Kossova vilayet the ground in many places was simply strewn with the bodies of women and children, that he had seen a living foot protruding from the ground and waving feebly, but had not dared to stop, as a Serbian officer was with him. As I was worked almost beyond my strength I did not, I regret now, see this witness and examine him, nor, in fact, attach much belief to the report, till a Serbian officer turned up at the dinner table, and related, with glee, the valorous deeds of the Serbians. "We have," he boasted, "annihilated the **Luma tribe.**" He described wholesale slaughter of men, women and children, and the burning of the villages. The Montenegrins chuckled as they gobbled their dinner. "Why did you do this?" I asked at last. "When I was there the people received me very well."

There was a shout of laughter. "Go there now look for your dear friends. You won't find a single one. They shot one of our telegraphists, and we sent enough battalions to destroy them. "The Moslem problem was to be simplified." "When the land is once ours," I was repeatedly assured, "there will be no Moslem problem."

Of the Luma tribe very few survived. The destruction of the whole Albanian race was the avowed intention of both Serbian and Montenegrin. The company at the dinner table varied from week to week; but on this point was always agreed.

corps were mobilized to hold Russia in check. Russia, being unprepared, was most anxious to preserve peace, and used her utmost efforts to induce Serbia to give way. But in vain, Serbia continued to refuse to comply with the demands of the Powers, and since Austria appeared determined not to enter into a European Conference before she had come to a settlement with Serbia, the outlook was dark.

Finally Serbia, realizing that Russia was not willing to champion her cause, began to profess herself ready to accept the decision of the Great Powers with regard to all the points at issue.

On December 4 news were published that the Ambassadorial Conference proposed by Sir Edward Grey would be held in London to consider and solve the pending difficulties. On December 21 the Ambassadorial Conference assembled in London under the presidency of Sir Edward Grey and an official notification was issued saying that the High Assembly recommended to their Governments and that the latter had accepted the principle of Albanian autonomy. Subsequently it became known that the Conference had recommended the neutralization of the whole of the Albanian coast line. The news was published simultaneously in the various European capitals, and was everywhere regarded as a clear indication of the accord with which the Great Powers were workings to bring about a definite and permanent settlement of the Albanian question.

The Greeks began to advance in Southern Albania from *Acarnania*. On November 3rd, they entered the town of *Preveza;* and towards the middle of the same month they occupied *Pentepegadia*. By November 16th the Greek Army had left Pentepegadia and began to advance on *Janina*. The garrison of the fortress was supposed to number about

25,000 men, and was rumored to be in favor of surrendering owing to lack of food.

So close did the fall of Janina seem that correspondents at Arta were almost afraid to undertake the short journey to Athens and back lest they should miss the entry of the Greek troops into the town. But Janina proved to be far more capable of resistance than any, save its Albanian defenders, had supposed. The campaign in southern Albania was only just beginning.

On December 4, 1912, the Greek fleet bombarded *Vallona* which is not fortified. Some of the shells fell between the Italian and the Austro-Hungarian Consulates. In view of the panic caused among the people, *Ismail Kemal Bey Vlora,* the President of the Albanian Provisional Government, at once addressed telegrams of protest to the Great Powers and to the Greek Government. They also landed troops to occupy *Sassano,* an islet which is the landing place of the cables from Italy to Albania, and which commands the entrance to Vallona harbor.

On December seven this incident evoked some comments in the Italian Chamber.

Marquis di San Giuliano, the Minister of Foreign Affairs replying to interpellations by *Signori Salandra and Galli* regarding the bombardment of Vallona and the occupation of Sassano by the Greeks, said that the Italian Government had declared to the Greek Government, in friendly, but firm terms that, while willing to respect the liberty of operations of belligerents, Italy never could consent to the Bay of Vallona, of which the island of Sassano was an integral part, belonging to Greece, or being transformed into a naval and military base. A similar step had been taken by Austria, with whom Italy was in intimate agreement. In conclusion the Minister said, "We have grounds for hoping that the question will be decided in conformity with the legitimate interests, and that our cordial relations with Greece will continue to expand and develop."

The semi-official explanation of the incident given at Athens was: "For several days the Greek gunboat *Pensios,* which was blockading the coast, noticed bodies of armed men on the shore. Fearing that she was about to be attacked, she fired several shells on them, whereupon the men waved a white flag and gave the ship to understand that they were not Turkish soldiers, and had no hostile intentions. It is pointed out, moreover, that none of the Greek projectiles took effect on the Albanians." Thus this incident came to an end. Meanwhile another division of the Greek army marched from Salonica and attacked, near Florina, the retreating Turkish troops which were defeated at Monastir plain by the Serbians, and pressed them to retreat farther. They succeeded finally in rallying at Kortcha, which they occupied in some strength. *Ali Riza Pasha,* after restoring the Turkish organization of Kortcha, marched south to Janina with some 20,000 regulars. *Djavid Pasha* was left with about the same number at Kortcha; but on December 13 or 14 he also retired upon Janina with 5000 men. The remainder of the Turks, two days later were attacked by the Greek cavalry at *Bihlishta* where the Hellenic troops concentrated from Florina and from Kastoria and advancing attacked the crest of the *Morava Planina,* and the *Tsangoni* gorge held by natives. The Greek attack was made on December 19th, and after suffering considerable losses, the Hellenic Army under General *Damianos* forced the defile and drove the Turks south and west beyond Kortcha, which was occupied in force. Part of the defeated army retired in the direction of Janina, being pressed by the Greeks.

The following is a statement of the last events which occurred in the district of Kortcha, made by Mrs. C. A. Dako, who was an eye witness. It gives but a bit of the unspeakable atrocities committed by the Greek troops upon the people of Southern Albania, which refused to deny their own nationality:

The entrance of the Turkish army in Kortcha reminded me of the locusts of Egypt at the time of the ten plagues with the exception that it did not devastate the city. What amazed us all was this, that though starved to death, still they only begged, nothing was taken by force. The Kortcha people gave them as much as they could to satisfy their hunger. Many that could not procure suitable food were fed on roots and grass. It was never expected that order would prevail with such a starved large army. The Turkish military authorities took possession of all the public buildings and used them, but private property was fully respected. They slept like dogs in the open air, though the weather was bad, the caves being their only shelter, the deep mud their mattress and the cold wind and rain their cover.

All were anxious, as well as myself to know what the future would bring. Different rumors were scattered; but we could not depend on them, for we were besieged and there was no communication with the outside world. The Kortcha people expected to be liberated, but by whom? It was a mystery. One night we were unexpectedly awakened by rifle shots, which lasted for five or six hours. We thought that a fight was taking place somewhere near Kortcha, and we were not entirely mistaken. The commander of the Turkish army had set fire to the ammunition that was in the outskirts of the city, and the small number of soldiers that were left there on guard, fought faithfully and bravely with the *avant-guard* of the Greek army. Most of them fell in the fight. There is a tragic incident of a young Moslem Albanian who fought heroically from a minaret in *Plassa* (a village two hours north of Kortcha), and stood until all his ammunition was used up. After he was captured and instead of being taken a prisoner and praised for his patriotism and heroism, his body was mutilated and thrown to the dogs. Then all the village of Plassa was burned down. This is what a Christian nation can do in the 20th century.

That same night the Moslem women of *Dishnitsa* (a small village three quarters of an hour north of Kortcha), had to flee to our city in a panic just as they had come out of their beds sore-footed with their nightdresses, dragging their children and old people along with them. They knew they were going to have the same fate as their neighbors of the nearby villages, which were devastated and where the Greeks committed unspeakable cruelties. Their homes were pillaged, some of them burned down and the rest destroyed.

For hours and hours Moslem Albanians were pouring in the city from the surrounding villages. It was the most lamentable sight that I ever beheld and hope this will be the last one written in the history of nations. Many pathetic incidents took place, which broke many a heart. We read in Matt. 29: 19-22, but no one can imagine the reality of the fact without seeing it. In the crowd, my attention was drawn by a tall, slender woman with a calm, but sad and pathetic countenance. I could not make out what was the reason she moved so slowly and peculiarly. Occasionally a deep sigh was heard and lifting her eyes you could see her lips moving; sometimes she had no control of herself, for tears were streaming down her cheeks. When she came nearer to me I found out the secret. Several were interested to know where her destination was to be; and we found out later in the evening that she had no place to go, but a corner in a street, where she bore her child.

When the invaders entered, they were welcomed with great enthusiasm by the people of Kortcha who hoped that the banner of the cross would bring joy and peace to the nation; but the events soon proved that their banner did not bring what it indicated; but instead cruelties, destruction, especially to the Mohammedan Albanian population.

The spoil that was brought by the army from the many destroyed and burned villages attracted our attention. The peace and respect of the private property which the city enjoyed during the stay of the Turkish army was trespassed by the *Christian* invaders. The *first* thing they *did* was to destroy all the Albanian element which they name as Albanian propaganda and traitors of the country. They started to persecute, imprison and exile all those Albanians who refused to say that they were Greeks.

As the public building could not hold them all, they entered private houses whether wanted or not. They made pillage everywhere they could and not a Moslem Albanian was left without being personally robbed and sent senseless to the ground. Right after the army was quartered, orders were issued that all the people should speak Greek because "Kortcha was a pure *Hellenic* city" and the effort was made to prove to Europe that it was so; though they knew that they were deceiving not only the Powers but themselves too. Mass meetings were forced with the aid of the bayonet; they got all the signatures needed to send to London and so prove that Kortcha, the educational and political center of Albania was Hellenic.

Pen can never describe the great misery and discontent which prevailed among our poor population.

Our school bore the American flag, but in spite of it they wished to make the same attempts which they tried in former years through their andarties, who are like swarming wasps in the city. One evening, just at midnight, I heard a knock at the gate. The knocks increased, but I could not make out who was knocking at this late hour of the night. My room is facing the street, and when I lifted up gently and very carefully one corner of the shade, I beheld four soldiers and four andarties; they knocked persistently for two whole hours; and as I was afraid they might climb the wall and accomplish easily their aim, I went and woke up the teachers to help me go and call the guards and man-servant, quartered up in the adjoining yard. So soon as they understood that we had men around the building they left.

Next day the government was notified and the four andarties were dismissed from the police force, for it was found out that they really had come to the gate, though they did not wish to acknowledge that they came with a bad purpose. An officer came to apologize. He was very much surprised that I dared to tell him that I was an Albanian and not Greek. He called me coward because I did not open the window to inquire their mission, but I gave him to understand that I was ready to die for my nation, but not in the way they planned.

The critical time for us was at Easter eve. Immediately after Mr. Kennedy was expelled from the country, when at our great surprise regular troops surrounded our school building. This lasted three nights, and all our friends with great anxiety watched constantly and came to our rescue, for rumors were scattered that they wished to burn us alive. What kept them back from fulfilling their evil purposes? It is not known.

The school continued its work until the end of May, 1913, when we were threatened that it was to be closed, and I sent to exile. We completed our work before any word could be sent me. In July I had to flee to Monastir for my life.

The above mentioned incidents are insignificant as compared with the other cruelties which I cannot mention on paper. The world must surely be amazed that nations calling themselves Christians can either through anger or greed commit such barbarous acts on their brethren. What we expected from the Turks we got in abundance from the Christians. Instead of liberty and peace, for which we fought for so many years, they brought all the debasing elements of their civilization with unbridled appetites and passion, which are a great disaster to our invaded places. Yes, the Balkan allies fought side by side simply for the devastation and extermination of our nation; and it is surprising when I say the plain truth, that the population, at present under the Serbian and Greek banners, are calling for the rule of the Crescent and not the Cross.

On December 20, 21 and 22nd the Turkish army reinforced by the greater part of the army which escaped from Monastir made a series of attacks on the Hellenic forces threatening Janina from the south. The chief attack was directed against the left wing of the Greek army. On the 21st an attack as made on the whole of the Greek front. On the 22nd the attack upon the centre was repeated.

The Greek predictions as to the approaching fall of *Bezhani* proved to be too optimistic, and the Turkish successes were probably more complete than the authorities at Athens chose to admit.

On December 29th a lively artillery attack accompanied by a furious attack by the Turks began at *Bezhani*. The Turks concentrated their forces on the right wing and assaulted the Greek forces. After some fierce fighting *General Sapoundzakis,* who had hurried up with reintorcements, succeeded in repelling the enemy and making a counter attack. The Turks, however, continued to make assaults all through the night, but were driven back with heavy losses.

New Year's day was ushered in by a bombardment. The garrison's artillery did not reply. At about three o'clock in the morning the Turks attacked the Greek center and left wing. Fighting continued throughout the month of January without very definite results. On January 20th the Greeks commenced a general attack on Bezhani, the key to Janina, but all this fighting proved of little effect. On March 4th a general attack on the fortifications of Janina was begun on a new plan. The crown prince ordered a concentrated bombardment of the enemy's positions and the Greek guns poured some ten thousand shells into the Turkish lines. The Bezhani first was bombarded by ten siege guns placed at *Kanata,* which were hidden from view by the ridge of an intervening hill. Its batteries did not reply at first, but later in the day returned the Greek fire, which by the evening had silenced six of them. In the meantime large bodies of Greek troops, advancing rapidly from the left approached the *Manohasa* heights. During the night the bombardment slackened, but on March 5th it was again resumed, fifteen thousand shells being fired during the day. The Greek troops on the left attacked the enemy, who fled towards Janina, closely pursued across the plain. By eleven A. M., *Bezhani* had been completely silenced and the eastern forts were in Greek hands. The town was surrendered finally on March 6th to *General Soutzes,* the commander of the Greek cavalry, by *Vehid Bey,* the brother of Essad Pasha. Then the cavalry entered the streets. The official entry of the Crown Prince and his staff into Janina took place at noon. The prince issued a proclamation to the inhabitants of Southern Albania guaranteeing to them "their lives, their honour, and their goods," but stating that any attempts to provoke disorder will be summarily dealt with.

Columns were sent to occupy *Arghirokastra,* and *Permeti,* 46 miles north of Janina. The bishop of Paramythia telegraphed to ask the Greek troops to be sent there; and by March 13, *Colonel Ipitis* wired from *Paramythia* as follows: "Following my proclamation in the name of the King of the Hellenes, the Crown Prince and the Government to the notables, *Beys* and *Agas,* regarding the submission of the inhabitants of southern Albania without distinction of race or religion, I am able to report the occupation and submission of the whole of southern Epirus as far as *Kalama* and beyond Philiates. I have disarmed the inhabitants. *Mehsim Dino,* the deputy in the Turkish Parliament accompanied by several Beys and Agas of *Castri* have made complete surrender.

Thus the Greek *official military* war against the Turkish troops in Southern Albania came to an end; and now they concentrated all their energy to force the inhabitants to renounce their nationality in favor of the Greek. But of this we will speak at length later on.

VI.

THE EUROPEAN IMPORTANCE OF THE ALBANIAN QUESTION.

THE Albanians took no part in the Balkan War. They were sure that the aim of the Balkan allies was to divide Albania and to abolish their national existence. On the other hand, they could hardly help the Turks; for an Ottoman victory would have delayed still more their freedom. But they did not remain inactive. As soon as the war broke out, they started to make the necessary preparations for a formal and solemn proclamation of independence, asking at the same time the Great Powers to recognize it, and admit the Albanian people, the most ancient people of the Balkans in the circle of the family of nations. We give the word to *His Excellency Ismail Kemal Bey Vlora,* the distinguished diplomat and the hero of this great National event to relate how this was accomplished.

The Grand Vizier, *Kiamil Pacha,* pressed me to stand by him and offered me a portfolio in his Ministry. In other circumstances I should have accepted this post of honor with pleasure, but now a higher duty forced me to decline it. My place was no longer there, and I owed my services entirely to my own country. Kiamil Pacha finally bowed to reasonings the urgency of which he could not but recognize; and we separated with mutual regrets. On my return journey I arrived at Bucharest, where there was a large Albanian Colony. As the result of a meeting we held there, fifteen of my compatriots decided to go back with me to Albania. I telegraphed to all parts of Albania to announce my arrival, and declared that the moment had come for us to realize our national aspirations. At the same time I asked that delegates should be sent from all parts of the country to Vallona, where a national congress was to be held.

At Vienna I received a telegram from a personal friend at

Budapest, who invited me to go hither in order to have an interview with a highly placed personage. My first visit at Budapest was to *Count Andrassy*, where I met *Count Hadik*, his old friend and former Under Secretary of State, who told me that the person I was to see was none other than *Count Berchtold*. I met the latter the same evening at Count Hadik's house. His Excellency approved my views on the national question, and readily granted the sole request which I made him, namely, to place at my disposal a vessel which would enable me to reach the first Albanian port before the arrival of the Serbian army.

As Vallona was blockaded by the Greek fleet, I was glad to disembark at Durazzo. There we found awaiting us two Greek warships, which had been there since the previous evening. Our captain was very anxious about us, not without cause, and we shared his concern. But the officer who came on board, after making a scrupulous examination, in the course of which he found nothing but a few arms in the possession of my companions, left me free to land, and our vessel continued her journey.

We found the people of Durazzo in total ignorance of all the events that had been taking place. Deceived by the sparse news which reached them through prejudiced channels, they believed that the Turkish army was victorious, that it was in occupation of Philippopolis, and was marching on Sofia and Belgrade. They did not know that the Serbians were at their very gates. Our arrival occasioned some excitement in the town which was fomented by the Turkish element, joined by a portion of the local population, consisting mostly of Bosnian immigrants, who spread the report that we were *agents provacteurs*. This special and local feeling had not prevented Durazzo and the dependent districts from appointing their delegates to the national congress; and these left for Vallona with me and my little band of Albanians from Bucharest.

We travelled on horseback, and before arriving at our first stopping place, I learned through a notable of the neighborhood, who came to meet me, that orders had been telegraphed by the Turkish Commander in Chief at Janina to the local gendarmerie to arrest me and take me to his headquarters. We accordingly changed our route and passed the night in another village. The next morning the chief of gendarmes who was to have carried out this arrest brought me a telegram from the same Commandant at Janina, which asked the local authorities to receive us

ISMAIL KEMAL BEY VLORA.

Blank in the original

with honor and do what they could to help us on our journey. This, however, far from calming our fears, rather confirmed the alarming news I had heard the previous evening; and so avoiding the route on which we were being watched, I took a safer one, and we finally arrived at Vallona. Here our reception was quite different from what it had been at Durazzo. A holy fire of patriotism had taken possession of my native town, and public enthusiasm and delight greeted us everywhere. In a short space of time I found myself surrounded by eighty-three delegates, Mussulmans and Christians who had come from all parts of Albania, whether or not they were occupied by the belligerent armies.

The Congress was at once opened. At its first sitting, November 15-28, 1912, it voted unanimously the proclamation of independence. The sitting was then suspended, and the members left the hall to hoist upon my house—the house where I was born, and where my ancestors had lived—amid the acclamations of thousands of people, the glorious flag of Scanderbeg, who had slept wrapped in its holds for the last 445 years.

It was an unforgettable moment for me; and my hands shook with hope and pride as I fixed to the balcony of the old dwelling the standard of the last National Sovereign of Albania. It seemed as if the spirit of the immortal hero passed at that moment like a sacred fire over the heads of the people.

On the resumption of the sitting, I was elected President of the Provisional Government, with a mandate to form a Cabinet. But I considered it proper that the Ministers should also be elected by the Congress, and so I waived this prerogative only reserving to myself the distribution of the portfolios. The Government having been constituted, the Congress elected eighteen members who were to form the Senate. I notified the Powers and the Sublime Porte of the constitution of the new State in the following telegram.

The National Assembly, consisting of delegates from all parts of Albania without distinction of religion, who have today met in the town of Vallona, have proclaimed the political independence of Albania, and constituted a Provisional Government entrusted with the task of defending the rights of the Albanian people, menaced with extermination by the Serbian armies, and of freeing the national soil invaded by foreign forces. In bringing these facts to the knowledge of your excellency, I have the honor to ask the government of his Britannic Majesty to recognise this change in the political life of the Albanian nation.

The Albanians, who have entered into the family of the peoples of Eastern Europe, of whom they flatter themselves that they are the eldest, are pursuing only one aim, to live in peace with all the Balkan States and become an element of equilibrium. They are convinced that the Government of his Majesty, as well as the whole civilized world, will accord them a benevolent welcome by protecting them against all attacks on their national existence and against any dismemberment of their territory.

This was a great blow, not only for Montenegro, Serbia and Greece, but also for Russia and France, which for years were supporting the former three states in their claims of keeping for themselves the respective Albanian territories, which they had already taken possession of, or were endeavoring to occupy. England, Italy, Austria and Germany[1] reminded them that the Balkan War was localized on the express and solemn agreement that the Balkan Allies were waging a war, not of conquest but in defense of the policy which was formulated and announced by Mr. Gladstone, *"The Balkans for the Balkan Peoples."* And as the claims of the Albanians to be one of these Balkan nationalities, indeed, the oldest of them all, could not possibly be denied, that Montenegro, Serbia and Greece were in the wrong when they attacked Albania. The antagonism between the two groups of the Great Powers became acute as time passed by. Both Austria and Russia mobilized. It looked dark for a moment. But finally the wise advice of England prevailed. An Ambassadorial Con-

---

[1] England's motives in supporting the claims of Albania were sincere. Italy's selfish: Austria's and Germany's criminal. It was, indeed, a great misfortune for the cause of Albania, the fact that Austria took the initiative to support the claims of the Albanians; for though she was right in supporting the just cause of this noble, but small nation, still her motives, with good reason, were suspected by all the Powers except Germany, under whose orders she was acting. The antipathy of the world towards Austria naturally was extended to the cause she was championing, and thus, Albania, instead of gaining, lost a great deal of her territory.

ference was called, which met on December 13th, in London, and resolved that the question of the status of Albania and the question of her boundaries should be decided by the High Assembly of the Great Powers. On December 20th, 1912, Europe solemnly recognized the independence of Albania, proclaimed by the Albanians themselves on November 28th, 1912. Further, the conference decided that the Albanian State be neutral and her neutrality was put under the joint guarantee of the Great Powers. The Ambassadorial Conference instituted also an International Commission of Control to administer the country till the arrival of its Sovereign, who was to be appointed also by the Great Powers. But in spite of this, the danger for an European conflagration was not over. The question of the boundaries of Albania was still pending, and this question proved to have the faculty of causing international complications.

But why is it that the Albanian question holds such an important place in the *Green Table* of the world? To make clear the study of the Albanian question in its details, we will give a brief presentation of the principle of nationality, which principle caused the first and the second Balkan war; then a summary statement concerning the interests and the policy of the Great Powers in the Balkans, and finally a statement concerning the policy of the Balkan States towards Albania.

The principle, *The Balkans for the Balkan Peoples,* was formulated and announced by the illustrious English statesman and diplomat, *William E. Gladstone* (1809-1898), with the purpose of checking the imperialistic ambitions of Russia and Austria, which were endeavoring to annex the European provinces of European Turkey to their respective Empires.

Turning now our attention to the beginning of the Balkan war, we see as already stated, that all the Balkan states have solemnly declared before the world that the purpose of their war against Turkey was not to conquer and subjugate any foreign race, but to free their own compatriots, the Bulgarians, the Serbians and the Greeks, who were suffering in Macedonia under the Ottoman oppression. In other words, it was a war undertaken for the defense of the *Principle of Nationality*. Indeed, this principle of nationality was often repeated in the press in the official communications, and by the statesmen of different countries in their speeches; and thus this great principle, the *Balkans for the Balkan People,* became the popular saying of the day.

It was on the express and solemn agreement of this very principle presented to the Great Powers by *President Poincairé,* that the Balkan war was localized and the Balkan allies were left alone to liquidate the *"Macedonian Question."* But shortly after, the Balkan Allies, intoxicated by the unexpected successes of their military operations, forgot their solemn engagements made with the Great Powers and began to manifest openly their real aims, of dividing *Albania* between themselves, a country which had no racial connection whatever with either of them.

To attain their aim they began a systematic press campaign against the Albanians, using all the brains and money at their disposal. They worked unceasingly to contradict the truth, by trying to promote the belief that the Albanians *lack National Consciousness* and therefore do not form a distinct nationality. Historical facts, however, of which I will mention but a few here, speak loudly against their contention.

Through the conquests of Alexander the Great, the Greek language, being a more cultivated language, and possessing a literature, was adopted as a general means of intercourse between the different nations of his wide Empire, which extended over the three continents then known, Europe, Asia and Africa.

Speaking of the *hellenizing effect* of the Greek language, *Niebuhr* says that Asia Minor began to be hellenized while as yet few Greeks have settled among them.

It is true that in *Macedonia, Epirus* and *Illyria* the Greek language was imported even earlier than this date; and it is clear that in the days of *Philip the Great* and *Pyrrhus*, the *courtiers, generals* and *statesmen* conversed in Greek, wrote in Greek and cultivated Greek literature; but this fact did not affect the people either socially or politically; they guarded intact; not only their language—which bears no affinity with either of the various dialects of the Greek —but also their customs, usages, and social, civil and military organizations.

Moreover, our ancestors, *the Illyrians, the Macedonians* and *the Epirotes* have not shown any sympathy for the Greeks. Two great historical events illustrate this. When the Persians started to fight Greece and when all the tribes of Greece united to fight the enemy, not only did the Macedonians, Epirotes and Illyrians refuse to join them, but they even became allies of the Persians in their war against Greece.

On the return of the Epirotes from Italy, in 274 B. C., Pyrrhus defeated *Antigonus* and became ruler of Macedonia and Epirus combined, though on his death the former revolted, and Alexander, son of Pyrrhus, now their king, declared war. From this epoch, there followed an alternation of disunion between the two people, of greater of short duration; but *neither* had recourse to Greece with a view to annexation or alliance.

But there is still another series of facts in favor of our opinion, viz., first, that while the Macedonians, Epirotes, and Illyrians intermarried among themselves, they never did so with the Greeks; and second, the fact that the Macedonians, Epirotes, and Illyrians were not members of the *Amphictyonic Council,* which was the political and religious center of all the Greek tribes.

When the Romans, irritated by *Perseus,* declared war, no application was made to the Greek republics for aid. This proves that the alliance, which had existed under Philip, by his admission into the *Amphictyonic Council* was purely personal and political. This had ceased with his death and the prior state of things had resumed its sway. On the other hand, *the Epirotes* and *Illyrians* who were *Macedonians* in race, language and sentiment, rushed as one man to the aid of Perseus and were involved in the common ruin which followed the defeat of *Pydna.* Macedonia was divided into four provinces under Roman supremacy, while Epirus was devastated, its inhabitants reduced to slavery, and its ruler *Gentius* carried to Rome to adorn the triumph of the conqueror.

The Roman Empire sent over large numbers of Roman citizens to colonize the country and to assimilate the inhabitants of the three Albanian provinces; and although Albania remained under their rule for a period of about six centuries, the Roman conquest and civilization wrought little influence in the social condition of the Albanians. They still retained their language and their national manners and usages, and remained a distinct people with *a distinct national consciousness.*

After the death of *Theodosius the Great,* in 395 A. D., the Roman Empire was divided between his two sons, *Honorius* and *Arcadius.* The latter took the Eastern Em-

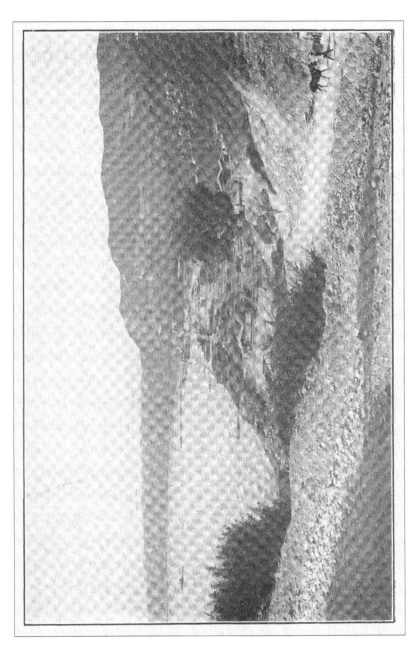

The port of Vallona or the Gibraltar of the Adriatic

pire, of which Albania became a part, included in the Illyrian prefecture.

The importance of the *Byzantine* culture and literature, in the history of the world is beyond dispute. They not only guarded for more than a thousand years the intellectual heritage of *antiquity,* but also called into life a peculiar medieval culture and literature of their own. They communicated the treasures of the old pagan as well as of their own Christian literature *to all* neighboring nations, especially through the Greek Church. Finally the learned men of the dying Byzantine Empire, fleeing from the barbarians (the Turks), transplanted the treasures of the Hellenic wisdom to the West, and thereby fertilized the Western peoples with genius of culture.

An important group of these emigrants settled in the village of *Moskopolis,* in the district of Kortcha, Albania, and thus the little village became a town of 60,000-70,000 inhabitants and for 350 years it boasted a famous school, a public library and a printing press.

The fact which we wish to emphasize is that while this powerful Byzantine culture and civilization came in contact daily with the Albanian people for a period of 14 centuries, it did not influence them much.

Beginning with the year 276 A. D., Albania was successively invaded by *the Goths, the Huns,* the Serbians, the Bulgarians and the *Normans* for a period of 12 centuries, but the influence wrought by all these upon the Albanian people amounts to almost nothing; they left as souvenirs of their incursions only a few geographical names.

In 1478 Albania became and remained till 1912 a part of the Turkish Empire, which inaugurated a system of oppression and persecution and deprived the Albanian people of the sacred right to educate themselves in their own language, while the foreign propaganda and intrigue had a wide open door and a free hand to divide and denationalize the Albanian nation. Special note must be made concerning the privilege given to the Greek Orthodox Church to organize "Greek communities," or *"milets"* out of the other nationalities which professed "the Greek Orthodox religion." And for many years the Hellenic kingdom has thrown dust in the eyes of Europe by confusing Greek religion with the Greek nationality and has prejudiced the national cause of Albania by adopting and making her own *Stamboul* fashion of calling the Albanians, who profess Mahomedanism, *Turks*, and those who profess Orthodoxy, *Greeks*.

In 1878, at the Congress of Berlin, the Greeks advanced claims to annex Southern Albania; but the Albanians rose like one man against their ill-founded and unjust pretentions and saved their land from their greed.

But the Greeks did not give up their hope, and after years of unscrupulous religious and political intrigue in 1897, declared war on Turkey with the purpose of getting Southern Albania, believing that its inhabitants *now* would welcome their army as liberators; but were bitterly deceived in their expectations. *E. M. Vogüé*, an eye witness, speaking of the Greek campaign of 1897 in Southern Albania, says:

"En Epire l'événement n'a pas mieux justifié les espérances des libérateurs. Les soldats du *colonel Manos* se sont avancés sur la route de Janina, ils y ont fait entrendre le cri d'indépendance; aucun écho n'a repondu sur un sol jalousement gardé par des Albanais. Ces clans defiants et beliqueux tolèrent par habitude la suzeraineté du Turc, ils ne recevront la loi d'aucun autre maitre; et on ne plaisante pas avec les Albanais. Les vieux Epirotes de Pyrrhus et l'Alexandre, l'Ali de Tépéleni et de Mehmet Ali n'ont pas dégénéré; ils restent les incomparables sergents qui assurèrent la victorie et maintinrent la domination de tous les conquerants orientaux."

In 1912-1913 the Greeks were forced to recognize that the inhabitants of Southern Albania were Albanians by race, language and customs; but they based their claims on the assumption that they were Greeks by feeling, adding that the sentiment is the decisive factor in matter of nationality.

The events that followed demonstrated fully that the inhabitants of Southern Albania are, as the rest of them, Albanians not only by race, language and customs, *but by sentiment also*. If they were truly Greek by feeling, why did 300,000-400,000 of them flee before the Greek army when they illegally invaded Southern Albania in 1914, just a few months before the outbreak of the European war and go to starve under the olive trees of Vallona? If they were truly Greeks by feeling, why did the Greek army massacre so many of those who could not get away; and, why did they devastate the whole country?

Not only the inhabitants of Albania itself could not be persuaded either by political oppression, or by religious intrigue, or by foreign propaganda of civilization and culture to abandon their national characteristics and national consciousness; but even those who emigrated into foreign countries did not do so, as it may be seen by the survival for centuries of the Albanian colonies in *Calabria*, Italy, and *Attica*, Greece.

But what do all these historical facts mean? Do they mean that the Albanians are incapable of civilization and progress? No. They simply tell us that the Albanian nation held itself *always* distinct from its neighbors, neither sharing their sympathies nor their aversions. They tell us that the Albanians *have rejected*, with an equal impartiality, the civilization of Greece, Rome and Byzantium. Moreover, they tell us that the Albanians have always considered the Greeks and Serbians as their hereditary enemies. Thy demonstrate that the Albanian nation is of a stock with *strong national consciousness,* that of being Albanian by race, language, customs and feeling, and therefore impossible to be assimilated; while they are keenly desirous to develop a civilization of their own; and their eagerness for civilization, culture and progress can be easily grasped if we only remember that during the first year of the Young Turkish *regime,* the Albanians held four national congresses, founded 66 national clubs, opened 34 day schools and 24 night schools, founded 15 literary societies and three musical societies, established four printing presses and issued eleven newspapers. In other words, they took all necessary measures for the enlightenment and uplift of the nation *in their own way.*

In view of these facts, it is erroneous to say that the Albanian nation lacks national consciousness. On the contrary, the Albanian nation gives us a unique example of how a small nation, without a written literature, without any schools and churches of her own, surrounded by so many and powerful foreign civilizations which endeavored to force themselves in, and politically oppressed for so many centuries, resisted successfully and survived them all.

It is not too much to say, therefore, that the *National Consciousness* of the Albanian nation is stronger than that of the other Balkan nations.

Speaking of the strength of the national consciousness of the Albanian people, *Mr. N. H. Brailsford* says, "Here at length is a race which neither religion nor education can corrupt."

England, Italy, Austria and Germany, rejected the view of the Balkan Allies, saying that the Albanians are not a distinct nation, and determined to support the claims of Albania. While the armies of Montenegro, Serbia and Greece were marching and penetrating Albania, the Italian and Austro-Hungarian ministers at Cettigne, Belgrade and Athens pointed out to their respective Governments that they could never agree to a division of Albania. That both Italy and Austria were determined that *Durazzo, San-Giovanni di Medua, Alessio Prizsen, Ipek, Jakova, Dibra* and *Ochrida*, as well as *Scutari* in the north; *Vallona, S-ti Quaranta Parga, Janina, Parivoli* and *Kortcha*, in the south, should remain integral parts of independent Albania.

Greece did not answer. She defied the four Powers, defending the rights of Albania, by disregarding the warning and by continuing the military operations, and penetrating deeply in Albania. Serbia answered the warning through Mr. Pasitch, the Prime Minister, saying:

> We feel strongly that it will be in the interests of neither the Albanians nor of Europe to insist on having an autonomous Albania, for the Albanians are neither ready, nor worthy of autonomy; they have no men to rule the country. Albania, if autonomous, shall always be a cause of disturbance in the Balkans. Under Serbian rule they will enjoy the fullest liberty; schools in their own language, religious freedom, and security for life and property to a degree they have never yet known.

The King of Montenegro appealed to Russia regarding the decision of the Powers, which gave Scutari to Albania, and *Mr. Popovitch,* the Montenegrin delegate in London, on February 27th, made public the following statement on behalf of his government:

> My Government has no reason to alter its views on the subject of the capture and the possession, already decided upon, of Scutari, and its environs. Scutari is a vital question for

Montenegro. The treaty of Berlin itself recognized the fact when it stipulated by a theoretical and ill-contrived provision that Turkey should give Montenegro access to the sea through her territory. The sacrifices we have made to attain this object are enormous. The diplomatists of the Great Powers, with Russia at their head, may come to any agreement they like among themselves, and on paper, but we shall see if their peoples allow us to be stifled. Our cause is just. All our allies are with us, as is the whole public opinion of civilized Europe. Heroism gave Montenegro its birth and so far has dowered it with life. If such be her destiny heroism will teach her to live. *This* is my last word.

Montenegro addressed this appeal to the people of Russia, believing that the Panslavits would agitate and force Russia to support them against the Powers which were defending the rights of Albania. "Russia is in alliance with France," they said, "upon whom she could call for support in these circumstances; and France being united with England by the closest understanding, England too, will step to support its claims."

Thus the question of Scutari, Durazzo and Janina became of menacing importance, for if Austria and Italy determined to defend the rights of Albania, Russia and France manifested themselves ready to support Serbia and Greece in their greed. England, being under no treaty obligation towards either of the two, refused to join them and thus saved the situation. Finally the statesmen of France and Russia realized that they had no legal right to claim the support of England unconditionally, and thus they began to be more conciliatory.

Furthermore, from the English point of view, the Balkan Allies had absolutely no title whatsoever to claim a single inch of Albanian soil, for as already stated, all the Balkan states solemnly declared at the beginning of the conflict to be waging a war in defense of the policy, *the Balkans for the Balkan People.* . . . And, as the claims of the Albanians to be a distinct nation by itself, could not be denied, England therefore, held that they made a mistake in extending their military operation in Albania.

Time has shown that Mr. Asquith was right in standing by *Mr. Gladstone's* policy, and that by standing for the formula, "*The Balkans for the Balkan People,*" he has preserved the peace of the world.

Before proceeding to consider the interest and the policy of the Great Powers in Albania, we must stop for a moment to say a few words regarding the *geographical* and *political importance* of this country. By its geographical situation, Albania commands the *Straits of Otranto* and controls the whole of the Adriatic Sea. While *Pola* controls the bottom of the Adriatic bottle, its neck is potentially dominated by Vallona. This *Gibraltar* of the Adriatic could be easily converted into a position strong enough to seal up the Adriatic Sea; and it is obvious that it would threaten the vital interests of all the states having outlets on it, if it is allowed to fall in the hands of a naval power, such as Italy or Greece. Besides, Vallona is the most superb natural port of the Adriatic. It has a wide bay with deep waters, and no rivers to sand it, and well protected by the island of *Sassano*. The southern side of the bay, called the *Dukati Gulflet,* is protected from all winds, and has a depth of not less than 60 feet, the maximum depth of the bay being 150 feet.[1]

---

[1] The following is the description of this important place by **Lear:**

Avlona lies in a recess or bay of the mountains, which here leave a level space of 2 m. or more between their base and the sea. The town is built for the most part at the foot of a crescent of rock, but the sides are dotted with houses; and at the two horns of this natural amphitheatre stand many conspicuous Dervish tombs of pretty architecture, surrounded by groves of cypress. From hence the eye looks down upon Avlona in its garden of plane and olive trees, its principle building, the

On the other hand, Albania holds a position which commands the shortest route[1] between Western Europe and the Near East. The Romans made use of this fact and built the celebrated road called *Via Egnatia,* which started from *Dyrrachium* and *Apollonia* and extended a distance of 500 miles to *Hebrus* in Thrace. The roads from Dyrrachium ascends the valley of the *Shkumbi* to Ellbasan, penetrates through a pass to the valley of the Black Drin, crosses the stream at Struga when it issues from the lake shore and passing through the town of Ochrida breasts a second mountain range and descends at last into the basin of Monastir, and meets there the other branch coming from Apollonia, at a place called *Clodiana.* Then the *Via Egnatia* passed over the mountains to *Heraclea* in Macedonia. It entered the plains at *Edessa,* and thence passed by *Pella* and *Thessalonica* to *Constantinople.* There were many other Roman roads in connection with the *Via Egnatia* and in the present day remains of them may be found both north and south of the Balkans.

It was through this road that the Roman troops were dispatched in time of need, and thus the Roman Empire was able to maintain her supremacy for centuries not only over the Balkan Peninsula, but over Asia Minor and Egypt.

These are in brief some of the most important considerations which for centuries have made Albania to be *the Master Key to the Near East;* the coveted apple between Italy and Austria and between the other Balkan nations.

---

fine palace of its Bey, and some good mosks which stand out in beautiful relief from the wide salt plain and gulf beyond. The Gulf shut in on one side by the long point of mountain called **La Linguetta,** and on the other by the island of Sassano has exactly the appearance of a lake; so that the effect of the whole picture is most complete and charming.

[1] The distance between Rome and Constantinople could be made via Vallona by a train-boat over the **Straits of Otranto** in 48 hours; while **via** Vienna it takes four days. It is impossible to overestimate the political and economical importance of this route.

While partially settled by the London Conference of 1913, the Albanian question still remains one of the most important problems waiting to be solved by the Supreme Peace Council assembled at Paris. The fact that the Allies and especially the United States of America, which so nobly has pledged itself to the great principle of nationality and self-determination is an assurance for the Albanians to hope for a *just* and *definite* solution, which will restore them national unity, will recognize their unprescribable right to govern themselves and develop a civilization of their own.

VII.

ALBANIA AND THE GREAT POWERS.

THE policy of the British Government in the Balkans has always been unselfish, sincere and impartial, her only purpose being to keep Austria and Russia from getting control of these important Turkish provinces. In all, the projects presented for the partition of Turkey, and there are a hundred of these,[1] England does not appear to be claiming any portion of the Balkan Peninsula.

In 1880, when it became evident that the integrity of the Turkish Empire could not be maintained in spite of the international treaty obligations, the British Government strove to create a strong living independent Albania, including within her boundaries *Kossova, Scutari, Janina* and the largest part of *Monastir* vilayet. *Lord Goschen* and *Lord E. Fitzmaurice,* both foreseeing the importance of the Albanian question, worked hard for this end. Had they succeeded many of the recent complications and much bloodshed and misery would have been obviated.

It is true that *Lord Beaconsfield* at the Congress of Berlin withdrew his objections regarding the boundary project proposed by the First Plenipotentiary of France, which was the interpreter of the Greek claims, but he has done it, saying that he would withdraw his objections in the presence of an unanimous vote of the other Powers, harmony being above all things desirable. These objections were made known to the public by Lord Beaconsfield himself on the 18th of July, 1878, when he presented his report to the House of Lords, saying that the demands of Greece were not only unjust, but

---

[1] Cf. **T. G. Djuvara, Cent Projets de Partage de la Turquie.**

extravagant. In 1912-13 the Balkan Allies, blinded by their ambition of dividing Albania between themselves, defying the views of the Great Powers, threatened the peace of Europe. It was through *Mr. Asquith* and *Sir Edward Grey* that this awful calamity has been averted from the world. In the course of the debate on the Address in reply to the King's speech, March 10, 1913, the question of the Balkan War came under discussion. In the course of *Mr. Asquith's* address, *Lord H. Cecil* interrupted the Prime Minister asking whether England had any agreement with France and Russia which bound her to support France in case of her being engaged in war with a Continental Power. Mr. Asquith at once replied that Great Britain had no understanding or engagements with France or any other Powers than those known to the House, and that under these agreements no engagements existed which bound England in any way to render military aid to France in any contingency whatsoever. Thus with a few quiet words, Mr. Asquith knocked the arms out of the hands of the French and Russian *Chauvinists* and checked the war fever which had overtaken Europe.

On Monday, April 7th, in reply to *Mr. Bonar Law, Sir Edward Grey* said:

We are a party to the naval demonstration against Montenegro, because we are a party with the other Great Powers to an agreement which the naval demonstration is intended to uphold. This agreement is that there should be an autonomous Albania. We willingly became a party to this, for the Albanians are separate in race, language, and to a great extent in religion. The war which is a proceeding against them has long ceased to have any bearing on the war betweer Turkey and the Allies, or to be a war of liberation.

The operations of Montenegro against Scutari, are part of a war of conquest, and there is no reason why the same sympathy that was felt for Montenegro or other countries contending for liberty and national existence should not be extended to the

Albanian population of Scutari and its district, who are namely Catholic and Moslem, and who are contending for their lands, their religion, their language and their lives. For these reasons his Majesty's Government has no hesitation in being parties to the agreement of the Powers about Albania. The agreement between the Powers respecting the frontiers of Albania was realized after a long and laborious diplomatic effort. . . . The making of the agreement was essential for the peace of Europe, and in my opinion, it was accomplished only just in time to preserve that peace between the Great Powers. That this agreement, if disputed, should be upheld by international action remains essential for the continuance of that peace. . . . because we know that the peace of Europe depends upon the maintenance of concord between the Powers most directly interested in this region, we have thought it right, and becoming a party to this agreement, we have undertaken the honorable obligation, to take part in the international action now proceeding to uphold it and make it respected.

At the London Conference of 1912-13, the national rights of Albania were stoutly defended by Sir Edward Grey, but the greed of her neighbors was too great, and he was able to save but part of Albania's territory.

On the day of the outbreak of the war in Europe, July 1914, the British House of Commons and House of Lords, spurred to action by *Hon. Aubrey Herbert,* discussed with indignation the atrocities committed by Greek troops in Southern Albania. Great Britain would have adopted decisive measures had not the war absorbed all her energies.

Since the European war broke out, the British statesmen have made many solemn declarations regarding the attitude of Great Britain towards the small nations. We will quote but two of these. On November 9th, 1915, when the war had already lasted more than a year and three months, Mr. Asquith on behalf of the British Government spoke the following memorable words: "We shall not pause or falter until we have secured for the smaller states of Europe their Charter of Independence, and for Europe itself and for the

KEY TO THE NEAR EAST

world at large, their final emancipation from the 'Reign of Force.'"

Regarding the Balkan Peninsula, worthy of note are the words uttered on Sept. 28, 1915, by the then Foreign Minister in the House of Commons:

"Our policy," said Sir Edward Grey, "has been to secure agreement between the Balkan states which would insure to each of them not only independence but a brilliant future based as a general principle on the territorial and political union of kindred nationalities. To secure this agreement we have recognized that the legitimate aspirations of *all* the Balkan states must find satisfaction. . . . The policy of the Allies is to further the national aspirations of the Balkan states, *without* sacrificing the independence of any of them."

It is not necessary to add to these quotations; for the Balkan policy of the British Government is the same since the time of Mr. Gladstone, *The Balkans for the Balkan People*. The Albanians know the spirit of impartiality of England, and they believe that the British delegates at the Peace Conference will insist for the impartial application of the formula, *the Balkans for the Balkan people;* for only thus the peace in the *danger zone* of Europe can be assured.

The Albanians came for the first time in contact with the Italians in the time of Scanderbeg under the following circumstances. In the fall of the year 1458, *Alphonse d'Aragon,* King of Naples, died. His son *Ferdinand,* being in difficulty with *Jean d'Anjou,* asked Scanderbeg's assistance. Availing himself of the official armistice which reigned at this time between his country and Turkey, the Albanian hero sailed for *Apoulia* with a thousand of his brave veterans in July, 1461, and delivered Ferdinand, who was seiged in *Barletle* by *Piccino,* and chased the latter, while the King was fighting *Sforza* in the province of Abruzze.

After this, Scanderbeg returned to Albania with part of his troops, and the rest settled themselves in the *Province of Otranto.* After the death of Scanderbeg, Albania being conquered by the Turks, a large number of Albanians emigrated in Italy and settled themselves mainly in *Calabria* and *Sicily.*

These Albanians have given to Italy a number of important public servants, the most illustrious of all these being *Francesco Crispi,* born in Sicily. And although they have kept their national customs and language, they have taken active part in the struggle for the national unity of their adopted country, and have gained an honorable place in the history of the emancipation of Italy.

From the day in which her unity was gained, Italy determined to defend the Adriatic against Austria's greed, which until then was the only mistress. Ever since that time the competition in Albania between Austria and Italy has been constant.

The outstanding personality in Italian politics from 1878 to 1896 was undoubtedly Crispi. He abandoned the policy of his predecessors, who had cast covetous eyes upon Albania ever since 1870, saying that "The Italian National Party desired the formation of a Balkanic Confederation, having as its capital Constantinople; that the Turks could have their place in this confederation if they wished to live as brothers with the Balkan nations, and not as masters over them; that the Sultan ought to go over to Asia."

After the death of this remarkable statesman and shrewd diplomat, the imperialistic policy of Italy was resumed by diplomats who are living in the past, and who have become champions of an old doctrine, a doctrine contrary to the national sentiment reigning at present throughout the world.

That Italian diplomacy has cast covetous eyes on Albania from some decades is evident from the following authorized statements. *Admiral Bettollo* in an interview given declared: "Concerning Vallona, Italy will never be willing to accept a great Power to establish itself there, directly or indirectly; and least of all, she will never be willing to yield in having this splendid position transformed into a basis of military operations. If Vallona must one day become such a military basis, then it will be only Italy which will be entitled to occupy, for if Vallona would be in the hands of another maritime power, then the efficiency of *Taranto and Brindisi* would be considerably diminished, with the *great* danger for our strategical situation in the canal of Otranto."

This policy of Italy was expressed also in diplomatic terms in May, 1904, not less clearer by *Mr. Tittoni,* then minister of foreign affairs, who said: "Albania has no great importance in itself. All her importance lies in her sea coast and ports, which will assure to Austria and Italy, in case when one of these two powers would be mistress, the uncontested supremacy on the Adriatic; but neither Italy can consent this supremacy to Austria, nor Austria to Italy. So, in case one of these two Powers desires to conquer it, the other will oppose it with all her might. This is the logic of the situation itself."

Italy would have used force of arms long ago to get possession of Albania, if Austria was not in her way. Thus *Consulta* made treaty agreements with Austria, as early as 1898 to preserve the *status quo* of Turkey in Albania which agreements were made integral parts of the treaty of the

Triple Alliance.[1] On the other hand to prepare her way for the future she adopted a policy of "peaceable penetration," in Albania.

The "peaceful penetration" was inaugurated by following Austria's and Greece's examples. Italy at once founded centres of intrigue in the most important towns of the Albanian coast. In Scutari, they established a "home for the aged," and opened schools there, where agents were trained for the Italian propaganda. In addititon to these institutions in *Scutari,* the Italians possessed schools at *Vallona* and at *Janina.*

In spite of the fact that Austria's propaganda in Albania was of an early origin, in spite of the fact that the Dual Monarchy had the upper hand in Albania largely through the Catholic Clergy, who were trained in Austria, nevertheless it is during recent years that the Italian propaganda made some progress. This progress is due to the fact that they came in Albania covered with a new robe of intrigue, unknown to the people. The Italians opened trading schools for boys and girls pretending to teach them carpentering, printing, tailoring, bookbinding, etc.

---

[1] L'Autriche Hongrie et l'Italie n'ayant en vue que la maintien autant que possible du **statu-quo** territorial en Orient, s'engagent à user de leur influence pour prevenir toute modification territorial qui porterait dommage à l'une ou à l'autre des Puissances signataires du présent traité. Elle se communiqueront à cet effet tous les renseignements de nature à s'éclairer mutuellement sur leurs propres dispositions ainsi que sur celles d'autres Puissances. Toutefois dans le cas où, par suite des événement, le maintien du **statu-quo** dans les regions des Balkans ou des côtes et iles ottomanes dans l'Adriatique et dans la mer Egée deviendrait impossible et que, soit en consequence de l'action d'une Puissance tierce, soit autrement, l'Autriche Hongrie, ou l'Italie se verraient dans la nécessité de le modifier par une occupation temporaire ou permanente de leur part, cette occupation n'aura lieu qu'après un accord préalable entre les deux Puissances, basé sur le principe d'une compensation reciproque pour tous avantage, territorial ou autre, que chacune d'elle obtiendrait en sus du **statu-quo** actuel et donnant satisfaction aux intérets et aux prétentions bien fondées des deux Parties.
(The Treaty of the Triple Alliance, Art. 7.)

KEY TO THE NEAR EAST

This treaty agreement suited the Italian diplomacy, beautifully for the time being. The Italian trade in the Ottoman Provinces favored by the equality of the tariff, was expanding more rapidly than that of any other country. On the contrary if these Turkish dominions were to fall under the rule or under the exclusive influence of Austria or Russia, or of the Balkan states, the Italian trade would soon be greatly reduced, if not entirely driven out from the Near Eastern markets. It was on the basis of these considerations that *Consulta* determined to support most strongly the programme of reforms in Turkey, believing that by so doing, the *status-quo* in the Balkans could be maintained, against the national aspirations of the Balkan nations, who were suffering under Turkish oppression, and who were struggling and fighting for their own independence. The Albanian revolution of 1909-1912 made it clear to everybody though, that the *Status-quo* in the Balkans could not be maintained any longer, and both *Consulta* and *Ballplatz* were forced to come together and revise their treaty agreements in regard to Albania. And since, it has been impossible for them to come to an agreement of dividing the country between themselves, they decided to support the programme of the Albanians. Their new agreement was made public by *Professor Baldacci,* who said, "Our formula is as follows, in the case the *Statu-quo* of Turkey cannot be maintained in Albania, then no other banner except the Albanian will be hoisted on the Shkipëtar town of Vallona."

It was on the basis of this agreement that Italy officially joined Austria in her representations at Cettigne, Belgrade and Athens, when it became evident that the Balkan Allies' purpose was the partition of Albania, and not the liberation of their brethren of Macedonia from the Turkish yoke. The great object of both *Consulta* and *Ballplatz* in desiring an autonomous Albania was to prevent either Power from acquiring possession of Vallona, the master-key of the Adriatic sea. From events which developed later on though, it is evident that Italy had a secret agreement with Greece regarding Southern Albania. For those who were acquainted with the secret policy of Italy, it was not a surprise to see the rare good grace with which Consulta swallowed the capture of Janina, the capital of Southern Albania, by Greece; to see how she dragged out the negotiations at the London Conference on the question of the southern and southeastern frontiers of Albania, and finally how she consented to hand over to Greece, the entire district of *Chameria,* which is purely Albanian. She trespassed even over the agreement of July 1, 1880, by which the *Thalweg* of the Kalama, a river flowing into the channel of Corfu was recommended by the Powers, as the suitable frontier between Greece and Albania.

But this is not all. After the Italian representative, on behalf of his Government, had signed the international agreement reached by the six Great Powers of Europe at the London Conference recognizing the independence of Albania, after signing the agreement regarding its boundaries, Italy started to fight this newly-born state, giving it a deadly stroke before it had time to get on its feet. It is not a secret of today that the criminal movement, under the manufactured term of *"Epirotian Movement,"* organized, supported and carried on by the Greek Government had not only the consent but even the support of the *Consulta.* And when it became evident that this movement was to fail, Italy organized the *"Mohammedan Movement,"* under Essad Pasha, combining it with the *Epirotian Movement* to fight the Albanian Government, giving as an excuse that she was fighting the *Mbret* of the Albanians, who, she said, was a tool in the hands of Austria.

When the European War broke out the treasury of Albania had available only $60,000. The Albanian Minister of Finances was sent to Rome to ask for another installment from the international loan of fifteen million dollars pledged to her by the Great Powers; but all efforts were useless, for Italy opposed her veto. Thus Albania was left in lurch by those who had sworn to befriend her. On Sept. 3rd, 1914, the *Mbret* as well as the members of the Albanian Government under lamentable conditions of which they were not responsible left the country turning over the affairs of the state to the *International Commission of Control* instituted by the London Conference.

Shortly after this, the agreement between Italy and Greece for the partition of Albania was renewed October 23, 1914, and put in practice immediately. Italy crossed the Adriatic and entered Vallona and Greece reoccupied simultaneously the Albanian districts of Chimara, Arghirokastra and Kortcha, which they call *Northern Epirus*. This event was widely commented upon by all the presses of the world criticising and protesting[1] against this act of Italy, to which she replied that "the occupation of Vallona was occasioned by the state of disorder then prevailing in Al-

[1] On December 30, 1914, the Albanian Society of Sophia, **Quendra Vllaznore**, addressed to the representatives of the six Great Powers signatairies of the London Agreement the following protest:
EXCELLENCE,
Les Albanais habitant la Bulgarie, tant Chrétiens que Musulmans, dans la réunion qu'ils ont tenue aujourd'hui ont pris la décision de s'adresser aux six Grandes Puissances, pour protester du plus profond de leur cœur contre l'occupation de Vallona par l'Italie. Cet acte, de la part d'une Puissance, signataire de la Conférence de Londres et approbatrice de la décision prise à Florence par la commission internationale des frontières méridionales albanaises, et juste à un moment où les autres Puissances se trouvent engagées dans la grande guerre européenne, nous parait comme une violation des droits des gens un mépris

bania; that it was aimed to safeguard the deliberations of the conference of London, Italy being the only Power that was not involved in the war; and that it was *purely* a provisional measure, meant not to be extended beyond the city of Vallona."

On May 4, 1915, Italy denounced her treaty with the Central Powers, and on May 23rd she formally entered in the war on the side of the Allies, blocking the entire seacoast of Albania, and leaving the people to starve. The following is the text of the resolution unanimously voted at meeting of the Albanians of America, held at *Faneuil Hall*, on Sunday, Nov. 4th, 1915.

The friends of Albania in *Faneuil Hall* assembled bespeak for this brave and oppressed nation, the sympathy and co-operation of the people and government of our republic. For 3,000 years, this race has defended its liberties, preserved its language and sought the blessings of freedom and peace. Since the outbreak of the European War, Italy, Serbia, Montenegro and Greece, all bound by solemn treaty to respect this sovereign state, created by the Great Powers of Europe, have for mere purposes of conquest invaded its territory, seized its flocks and crops, burned its villages, put its people to the sword and left starvation and disease in their pathways. Against this cruel injustice no nation of Europe raises its voice. Our great Republic has sent only one small schooner with food for a sister nation which defenseless and without fault is perishing of hunger. We solicit a part of the American Charity for the relief of this helpless people.

We expressly request the Government of the United States to

---

des traités et une action contraire à l'humanité. Nous protestons donc avec indignation et nous nous addressons aux ambassadeurs des six grandes Puissances signataires de la Conférence de Londres, avec prière de communiquer la présente protestation à leur Cabinets respectifs.

Veillez agréer, Excellence, l'expression de nos plus respectuenx sentiments.
17/30 Décembre, 1914.
Au nom des Albanais,
Le Président de la Société
"Qendra Vllaznore"
(Signe) Kr. Ilia.

KEY TO THE NEAR EAST

protect us against the official declaration by Italy of a blockade of the whole Albanian coast. This state is neutral and has no government to protect it; the blockade is unlawful, unprecedented, destructive of the commerce of the United States and the Freedom of the seas. For this nation, the most ancient of Europe, whose love of freedom and independence is as keen as was that of our revolutionary forefathers, who spoke from this hall, we especially ask the study and sympathy of the United States Government to the end that when peace is made in Europe, it shall exercise its offices to secure recognition, opportunity and freedom for this oppressed race.

Towards the end of the year 1916, France to put an end to the Pro-German intrigues of King Constantine, drove the Greeks out from the district of Kortcha and in co-operation with the Albanians under their brave leader *Th. Gërmënji*, occupied the town of Kortcha and its district, lowering the flag of Greece and hoisting the Albanian standard at the wild manifestation of the inhabitants.

Fearing that France might extend her occupation behind the district of Kortcha, Italy began at once to advance and occupy the rest of the territory assigned to Albania by the London Conference. On June 3, 1917, *General Ferrero* read before the people of Arghirokastra the following proclamation:

"To all the people of Albania, today June 3, 1917, the happy anniversary of the establishing of Italian constitutional liberties, we, *Lieut. Gen. Giacinto Ferrero,* commanding the Italian corps of occupation in Albania, by order of the Government of King Victor Emmanuel III, solemnly proclaim the unity and independence of all Albania under the aegis and protection of the Kingdom of Italy."

This proclamation made a revolting impression not only upon the Albanians, but among all circles who have at heart the great principles of nationality and self-determination. The reason is evident, for if this proclamation be shorn of its flowery phrases, the fact remains that without the knowledge of the Allies, Italy established its supreme authority over Albania, thus proving to the world that as far as she is concerned the pact of London of 1913, of which she was a party, recognizing the independence of Albania was merely a *"scrap of paper."*

Mr. *Isaac don Levine,* writing for the *New York Tribune* and commenting on this act of Italy, said:

"One day last month an international crime was committed in Europe. The Government of a certain power, without consulting its Allies, assumed power over a neighboring country. The power was Italy; the victim Albania."

On Nov. 23, 1917, *Leon Trotzky,* the Bolshevist Minister of Foreign Affairs, published the secret treaty which Italy made with Russia, Great Britain and France signed in April 26, 1915, three weeks before the entrance of Italy in war. The following is the text of this treaty, and from which everybody can see how great are the imperialistic claims of Italy in Albania, and elsewhere, if she is allowed to have her own way, which we have good reason to doubt:

The Italian Ambassador in London, *Marchese Imperiali,* on instructions from his Government, has the honor to communicate to the Secretary of State for Foreign Affairs, *Sir Edward Grey,* to the French Ambassador, *M. Cambon,* and the Russian Ambassador, *Count Benckendorff,* the following memorandum:

1. The Great Powers of France, Great Britain, Russia, and Italy shall without delay draw up a military convention by which are to be determined the minimum of military forces which Russia will be bound to place against Austria-Hungary in the event of the latter throwing all her forces against Italy. This military convention will also regulate the problems relating to a possible armistice, in so far as these do not by their very nature fall within the competence of the Supreme command.

2. Italy on her part undertakes to conduct the war with all means at her disposal in agreement with France, Great

KEY TO THE NEAR EAST 147

Britain and Russia, and against the states which are at war with them.

3. The naval forces of France and Great Britain will lend Italy their active co-operation until such time as the Austrian fleet shall be destroyed, or till the conclusion of peace. France, Great Britain and Italy shall in this connection conclude without delay a naval convention.

4. By the future treaty of peace, Italy shall receive the *Trentino*, the whole of *Southern Tyrol*, as far as its natural and geographical frontier, *the Brenner;* the *city of Trieste* and its surroundings, the county of *Gorizia* and *Gradisca*, the whole of *Istria* as far as *Quarnero*, including *Voloska* and the Istrian Island, *Cherso* and *Lussin*, as also the lesser islands of *Plavnik, Unia, Canidoli, Palazzuola, S. Pietro Nerovio, Asinello* and *Gruica*, with their neighboring islets.

Note 1. In carrying out what is said in Article 4, the frontier line shall be drawn along the following points: From the summit of *Umbrile* northward to the *Stelvio*, then along the watershed of the *Rhaetian Alps* as far as the sources of the rivers, *Adige* and *Eisach*, then across the Mounts of *Reschen* and *Brenner* and the *Etz* and *Ziller* peaks. The frontier then turns southward, touching Mount *Toblach*, in order to reach the present frontier of *Carniola*, which is near the Alps. Along this frontier, the line will reach Mount *Tarvis* and will follow the watershed of the *Julian Alps*, beyond the crests of *Predil, Mangart* and *Tricorno*, and the passes of *Podberdo, Podlansko* and *Idria*. From here the line will turn in a southeast direction towards the *Schneeberg* in such a way as not to include the basin of *Save* and its tributaries in Italian territory. From the Schneeberg, the frontier will descend toward the seacoast, including *Castua, Matuglia* and *Volosca*, as Italian districts.

5. In the same way Italy shall receive the province of *Dalmatia* in its present extent, including further to the north *Lissarika* and *Trebinje* (i. e., two small places in southwestern *Croatia*), and to the south all places as far as a line starting from the sea close to *Cape Planka* (between *Trau* and *Sebenico*), and following the watershed eastward in such a way as to place in Italian hands all the valleys whose rivers enter the sea near Sebenico, namely, the *Gikola, Krka*, and *Butisnjica*, with their tributaries. To Italy also will belong all the islands north and west of the Dalmatian coast, beginning with *Premuda, Selve, Ulbo, Skerda, Maon, Pago* and *Puntadura*, and further north and

reaching to *Meleda*, southward with the addition of the islands of *S. Andrea, Busi, Lissa, Lesina, Tercola, Curzola, Cazza*, and *Lagosta* and all the surrounding *islets* and *rocks*, and hence *Pelagosa*, also, but without the islands of *Grande* and *Piccola, Zirona, Buje, Solta* and *Brazza*.

The following shall be neutralized: (1) The whole coast from *Cape Planka* on the north to the southern point of the Peninsula of *Sabbioncello* on the south, this Peninsula being included in the neutral zone. (2) Part of the coast from a point 10 Kilometers south of *Raguslavecchia* as far as the River *Vojussa* on the south, so as to include in the neutralized zone, the whole gulf of *Cattaro*, with its ports, *Antivari, Dulcigno, S. Giovanni di Medua*, and *Durazzo* with the reservation that Montenegro rights are not to be infringed in so far as they are based on the declarations exchanged between the contracting parties in April and May, 1909. These rights being recognized solely for Montenegro's present positions, they shall not be extended to such regions and ports as may in the future be assigned to Montenegro. Hence, no part of the coast which today belongs to Montenegro shall be subject to neutralization in future. But all legal restriction regarding the port of *Antivari*, which Montenegro herself gave her adhesion in 1909, remain in vigor. (3) All the islands not assigned to Italy.

Note 2. The following districts on the Adriatic shall, by the work of the Entente Powers, be included in the territory of Croatia, Serbia and Montenegro. To the north of the Adriatic the whole course beginning at the *Gulf of Volosca*, near the frontier of Italy as far as the northern frontier of *Dalmatia*, including the whole course today belonging to Hungary. The whole course of *Croatia*, the port of *Fiume*, and the small ports of *Nevi* and *Carlopago*, and in the same way the islands of *Veglia, Pervicio, Gregorio, Kali*, and *Arbe*. To the south of the Adriatic where Serbia and Montenegro are interested the whole coast from *Cape Planka* to the river *Drin*, with the very important ports of *Spalato, Ragusa, Cattaro, Antivari, Dulcigno*, and *S. Giovanni di Medua*, as also the islands of *Grande* and *Piccola Zirona, Buja, Solta, Brazza Cikljan* and *Calamotta*.

The port of Durazzo can be assigned to the independent Mohammadan state of Albania.

6. Italy shall obtain *in full ownership*, Vallona, the island of *Sasseno* and territory of sufficient extent to assure her against dangers of a military kind approximately between the river

KEY TO THE NEAR EAST

Vojussa to the north and east, and the district of *Chimara* to the south.

7. Having obtained *Trentina* and *Istria* by Article 4, *Dalmatia* and the Adriatic Islands by Article 5, and also the Gulf of Vallona, Italy undertakes in the event of a small autonomous and neutralized state being formed in Albania, not to oppose the possible desire of France, Great Britain and Russia to partition the northern and southern districts of Albania between Montenegro, Serbia and Greece. The southern coast of Albania from the frontier of the Italian territory of Vallona to *Cape Stilos* is to be neutralized.

To Italy will be conceded the right of conducting the foreign relations of Albania; in any case, Italy will be bound to secure for Albania a territory sufficiently extensive to enable its frontiers to join those of Greece and Serbia to the east of the Lake of Ochrida.

8. Italy shall obtain full possession of all the islands of the *Dodecannese* at present occupied by her.

9. France, Great Britain and Russia recognize as an axiom the fact that Italy is interested in maintaining the political balance of Power in the Mediterranean and her right to take over when Turkey is broken up, a portion equal to theirs in the Mediterranean, namely, in that part which borders on the province of *Adalia*, where Italy had already acquired special rights and interests laid down in the Italo-British convention. The zone to be assigned to Italy will in due course be fixed in accordance with the vital interest of France and Great Britain. In the same way, regard must be had for the interest of Italy, even in the event of the Powers maintaining for a further period of time, the inviolability of Asiatic Turkey and merely proceeding to map out spheres of interest among themselves. In the event of France, Great Britain and Russia occupying during the present war, districts of Asiatic Turkey, the whole district bordering on Adalia, and defined above in greater detail shall be reserved to Italy, who reserves the right to occupy it.

10. In *Libya*, Italy obtains recognition of all those rights and prerogatives hitherto reserved to the Sultan by the Treaty of *Lausanne*.

11. Italy shall receive a military contribution corresponding to her strength and sacrifices.

12. Italy associates herself with the declaration made by France, Great Britain and Russia by which the Mohammedan

holy places are to be left in the possession of an independent Mohammedan State.

13. In the event of an extension of the French and British colonial possessions in Africa at the expense of Germany, France and Great Britain recognize to Italy in principle the right of demanding for herself certain compensations in the form of an extension of her possessions in *Eritrea, Somaliland, Libya* and the colonial districts bordering on French and British colonies.

14. Great Britain undertakes to facilitate for Italy without delay and on favorable conditions the conclusion of a loan in the London market, amounting to not less than £50,000,000.

15. France, Great Britain and Russia undertake to support Italy in so far as she does not permit the representatives of the Holy See to take diplomatic action with regard to the conclusion of peace and the regulation of questions connected with the war.

16. The present treaty is to be kept secret. As regards Italy's adherence to the declaration of September 5, 1914, this shall only be published after the declaration of war by and upon Italy.

The representatives of France, Great Britain and Russia, having taken cognition of this memorandum, and being furnished with powers for this purpose, agreed as follows with the representative of Italy, who was also authorized by his Government for this purpose:

France, Great Britain and Russia declare their full agreement with the present memorandum presented to them by the Italian Government. With regard to Points 1, 2, and 3 (relating to the co-ordination of the military and naval operations of all four powers), Italy declares that she will enter the war actively as soon as possible, and in any case not later than one month after the signature of the present document on behalf of the contracting parties.

(Signed in four copies, April 26, 1915.)
Edward Grey, Jules Cambon, Imperiali, Benckendorff.

At present, Italy is insisting that the Supreme Peace Council assembled at Paris should sanction this treaty, and also the claim of Italy to have the protectorate over the small part of Albania, after she takes for herself Vallona and its surroundings, and after Greece and Serbia and Montenegro take their respective gift of property coming from the *Consulta*, which does not belong to her, in spite of the wise advice, given to them by *President Wilson* to put a bridle on their greed.[1]

Before closing this section, it is necessary to state briefly that Italy's foreign policy aims to secure control of both shores of the Adriatic, to strengthen her position on the Mediterranean at the expense of others, excluding from the sea *the Albanians, the Slavs, the Magyars, the Austrians,* etc. defying both the principle of nationality and self-determination for which so much human life and property has been sacrificed. Even, if we admit that the interested parties will not be able to oppose Italy's claims, which is a daring assumption to make, the Italian people, and the Italian soldier who so bravely fought to liberate his subjugated brothers of *Trieste* and *Trentino*, would hardly be reconciled to such an imperialistic policy of the *Consulta*. So whatever she might get now, that does not belong to her, it will be only temporary; the trend of thought and feeling of the present age being, liberty to all people, great or small.

Modern France came for the first time in contact with the Albanians on May 26, 1797, when *Venice* capitulated to the French troops, and when France took possession of the

---

[1] The following is the text on one of the many petitions addressed by the Albanians to President Wilson while in Rome, and which is self-explanatory:

In the name of eighty thousand Albanians residing in free and liberty-loving America, who represent the nation that has no freedom of expression, we come to appeal to the great man of the world to intervene with the Italian Government to unite fully with your great and sacred principles, in laying a just foundation for our long suffering nation that it may enjoy in the new era of the world complete independence without any protectorate and with its ethnographic and natural boundaries.

(Signed) MISS P. D. KYRIAS,
CHRISTO A. DAKO,
MIHAL GRAMENO.

Ionian Islands and the town of *Preveza* and *Vonitza* of the Albanian coast.

On July 5, 1797, *General Roze* was sent to Janina to fraternize with *Ali Pasha Tepeleni,* and to hand him the French colors. The latter received the *envoyée* of France with consummate honors, and while receiving the French colors, he expressed in unmistakable terms his admiration and love for France and its people.

It was during this time that the French Military authorities were able to get acquainted with the special qualifications the Albanians possessed of becoming consummated soldiers, and at their recommendation France established an Albanian regiment of 3254 men and 160 officers and put under the command of *Major Mignot,* making it part of her army operating in *Orient.*[1]

The dealings which France had with Ali Pasha, especially after it accredited the great scholar *Pouqueville* to his person, made it evident that in fact France had acknowledged the independenee of Albania, whose capital, at that time, was Janina.

During the Crimean War, at the request of *Marshal Pelisser, Bib Doda,* the hereditary Prince of the Mirdites, for the services rendered to the cause of the Allies, was nominated *Pasha* and *Brigadier General.* Ever since, the Mirdites have made repeated appeals to the French *protection,* which was never denied them.[2]

Mr. Aubaret, a French consul, was *Bib Doda's* adviser, who in 1868 was nominated to be the executor of the

---

[1] Cf. **August Boppe, L'Albanie et Napoleon,** Paris, 1914.

[2] In Albania in virtue of the treaties intervened between Turkey and Austria in the eighteenth century, confirmed by the circular of the **propaganda** of 1888, the Dual Monarchy got the protectorate over Mirdita. Thus, by treaty agreements Austria had the **protectorate,** while France, by tradition and custom, had the **protection** over the Mirdites.

testament of the Albanian chieftain, placing at the same time his children under the protection of France. *Prenk Bib Doda,* the present chieftain of the Mirdites, was but nine years old, and with the assistance of the French consul, his cousin *Dhone* was designated acting governor of Mirdita till he becomes of age. It was during the time of *Dhone* that the Turkish by means of intrigues occupied Mirdita and made an attempt to abolish its privileges. But the French Ambassador intervened at the Porte; and Essad Pasha, the Governor of Scutari, received order to evacuate Mirdita.

In 1878, at the Congress of Berlin, France in common accord with Austria made an intervention in favor of the Mirdites. The thirteenth protocol of the treaty of Berlin contains the following clause: "The people of Mirdita will continue to enjoy their privileges and their immunities *ab antiquo.*"

But while France was thus defending the privileges of the Mirdites, *Mr. Waddington,* her first Plenipotentiary, opposed most strongly the English proposal for an independent Albania, on the principle of nationality, giving her a boundary on ethnographic basis, becoming the champion of the Greek claims at the expense of Albania. And why so? Was it because Mr. Waddington believed that Greece's claims were just? Was it out of admiration he had for the old culture of the Hellenes with whom the present Greeks have no racial affiliations whatsoever?

No. The foreign policy of the different European countries, at least so far, has been a matter of business, not of sentiment. France has become the champion of the Greek claims on Southern Albania, because by so doing she is fighting her adversary on the Mediterranean, Italy. She herself, being far from such an important strategical position as is the channel of Corfu, or of *Vallona,* helped Greece whom she regarded as her friend.

I speak in the past for the events which developed during the European War fully proved that Greece is not a sincere friend of France. The failure of the Allies on the Salonica front was due mainly to the unfriendly attitude of the Greeks towards France and her Allies.

On the basis of these facts, and on the basis that Italy can be prevented from getting possession of Vallona and of the channel of Corfu by the restoration of a strong and independent Albania, the Albanians hope to believe that France, which has sacrificed so much for the noble cause of *Liberty, Fraternity* and *Equality,* will cease to support the unjust claims of Greece, giving a helping hand to *Albania,* especially as she herself has been an eye-witness of the Greek intrigues and of the crimes and atrocities committed by them upon the Albanian nation.[1]

July 3, 1866, is the date when *Austria,* defeated by the Prussians, was forced to turn definitely her eyes from the Rhine towards the lower course of the Danube and the Balkans. Prussia not only did not oppose this new policy of Austria, but on the contrary helped her, for by so doing

---

[1] The following is the address of **Colonel Descoin,** the Commander of the French troops, which occupied Kortcha in December, 1916, hoisting the Albanian flag on the Governmental Buildings. "Shkipetars, my friends until December, 1912, you suffered under Turkish regime; in May, 1913, it was the Greek army that **mistreated** you, then until March, 1914, you became familiar with the inconveniences of Greek Civil Administration. In Dec., 1915, it was again the Greek military occupation. In October, 1916, it was the Greek royalist Civil administration, and in November, 1916, the Venezelist, followed in Dec. by the French military occupation with Greek civil authorities. You ought to have enough of all these experiments, and I have a very simple suggestion to make to you. Why don't you govern yourselves? You are Albanians. Be Albanians, then, and nothing else. Cease all intrigues and occupy yourselves with your own self-government. French troops are here to defend the territory, that's all. Be honest men, I'll be the Gendarme."

KEY TO THE NEAR EAST

Bismarck was accomplishing two purposes, viz., Austria by directing her forces toward Southeastern Europe ceased to be a rival of Germany; on the other hand through the advance of Austria's influence in the Balkans, he was preparing the way for the *Mittel European* scheme.

If one remembers that Albania is the *mistress* of the route to lead Austria to Salonica and the mistress of the Adriatic, out of which the Dual Monarchy intended to make an Austrian lake extending her Empire from Trieste to the Albanian coast, thus making herself mistress of the beautiful seaports of *Antivari, San-Giovanni di Medua, Durazzo* and *Vallona,* then he will easily understand why Austria displayed such a wide and strong propaganda in Albania. The agents of Austria have worked hard to raise and foster ill-feelings between Christians and Moslems, aiming to divide the Albanian nation and delay as long as possible any national movement leading to independence.

The Austrian propaganda was greatly strengthened by the establishment of schools. In 1842 the first Austrian supported school was opened in Scutari. About the same time, on the basis of a treaty agreement between the Dual-Monarchy and Turkey Austria was recognized as the protector of the Roman Catholics in Albania. Later the Austrian schools increased in number, the purpose being to use them as centres of intrigue for Austrian propaganda.

The greatest opposition to the English proposal made in 1880 for the erection of a strong living independent Albania came from Germany and Austria.

It was natural, therefore, for all those who were acquainted with Austria's Balkan policy, to be amazed with Austria's Balkan policy; to be amazed with her attitude of 1912, when she took the initiative to recognize the independence of Albania; and, to press her demand addressed to Serbia to evacuate Scutari, so far as to bring all Europe to the verge of war. Although, this time, she was supporting the right cause of the most ancient people of the Balkans, her motives were rightly mistrusted by everybody. Her real purpose was to break the Balkan Alliance and keep the state of unrest in the Balkans till she was ready to make the attack, for which Germany and Austria were preparing for some decades.

Russia and Turkey are old enemies. The dismemberment of Turkey,—of which Albania was a part until 1912,—can be justly understood only by reviewing in brief the history of the Russian intervention in the interior affairs of the Ottoman Empire.

In 1711, *Peter the Great* had proclaimed himself the protector of the Sultan's Christian subjects, with the purpose of finding a pretext to interfere[1] in the interior affairs of Turkey and thus hasten the dismemberment of the Ottoman Empire. Peter's action in this matter received full indorsement from *Catherine II*. She insisted on having it inserted in the treaty of *Koutchouk Kainardji*, Bulgaria, concluded in July, 1774, after the Turkish troops were completely routed by the Russians, in a war which began in 1768 and lasted until 1774.

The declaration of war came from the Sultan and was caused by the interference of Russia in the affairs of Poland, which resulted in its first partition. During this war, the whole of the country between the *Danube* and the *Dnieper* fell into the hands of the Russians; Crimea was conquered, and in 1770 the Turkish fleet was defeated in the *Bay of*

---

[1] The Russians based their claims of interfering in the internal affairs of the Ottoman Empire upon the decree issued by Sultan Mahomet II which recognized the Patriarch of Constantinople, not only as the religious head, but also as the civil chief of the **Roum Milleti**, by arguing that the greatest part of the Sultan's subjects are Greeks and that the Greeks are Russians.

Chesme by the Russian navy. The Russian interference in the internal affairs of Turkey, under the pretext of defending the Christian subjects of the Sultan led to numerous wars, involved the Great Power of Europe in many painful complications, for while Moscovit Empire was aiming at the destruction of the Ottoman Empire, England, France and later Austria and Germany were endeavoring for the preservation of its integrity. For centuries Russia has promoted her boundless ambition, but failed to accomplish its goal, that of attaching to the Slav Empire all the Christian peoples of the Balkans, regardless of their nationality, and conquering Constantinople.

Prince Gortchakof (1798-1883), realizing that the *principle of nationality*, which was just budding, was to be the great principle for the reconstruction of Europe, reshaped Russia's Balkan policy so as to be on the *surface* in agreement with the trend of thought and feeling of the coming ages. Accordingly, the *Tzar* of Russia ceased to conduct the destinies of the Balkan peoples in the name of *"The Orthodox Faith,"* and began to work on the basis of this new great principle, with renewed energy, in the name of *Pan-Slavism*, as they liked to call it. At once an inflaming propaganda was kindled and spread through the Balkans, under the auspices of the new Russian Ambassador at Constantinople, *General Ignotief*, who was a consummated *Panslavist*, by the Society of the Friends of Natural History of Moscow. The result of these vast and enkindling efforts in favor of their Slavic peoples in the Balkans led Russia again to armed conflict with Turkey. On April 24th, the Emperor of Russia issued the manifests from *Kisheneff*, declaring war on Turkey. After a few months the Russian armies stood victorious before the gates of Constantinople. But then England, on the basis of formal and solemn declaration made by Russia, that the acquisition of Constantinople was excluded from the views of the Emperor, intervened and saved the Turks from being driven out of Europe. Russia had to content herself with the provisions of the treaty of San-Stefano, of which mention was already made; but it is not out of place, to emphasize here once more that Russia, through severing a great portion of the territory of Albania, grafting it to the new principality of Bulgaria, tacitly recognized the prospect for the erection of an Albanian independent state.

Shortly after, England, Germany and Austria manifested themselves against the provisions of the San-Stefano treaty and summoned Russia to submit it for revision to a European Congress. The result of this interference was the treaty of Berlin, by which a great portion of the territory inhabited by Albanians was restored to Turkey.

Needless to say, this was a great blow for Russia and its satellites. But they did not give up their claims and aspirations. They resumed the practice of their propaganda with new vigor, and the consequence of it was the *Balkan League* and the war, which they declared on Turkey on October 9, 1912, the official aim of it being the liberation of their respective brothers of Macedonia from the Turkish oppression. The unfortunate thing regarding this act of the Balkan Allies was that their appetite for new territory increased as they ate. They did not confine their claims to the territories inhabited by people of their respective races, but blinded by their unexpected easy success insisted on the partition of Albania. In this claim they were strongly supported by the Government of the Tsar, their patron. The consequences of this imperialistic policy was the second Balkan War between the petted children of Russia themselves, besides bringing all of Europe to the point of an armed conflict.

VIII.

ALBANIA AND THE BALKAN STATES.

HE author of the imperialistic policy of Greece is *Count J. Capodistrias,* a Russian diplomat, who became the president of Greece after her independence. In capacity of chief administrator of his state he addressed on March 31, 1828, to *Emperor Nicholas* of Russia, a letter by which he submitted the following project for the political reconstruction of the Balkan Peninsula: First, the erection of the kingdom of *Dacia,* composed of *Wallachia* and *Moldavia;* second, the erection of a *Serbian* kingdom formed of *Serbia, Bulgaria,* and *Bosnia;* third, the erection of a *Macedonian* kingdom, composed of *Macedonia,* of *Thrace,* the islands of *Prototides* and the islands of *Imbros, Samothrace* and *Thassos;* fourth, the erection of an *Hellenic* kingdom formed of *Greece* from *Peneus* to the town of *Arta,* and of the neighboring islands. Constantinople, with a hinderland of 13-14 miles in radius to be proclaimed free city, and capital of the confederation of the preceding five states, where the Congress of this confederation was to meet.[1]

---

[1] It is worthy of note that **Count J. Capodistrias** includes Bulgaria in the kingdom of Serbia, and that while the President of Greece does not claim for his country neither Thrace, neither Macedonia, neither Epirus, neither Albania, nor a number of the islands, nevertheless his **arrière pensée** was even more pretentious. Of the five future states, three were to become **Greek,** and these will assure, he thought, the hegemony of Hellenism in the Balkan Confederation. Besides it must not be overlooked, the fact that Principalities of the Danubian Kingdom of **Dacia** were to be administered by Princes coming from **Phanar.** Capodistrias evidently counted on the assistance of the "**hellenized**" kingdom of Dacia. Thus from the five parties represented at the Congress of Constantinople, only one belonged to the dreaded Slavs of the Balkan Peninsula. At present we find ourselves to be far from the political schemes begot by the vivid imagination of the President of Greece, and we are afraid that after a while we will still be farther away.

Dr. A. C. Dandolo,[1] in 1853, taking up this project of President Capodistrias, revised it and enlarged it and presented it in the following form: First, the reconstruction of the kingdom of *Greece* with *Thessaly,* up to the gulf of Cassandra with Salonica and Mount Athos; second, the erection of a kingdom of *Epirus,* including *Roumelia, Adrinople,* up to the Black Sea and Mount Enos, the islands in the neighborhood of these places; third, the reconstruction of the *Roumanian Kingdom,* composed of *Wallachia* and *Moldavia* up to the frontiers of Austria and Russia of that epoch; including besides, *Serbia, Bosnia, Herzegovina* and *Montenegro;* fifth, the erection of a kingdom formed of the island of *Cypress, Samos* and the others in the neighborhood. Constantinople, as in the project of Capodistrias, should be proclaimed a free Greek city. This imperialistic idea has inflamed the imagination of the Greek publishers, to such a degree that even today, it has not disappeared from their minds.

What methods the Greek Government and its agents have employed to reach the goal of this creed of political faith and how hard they have worked for it, has been stated in the preceding pages, and we will resume the narrative of their further endeavors when we will come to consider the work of the London Conference and *"The Epirotean Movement."*

In the Balkans, besides the Albanians, Bulgarians, Greeks, Serbians, Jews, there is another interesting people, the *Roumanians* of Macedonia or the *Kutzo-Wallachians,* as they are called by some countries. These Roumanians, living on the right side of the Danube, are the descendants of the aboriginal Thracians, who amalgamated with the

---

[1] Cf. **Dr. A. C. Dandolo, Quelques mots sur la question d'Orient;** Corfu, 1853.

KEY TO THE NEAR EAST 161

Latin colonists and adopted their language. There is a strong resemblance between the language of the Macedonian Wallachians and that of the inhabitants of Roumania, although they are separated from each other by a wide belt of other races, mainly by the Bulgarians and Serbians. The Wallachians of Macedonia are very much scattered, their chief settlements being in the *Pindus* range, and in the neighborhood of *Monastir, Metzova, Kortcha, Krushova, Vodena,* etc. They are an extremely intelligent, fine-looking people of considerable business ability. Their towns and villages, which are usually found on the summits of hills, are more solidly built than those of the Bulgarians, Serbians and Greeks. Krushova, which suffered heavily during the Bulgarian uprising of 1903 was a notable instance. But in spite of their love of well-built stone houses, the Wallachians have strongly ingrained nomadic habits, and in summer time their towns are for the most part abandoned by all the able-bodied males, who wander about the country as itinerant *kiradjis* (dealers in and hirers of horses). Many of them are men of substance and have business connections with all the important centers of the Balkans and Austro-Hungary. According to some authorities, they are not more than 50,000, whereas Roumanian patriots affirm them to be at least half a million. Probably they amount to about 100,000. They have usually kept on good terms with the Albanians and the Turks, who, until the last rising, treated them better than their other Christian subjects. They attended to their trade and took little part in political movements. For a long while they were considered as Greeks, whose language they speak as well as their own. The Greek party still counts them as members of their own race in their statistics of Macedonia.

But with the growth of the national consciousness among the other Balkan peoples, it was natural that the Wallachians, too, should follow suit. The honor of being the pioneer of their national movement, and first to conceive of a community between the Roumanians of Roumania, belongs to *Apostol Margarit,* born in Monastir. He devoted the early years of his life to business and accumulated considerable wealth. Then he went to Bucharest, where he was fired with the idea of awakening a feeling of nationality among his fellow countrymen. In 1865, he returned to Macedonia, and set to work to carry out his plan. He determined to detach the Wallachians from the Greeks, to revive their language and to agitate for an *autocephalous Church,* like the Bulgarians, and deliver them from the unbearable yoke of the *Phanariot Clergy.*

In his patriotic endeavors, Margarit was most sympathetically supported by the Albanians, high officials at Constantinople, and by the Albanian people in all their centres of activity.

For some time, the Government of the independent kingdom of Roumania supported this movement of the Wallachians with a great deal of zeal and funds, although they fully realized that the Wallachians could not form an independent principality of their own, on account of being so small a number, and on account of the fact that they were not a compact mass, but scattered throughout Macedonia and Albania.

Living in the region of Pindus, where they form the bulk of the population, by the memorandum, which their duly accredited delegates presented to the Ambassadorial Conference of London, the Wallachians expressed their warm desire of associating their political life with that of the Albanians. They begged for the incorporation of the territory they inhabit, within the limits of the independent state of Albania, and were heartbroken to see their mother country consenting that they should become a part of the kingdom of Greece, from which they have so long suffered, in exchange of other compensations, which they were unable to see and appreciate.

Beginning with the year 276 A. D., the country of the Mountain Eagle was invaded by the *Visigoths,* under their leader *Alaric,* and by the *Ostrogoths,* under their leader *Tottila.* The Albanians, to save their language, their traditions and their customs, so dear to them, retreated into the mountains, and here they gradually dropped whatever influence of Roman civilization had entered into their life, during the last five centuries, which they thought would threaten their national existence.

But the *Goths,* after a sojourn of a few decades, began to leave Albania and go to Italy. Thus the lowlands of the country were left open, when a new race of intruders, the Serbians, began to cross the Danube, about 550 A. D., and occupy them. In overwhelming numbers, they poured in, following the scattered bands of their own race, which preceded them some three hundred years before.

In the first half of the seventh century, the Serbians were officially recognized by *Emperor Heraclius,* who persuaded them to turn their forces against the *Avars,* their common enemy.

Shortly after, they founded an Empire of their own, within the frontiers of the *Byzantine Empire,* composed of the territories known today by the name of *Serbia, Montenegro, Bosnia, Herzegovina, Dalmatia* and *Northern Albania,* with *Ragusa* as their capital.

The Albanians *nominally* passed from the authority of the Emperors of the Lower Empire, to that of the Serbians, and from that of the Serbians to that of the Bulgarians, and back again. But it was only the lowlands and the towns that changed hands; the mountains remained always in the possession of their aboriginal inhabitants, the Albanians. In 1241, after the death of *John Assan*, the hegemony in the Balkans, passed to the Serbians, who at this time were ruled by the great Tzar of the *Nemanja family*. It was during the time of *Tsar Dushan* that the Serbians penetrated deeply in Albania enlarging the frontiers of their Empire up to Prizren, Scutari and Durazzo in Albania.[1]

"Empires came and went, and passed over the Albanian as does water off a duck's back." During the Turkish *regime*, descending from their mountains, the Albanians pressed the Serbians to move back eastward and they occupied again the land which for thousands of years had been theirs.[2] History records two great Serbian emigrations *en masse*. In 1680, the Serbian Patriarch, at the head of 100,000 people of his race, moved from Albania and established themselves to *Carlowitz,* in Hungaria. In 1730, another crowd of 30,000 emigrated, following the same route as their predecessors. Those of the Serbians who

---

[1] **Mr. Wadhan Peacock**, in his interesting book, **Albania, the Foundling State of Europe**, says: "The Serb, though a plausible and soft spoken individual when he has not got the upper hand, is at heart a savage, and the Thrako-Illyrian tribes, who were driven out of Thrace and Macedonia to the highlands of Epirus and Southern Illyria, were the sterner remnants of a population which had seen old men, women and children massacred, and homesteads burned by the invader. Then began that undying hatred between the Shkypetars and the Serbians, which is bitter even today, for the Albanian still looks on the Slav as the intruder and the destroyer of house and home. This explains why the modern Albanian has always been more friendly with the Moslem Turk than with the Christian Slav. The brutalities committed by the Turks were trifles compared with the atrocities of the Slav."

[2] The Serbians conquered and held the country for a few centuries; but now they are only a scattered remnant, and this remnant only exists because it has been **persistently** supported and incited to **assert** itself from without.

remained in the country were assimilated by the bulk of population. Soon after Serbia regained her independence, the Serbian *Chauvinists,* under the auspices of their brethren of the north, who were anxious to get possession of the Albanian Adriatic Sea Coast, started a propaganda with the purpose of re-establishing *Tsar Dushan's Empire.* For the last three fourth decades, the Serbians and the Albanians in the eastern part of the Kossova Vilayet have lived together in a continuous state of warfare. So strong has been the strife between the two races that all the Albanian population of the district of *Vrania,* ceded to Serbia by the treaty of Berlin, had been obliged to retreat thence to the vilayet of Kossova, and in the process of this forced expatriation, there were wholesale evictions and uncompensated confiscations of estates. This state of feud between the Serbians and the Albanians is still going on, both races claiming that the country is theirs, each one giving her own arguments. But of these a fuller statement will be given when we come to consider the work of the London Conference of 1913, regarding the frontiers of Northeastern Albania.

At the end of the seventh century, Central and Southern Albania were provinces of the Byzantine Empire, and *Nikopolis* and *Durazzo* were their respective capitals. Both these cities were conquered by another race of people, the Bulgarians, who invaded the country in 679 A. D., following the Serbians. The Bulgarians came into the Balkan Peninsula from Asia through *Bassarabia.* They, like the Turks, were a fighting race; but whereas the Turks have always kept apart from European life and civilization, the Bulgarians became Christians as early as 864, during the time of *Boris;* and after a few decades were slavonized (914-927 A. D.), adopting the speech and the customs of the people, which they turned out of the eastern lands of the Balkan Peninsula. Under the leadership of *King Simeon,* they established an Empire in the interior of the Byzantine Empire, which was nominally ruling over these territories. The Bulgarian Empire of *Tsar Simeon* extended right across the northern part of the Balkan Peninsula, displacing that of the Serbians, who were defeated and subjugated. Albania was also made part of the Bulgarian Empire, but again it was only the lowlands and towns, and not the mountains, which were nominally conquered. Soon after the death of Tsar Simeon (927 A.D.), the Bulgarian Empire broke to pieces. His successor, *Shishman,* and the son of the latter, Samuel, were able to keep the western portion with Ochrida as the capital for a little longer. In 1018, Emperor Basil II, surnamed the *Bulgaroktonus,* defeated the Bulgarians and utterly destroyed the Empire of Tsar Simeon. Thus Albania passed again under the nominal sway of Byzantium.

After the treaty of Berlin of July 13, 1878, the Bulgarians who were the *avant-guard* of the *Pan-Slavistic* ambitions in the Balkans, extended their propaganda behind the Macedonian borders over some districts of Albania, which they claim as their own, on the basis that they were parts of Tsar Simeon's Empire. This Bulgarian propaganda, backed up by churches and schools, extended as far southwest as Kortcha, which as has been already stated, was the cradle of the educational and national movement of Albania.

IX.

EUROPE STRUGGLING TO SAVE HER CHECKER BOARD.

IT has been stated in the preceding pages how and for what purpose the Ambassadorial Conference of London of 1912-1913 was called, and the provisions it made on December 20, 1912, regarding the status of Albania. Now we are ready to discuss intelligently the question of the boundaries of Albania, which was left to be settled in the following sittings.

When the Ambassadorial Conference met to consider and draw the boundaries of the new state, three projects were laid before the *High Assembly* of the six Great Powers. Realizing that their original wish of dividing Albania could not be carried out, the Albanian problem being taken from their hands, the Balkan Allies endeavored to make out of it, a small and weak principality with a large *irredenta*, so as not to be able to maintain and exist.

On the north, the frontier proposed by the Montenegrin Government started from the Adriatic sea-coast at the mouth of the *Mati River*, about half-way between *Alessio* and *Cape Rodini*, and then went north and northeast nearly to the Drin.

By this project, the Montenegrins were depriving Albania of *Scutari*, its northern capital, which is inhabited exclusively by *Shkipetars,* and of all the plain surrounding it; of the mountains, inhabited by the Malesori Roman Catholic clans, and a number of other tribes, half Roman Catholic, and half Moslem; and also of the district of *Dukaghini, Luma, Ipek, Jakova* and *Prizren,* all of which are inhabited in immense majority by Moslem Albanians.

In favor of their claims to sever from Albania the district of Scutari, Ipek and Jakova, the Montenegrins appealed to the historical argument, saying that all the territories of these districts were parts of the Serbian Kingdom of *Zeta*, of which the present kingdom of Montenegro is the legitimate inheritor. The last version of their claims on Scutari was issued on January 27, 1919, by King Nicholas, who said:

"We must have Scutari. We have taken it three times with our swords, and each time it has been snatched away from us in order to fetter the susceptibilities of Austria, which has now ceased to exist. Scutari is ours ethnologically, historically and geographically."[1]

The Serbians and the Bulgarians were equally preposterous in their demands. They claimed the entire upper and middle course of the Drin, including the watershed on the east of the mountains of Central Albania, down to the mountain west of lake Ochrida.

This proposed boundary cut Albania in two, annexed districts *purely* Albanian, and deprived the new state of any outlet to the hinderland of the east.

In support of their claims, asking to incorporate half of the territory of northern Albania, the Serbians advanced the historical and sentimental argument. They said that they must have the plains of *Kossovopolie*, for it was here that the Serbian kingdom was finally defeated and Tsar *Lazar* slain by *Sultan Murat*, on June 15, 1389. They added saying that they must have *Prizren*, for Prizren was the capital of the Serbian Empire of the great *Tsar Dushan*, in the fourteenth century.

Speaking of these regions, as well as of those of *Scutari*,

---

[1] Compare this with the Russian official statement of April 10, 1913, at the end of the volume.

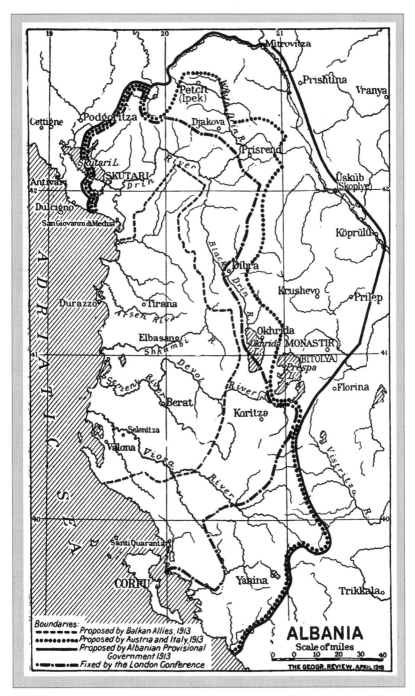

Sketch map of Albania, showing the various proposed boundaries and the boundary drawn by the London Conference (1912-1913).

Previous page:

FIG. 1—Sketch map of Albania showing the various proposed boundaries and the boundary fixed by the London Conference of 1913. Scale, 1:2,900,000. The boundaries are based on a map, 1:3,400,000, accompanying C. A. Dako: "The Independence of Albania a Necessity for International Peace, *Ylli Mengjezit* (*The Morning Star*), Vol. 1, No. 6, April 2, 1917, pp. 161-168 [an Albanian fortnightly published at Boston, Mass.]. For a somewhat different interpretation of the proposed boundaries, see the map (Pl. 33), 1:1,500,000, accompanying Antonio Baldacci: Der neue albanische Staat und seine Grenzen, *Petermanns Mitt.*, Vol. 59, 1913, Part 1, pp. 221-222.

Ipek, Detchani and *Jakova*, which were to be incorporated in Montenegro, the Serbian memorandum said, "The Serbian nation refuses to make any concession; it is an impossibility to come to any transaction of compromies. Indeed, there is no Serbian Government who will dare to do so."
The Greeks were no less exacting than their Allies. They drew their boundary line from *Gramola*, a point on the shore, half-way between *Dukati* and *Chimara*, and thence east to the fork of the river *Voiossa*, near *Klisura*, leaving *Tepeleni* to Albania. Thence the line went northeast by north to the proposed Serbian line southwest of lake Ochrida, cutting off from the new state provinces that are *purely* Albanian.

In support of their claims, the Greeks, in their turn, presented the following arguments. In Janina, the population, the commerce, the culture, are entirely Greek. At the proposal of the French Government, in 1878, the Congress of Berlin recognized the Greek claims advanced for Janina.

Geographically and economically, the possession of Janina leads to that of *Santi-Quaranta*, which in its turn commands that of *Chimara* on the sea-coast, and *Arghirokatra* in the interior. Indeed, all this region has no smooth road of communication except by way of Santi-Quaranta and Preveza, and it is at Santi-Quaranta only that the large ships can dock.

Ethnographically speaking, out of the 476,168 people inhabiting these territories, the Greek contention is that 316,651 are Greeks, 154,413 Mohammedans, and 5,104 Jews.[1]

Besides the above-mentioned arguments the Greeks say that in the districts they claimed to annex, there were

---

[1] It is important to keep in mind the fact that these figures are taken from the Turkish statistics of 1908, which classified their subjects, not according to their respective nationality, but according to their religious beliefs.

733 "Greek Schools" for boys and girls, out of which 3 *Gymnasia* for boys, one for girls, conducted by 927 teachers, and attended by 28,850 pupils; that is, by 9.2% of the population.

The boundary proposed by Italy and Austria followed the existing frontier between Turkey and Montenegro, as far as a point north of *Gussinje* and *Plava*, where it made a sudden loop to the south to include those two places in Montenegro. From *Gussinje* and *Plava* the line ran to the north to keep *Ipek, Jakova* and *Prizren* in Albania, but it left to the Slav the district known as *"Old Serbia,"* which is inhabited *almost* entirely by Albanians, and took from the new state *Kossovopolie, Ferizovik, Uskup*, and all the adjacent lands. From the summit of the *Shar-Dagh*, just east of *Prizren*, the proposed frontier ran almost due south between the lake of Ochrida and Prespa, giving *Dibra*, and the whole valley of the Black Drin to Albania. South of lake Prespa, the line bent a little to the east, following the Albanian claim very closely and reached the Greek frontier slightly to the east of *Metzova*, at the frontier of the late vilayets of Janina and Monastir.

The project of the Albanian Provisional Government demanded all the lands in the west of the Balkan Peninsula that are inhabited by a majority of Albanians and were till recently under the rule of the Sultan. The boundary can easily be followed on any map.

On the north, it kept from the *Boiana River* to the existing frontier between Turkey and Montenegro till it reached the *Sanjak* of *Novibazar*, south of Berana, whence it followed the course of the River *Ibar* to Mitrovitza. The boundary included the railway line as far south as *Kupruli* taking in *Ferizovik* and *Uskup* (whose inhabitants are in the great majority Moslem Albanians with about 25% of

Bulgarians and 7% of Serbians). The town was taken over in April, 1912, by the Albanians from the Turkish Government. From *Kupruli,* the project of the Albanian Provisional Government ran south to the angle of the Monastir railway near Florina, between the lakes of *Prespa* and *Ostrovo,* and then struck east, leaving out *Kastoria,* to a point nearly south of lake Prespa, whence it ran due south to the Greek frontier.

In reply to the arguments advanced by the greedy neighbors of the north, Albania presents the following considerations. Historically speaking, the Albanians have the upper hand in the Peninsula. They are the oldest, indeed the original and autochthonous inhabitants of the whole of the Balkan Peninsula. On historical grounds, they could claim the whole of Greece, Bulgaria, Serbia, Montenegro and Dalmatia. But they do not believe in the historical argument. For it is against the sacred principle of nationality and self-determination.

If the Serbians have a sentimental claim on the plain of *Kossovopolie,* the Albanians have a stronger sentimental claim to this region. In this field the Albanians fought against the Turks as allies of the Serbians in 1389. Later they, under *Kara Mahmoud Pasha* of Scutari, the semi-independent ruler of northern Albania, defeated the Sultan's army in 1786. Furthermore, it was at *Ferizovik* that the Albanians proclaimed their independence from the tyranni-

---

[1] In his book, **Albania, the Foundling State of Europe,** speaking of the boundary project presented to the London Ambassadorial Conference, **Mr. Wadham Peacock** says: "This attempt at the delimitation of the boundaries would, no doubt, have been accepted by Europe if the Albanians were strong enough or popular enough to command a propaganda such as has been worked by the friends of the Greeks, the Bulgarians and the Serbians, for it included the country in which the Albanians are undoubtedly in the majority, and in which the other nationalities have only maintained themselves by the most unscrupulous religious and political intrigues."

cal rule of *Sultan Hamid*, July 15, 1908. It was at *Uskup* that the Albanians gave, April 1912, the deadly stroke to the Young Turks.

The map of the Balkans was to be reconstructed, not on the basis of what her lands were a thousand years ago, but on the basis of what they are *now*. And at present the district of *Scutari, Ipek, Detchani, Jakova, Prizren, Dibra, Mitrovitza, Uskup, Kupruli, Perlep, Monastir, Resna, Ochrida* and *Struga* are Albanian.

In regard to Scutari, the Russian Official statement issued on April 10, 1913, says:

> Scutari is a purely Albanian town and the seat of a Catholic Archbishop. This has been fully confirmed by reports from the Russian vice-consul in Scutari, who has adduced facts to show that the Montenegrins play an essentially military *role* and have proved incapable of assimilating several thousands of Mussulman Albanians, who have been established in Montenegro for 35 years.
>
> Consequently the annexation of a portion of the Sandjak of Scutari would only weaken Montenegro considerably, as it would swell the scanty Montenegrin population with an influx of 100,000 men, foreigners to them in religion, blood and language, and Montenegro would thus be threatened with the fate of becoming a Montenegrin Albanian.[1]

The thoroughly non-Slavic character of Kossova, called by the Serbians *"Old Serbia,"* can be seen by the following impartial testimonies.

Miss Durham says, "Kosovoplain is now by a very large majority Moslem Albanian. . . . Albanian predominance is proved by the fact that so far as my experience goes, and I tried repeatedly, the Albanians are almost solely *Albanophone,* whereas the scattered Serbians usually speak both

---

[1] See the full text of this important Russian official document at the end of the volume.

languages and when addressed in Serbian, *often* replied *at first* in Albanian."

Mr. N. H. Brailsford, speaking on the same subject, says, "In the two districts of *Prizren* and *Ipek* there are no more than 5,000 Serbian householders, against 20,000 to 25,000 Albanian families. In all *"Old Serbia"* there are as many Serbian families as there are Albanian families in *Ipek* and *Prizren* alone."

Mr. *Gabriel Louis Jaray,* speaking in his book *L'Albanie Inconnue,"* of the ethnography of Northern Albania, says, *"Prizren, Ipek* and *Jakova* are *par excellence* Albanian towns."

Besides, there is a traditional feud between the Serbians and the Albanians which would render the peaceable administration of the country under a Serbian hegemony impossible. Far from considering them as his superiors in culture, the Albanians have learned to despise and to exploit them as his villeins.

In answer to the fallacies manufactured and used by her southern insatiable neighbor, Greece, Albania advances the following facts. The fact that *Epirus* geographically is an integral part of Albania can be easily verified on any map. The rivers of *"Epirus"* all empty into the Adriatic on the Albanian coast.

Generally speaking, the thoroughly non-Greek character of the Albanian territories claimed by the Greeks under the name of *"Epirus"* can be seen by the following testimonies. *Edward Brerewood,* writing in 1625, says, "But at this day the Greek tongue is very much decayed, not only as touching the largenesse and vulgarnesse of it, but also on elegance of language. For, as touching the former, the *natural languages of the countries* have usurped upon it so, that parts in which Greek is spoken at this day are, in a few words, but these: First, Greece itself, excepting *Epirus* and the part west of Macedonia. . . . likewise in the isles west of *Candia,* and along the coast of *Epirus* and *Corfu.*"

Viscountess Strangford, travelling in 1863, states, "we started on June 1, intending to make Janina, the capital of Southern Albania, our farthest point. . . . As we had divided upon the plain into three or four different parts, the first thing to be done when we had reached *Delvino,* was to find each other, but this was not accomplished until we had wandered far and wide, loudly shouting and inquiring from every man, woman and child we could see. We were decidedly in difficulties, for it was the hour of the mid-day sleep, and our inquiries were made in Greek, while the seeming answers were given in Albanian, neither party in the least understanding the other."

The official geographical maps of the eighteenth century of England, Germany and Austria called the portion of the country between *Voiossa* and the Gulf of Arta,—named by the Greeks *"Epirus," Southern Albania.* Again in the latter part of the eighteenth century, a commission was sent to measure the shores of the Adriatic. This commission calls the above-mentioned territory, *Southern Albania.*

Mr. Mavrommati, the Greek consul at Scutari, writing in *Akropolis* thirty years ago, states, "Ethnically Albania can be divided in five zones: First, *Southern Albania,* which extends from the *Greek frontier* up to the *Shkumbi* river; second, *Central Albania,* which extends from *Shkumbi* up to *Matti;* third, *Northern Albania,* which extends from *Matti* up to *Montenegro;* fourth, *Northeastern Albania,* which embraces *Novibazar, Prizren, Prishtina,* etc.; and fifth, *Western Macedonia,* from the Ochrida and *Prespa lakes* up to *Monastir* and *Perlep."*

Considering specifically some of the most important towns of this region, we can say: First, in regard to Janina in the fifteenth century, when Janina was attacked by the Turks, its fortresses were defended by Albanians and *not* by Greeks. This is proved by the history of the Ottoman Empire, written at that time, which says, that after Janina was besieged, three thousand heads of *Albanians,* inhabitants of Janina, were used to make a pyramid of trophy. Janina is called by the best impartial authorities, the capital of Albania. Here were the headquarters of Ali Pasha of Tepeleni, the independent ruler of Southern Albania, to whose court diplomatic representatives from England and France were accredited. In 1878, Greece begged Europe for a rectification of her northern boundary, but by the same assembly, Janina was officially declared as belonging to Albania, and so was left to her.

The great French Consul, *Laurent Pouqueville,* speaking about Arghirokastra, says, "There are in Arghirokastra about 2,000 Moslem Albanian families. The Bishop complained that there were only sixty Christian families thrown aside the plains out of town."

Mr. Paparousi, professor of History in Constantinople, Greek by nationality, published in May 4, 1910, in the *Neologos,* an article, and with authoritative and historical documents proved that *Epirus* has never been a part of Greece, but on the contrary, has been always an integral part of Albania.

The report of the foreign representatives of Monastir vilayet, and especially that of the *Swedish chargé,* for the reorganization of the Macedonian *gendarmerie,* prove fully that the inhabitants of Kortcha town and district are *purely* of Albanian nationality.

The people of the district of Kortcha number 132,000, of which 100,000 are Moslem Albanians, and 32,000 Orthodox Christians, Albanians and Wallachians. The city of Kortcha itself has a population of 22,000, of whom there was but one resident, Greek by nationality, the Bishop sent there by the Patriarchate to *anathematize* all those who, refusing to call themselves Greeks, work for the uplifting of their Albanian nation. But in spite of this ecclesiastical and school propaganda made with such great sacrifices by the Greek Patriarchate, the inhabitants of Kortcha district have always conserved their national consciousness, as the rest of their fellow countrymen throughout the country, their language and customs. Under the Turkish *regime*, when their nationality was denied to the Albanians, and when they were persecuted, Kortcha had the first Albanian schools, and always has been the centre of gravity of the Albanian national aspirations, with its schools, papers and societies. Kortcha is also the headquarters of the famous *Orthodox League*, whose purpose is to emancipate the Orthodox Albanians from the yoke of the Greek Clergy.

During the young Turkish regime, Kortcha has manifested anew its national aspirations by a meeting of 12,000 men, held against the young Turk scheme to force the Albanians to write their language with the Arabic characters, instead of the Latin. All the foreign consuls are witnesses of the spontaneous national manifestations as well as of the bloodshed in the summer of 1911 by the young Christian Albanians who fought for their liberty. They also are witnesses of the firm stand of the people of Kortcha during the summer of 1914, and how stubbornly they fought the Greek army who attacked the place like the *Huns* of

KEY TO THE NEAR EAST

the middle ages committing unspeakable atrocities with the purpose of forcing them to deny their nationality and claim union with Greece.

The claim of Greece to "Epirus" rests on a hoary confusion. She has been throwing ashes in the face of Europe for centuries by calling every "Orthodox Christian," Greek, defying the facts of the case. The majority of the population of the regime claimed by Greece is Moslem Albanian, while the Christian minority, though members of the Orthodox Church, is Greek neither by race, language or sentiment. The Christian inhabitants of southern Albania, or "Epirus," are "Greeks" only in the sense that the Roumanians, the Bulgarians and the Serbians were Greeks a century ago, when they had the misfortune, too, of being under the jurisdiction of the *"Orthodox Church"* of Constantinople. In fact, all of them are Albanian by blood, language, customs and feeling, and for centuries have proved to be impossible of assimilation.

In spite of the fact that there were three different parties, each one presenting its own claims, the problem of drawing the boundaries of Albania, in itself, would have been comparatively speaking, not a difficult one, if all the Powers would have accepted *Great Britain's* point of view, of applying impartially the principle of nationality in every region under consideration. But the representatives of the Great Powers assembled in Conference at London, not to solve the problem, but on the contrary with the firm determination to save their *checker board,* which they have played for decades.

On March 26, Sir Edward Grey, chairman of the Conference and the Ambassadors of the Great Powers accredited to the court of *Saint James,* on behalf of their respective Governments formally accepted the delimitation of the northern and northeastern frontiers of Albania, which had been adopted on March 22, after a prolonged wrangle between Russia and Austria. This frontier was drawn so as to leave the Taraboshi ridge to Albania, but a great part of the province of *Gusinje* and *Plave,* the important towns of *Ipek, Jakova, Prizren* and *Uskup,* the whole plains of *Kossovopolie,* inhabited in immense majority by Albanians, the town of *Perlep, Monastir, Resna, Ochrida,* and *Struga,* were all cut off from Albania.

On April 7, Sir Edward Grey, in his statement made in the House of Commons, said in part:

"The agreement of the Powers respecting the frontiers of Albania was reached after a long and laborious diplomatic effort. It was decided that the littoral and Scutari should be Albanian, while Ipek, Prizren, Dibra and after much negotiation Jakova should be excluded from Albania. This agreement was essential to the peace of Europe, and had been reached only just in time to preserve the peace between the Great Powers.

Naturally the Albanians were deeply grieved with this unjust decision of the London Conference and the people of *Gruda* and *Hoti* have immediately informed the Admiral at Scutari that they would not become Montenegrin subjects.

On October, 1913, under the pretext of quelling the uprising of the Albanians of the Dibra district, Serbia returned to Albania. With an army of sixty thousand men, she laid waste the districts of *Dibra, Struga, lake Ochrida* and *Goloberda,* in Central Albania, and *Gashi, Krasniku* and *Valbona,* in Northern Albania, killing and burning to death eight thousand men, women and children; destroying one hundred villages, and making homeless one hundred and twenty-five thousand persons. The purpose of the attack being to complete her work of destruction, which she began with the opening of hostilities, and was unable to finish when she marched her troops away from her coveted, *"Open window to the World,"* and thus give a stroke to the newly-born state before it could get on its feet.[1]

In spite of the assurances given, that the question of the southern and southeastern frontiers of Albania will be settled in a shorter length of time, the Great Powers contemplating to base their work upon the agreement[2] of July 1, 1880, nevertheless this question remained open till December, 1913. After a long wrangle, this time, between France and Italy the Ambassadorial Conference decided August 10, 1913, that the boundary between Albania and Greece should run from the Eastern limits of the Kortcha district, leaving Kortcha to Albania, to the *Cape of Ftelia*. For the delimitation of the frontier between these two points, the Ambassadorial Conference appointed a mixed Commission to go on the spot and draw the line, taking as a basis the language and sentiment of the inhabitants.

It took the commission three months to get ready to start. Finally they met in Monastir, and in October, in 1913, they proceeded. In studying the conditions and in trying to find out the true feeling of the inhabitants, they met with many difficulties and unpleasant experiences from the agents of Greece. The British delegate who was suspected of favoring the Albanians, was fired at by a Greek woman while in Arghirokastra.

---

[1] Cf. **The Cause of Albania's Trouble, by W. W. Howard. The Christian Work and Evangelist**, pages 480-481, 1914.

[2] In virtue of the Agreement of July 1, 1880, the Great Powers signatories of the Treaty of Berlin, recommended to the Sublime Porte, the Thalweg of the Kalama, a river flowing into the channel of Corfu, as a suitable frontier between Greece and Albania.

Meanwhile, European diplomacy intervened and asked the commission to draw the boundary not on the basis of their investigation and study, but on the basis of a compromise, which the Great Powers of Europe arrived at to suit their own affairs, and so the boundary was drawn as follows: "The southern boundary starts from a point between the village of *Tushemishti* and the Monastery of St. Naum, and strikes towards the southern extremity of the Prespa lake; then following the eastern boundary of the Kortcha district passing not far from Kastoria, whence almost in a straight line goes as far as Leskoviki. Another almost straight line directed from northeast to southwest ends at Cape Stylos. This boundary includes *Kolonia, Permeti* and *Arghirokastra,* with all its valley in Albania, while *Konitza,* the district of *Pindus, Janina,* the capital of south Albania, and the whole province of *Chameria,* almost exclusively inhabited by Albanians, to Greece. Thus the representatives of the Great Powers, faithful disciples of the "Old School diplomacy," ignored the interest of the people, and drew an Albania on the map, which shut the Albanians in the narrow mountains, "the most ancient race of the Balkans and of Europe, being forced to yield towns and low lands to the Serbians and the Greeks, and starve on the ridge of sterile crags."[1]

Again the European diplomacy, instead of asking Greece

---

[1] In his book, "**Albania, the Foundling State of Europe,**" speaking of the boundary drawn by the London Conference, Mr. Wadham Peacock says, "From the cynical way in which large populations of Albanians are ignored and handed over to their hereditary enemies, it is obvious that the Great Powers are not over anxious to found an Albanian principality which could have a reasonable chance of success. The nascent Albania is cut down to a minimum, and if Europe had wished to make the new state dependent on Austria or Italy, she could hardly have set about it more effectually. . . . There is not much future for an Albanian of this sort; but the Shkipetars are a dogged race who have survived many tyrants, though so far they have only had to face death by the sword and not strangulation by the red tape of a bureaucracy."

KEY TO THE NEAR EAST 181

to evacuate the territories assigned to Albania, as it was decided at their session of August 10, 1913, she granted to Greece first one month, then another, changing it from December 31, 1913, first to February 1, 1914, then to March 1, 1914, giving Greece plenty of time to complete her intrigues and preparation for the *"Epirotian tragedy,"* which she was planning to play. The last diplomatic pourparlers between the Great Powers and Greece regarding the evacuation of these regions by the Hellenic troops are worthy of record for they help one to understand the events which followed later.

On February 13, 1914, the representatives of the Great Powers presented to the Greek Government a collective communication regarding southern Albanian frontier and the Aegean islands. The Powers intimated that they had decided to give Greece the islands occupied by her, with the exemption of *Tenedos, Imbros* and *Castellorizzo.* The islands will not be definitely handed over to Greece until the Greek troops have evacuated the territory assigned to Albania by the London Ambassadorial Conference, the Hellenic Government undertaking to offer no resistance, either directly or indirectly, to the wish of the Powers. The evacuation of Albania, the note said, will be begun on March 1, at Kortcha, and will be concluded about March 31, 1914.

In its reply, handed on February 21, the Greek Government, while regretting the necessity of evacuating southern Albania and the Aegean islands, Imbros, Tenedos and Castellorizzo, agreed to comply with the decision of the Powers. The Hellenic Government, at the same time, stated that orders will be given to the Greek troops to evacuate the territories assigned to Albania in due time, handing them over to the Dutch officers, appointed by the Powers for the organization of the Albanian *gendarmerie;* and *solemnly* declared that they will offer no resistance either directly or indirectly to the wish of the Powers.

The Greek reply, however, proposed a rectification of frontier near *Arghirokastra* on ethnological grounds in favor of Greece, and offered in exchange a long, but narrow, strip of coast line between *Ftelia* and *Cape Pagania,* as well as a million dollars. The Greek note concluded, remarking that the frontiers of the Turkish *kaza* of Kortcha, which was accepted as forming part of the new international boundary by the Powers, are neither scientific nor definitely established. The Greek Government expressed the hope that this point will be settled upon a reasonable basis, and *proposed that the Hellenic troops should withdraw only to the "natural frontiers"* of the *kaza, pending a definite settlement.*

Before leaving this chapter, we must add that during the Greek occupation of southern Albania, the Greek military authorities organized in all parts of the country "sacred regiments of volunteers," formed mostly of Cretans. The Christian-made population between 15-55 years of age being forced to enroll, drill and swear in the presence of the bishop that they would die to incorporate these territories to "mother Greece."

Just what the Greek Government has determined to do with these "sacred regiments of volunteers," having their headquarters at "the natural frontiers" of the *kaza* of Kortcha will be fully appreciated when we come to consider the attacks of the Greeks disguised as "Epirotes."

Let us go back and hear the report of His Excellency, *Ismail Kemal Bey Vlora,* regarding the Provisional Government of Albania.

I had one dominant thought, now that I was given presidential power, continues Ismail Kemal Vlora, and that was to reorganize the small extent of country that remained to us, to show the Great Powers that Albania was capable of governing herself and deserved the confidence of Europe. As to the future Sovereign, the interest for the moment did not lie so much in the choice of his personality as in the principle which was to decide the choice between a European and Mussulman prince. My own views frankly favored a Christian and European; and in this I was supported by all the Albanians as well as by the political considerations that had to be taken into account. Only a European Sovereign could properly guide us in the great European family we were entering. The question of religion did not enter into consideration in this preference for a European, since all the three cults practiced in the country—Mussulman, Catholic and Orthodox—had equal and complete liberty, no rivalry or pre-eminence being possible.

The Sublime Porte, immediately on receiving our notification of independence, set itself in opposition to our aspirations. The Grand Vizier, in a telegram replying to my note, tried to impose on us, as Sovereign, a member of the Imperial family. According to him, Albania could only be saved by being the vassal of the Ottoman Empire, with a Prince of the Imperial family. On what Power, he asked, did she expect to rely? On Austria? On Italy? Let her not forget, he added, the example of the Crimea, for which independence under the protection of Russia was but the prelude to complete subjection. My reply was that Albania relied neither on Italy nor Austria, but on the rights of the Albanians to exist and have a nationality of their own, as well as on the duty of the Powers to respect nationalities. I added that Turkey could not but be a bad advocate of the cause of free nationalities, and that Albania would prefer to defend her cause herself, but that, on the other hand, when the final solution came, she would do all she could to prevent the new situation from being an obstacle to good relations with the Sublime Porte. So ended what I may call the first candidature to the Albanian throne, which was followed by others that had no weight at all with the Albanians, who placed their confidence in the Great Powers. In spite of this attitude of the Porte and of the menace of the Turkish armies, which still occupied a portion of the country, we spent our time in organizing the administration, and maintaining order in the portions left to us. The silence of the Great Powers, and their indifference in face of Serbia's invasion and devastation of our land, as the same time Greece was blockading and bombarding the town of Vallona and the littoral, disgusted us. A little later, the Greek fleet having cut the cable which was the only channel of communication with the outside world, we were completely isolated and deprived of all knowledge of what was taking place beyond our borders.

One evening towards the end of March, 1913, we learned that a vessel flying the British flag had anchored in the port and announced that the blockade was suspended. We naturally were delighted with the news. Next morning I learned that this vessel was the yacht of the *Duc de Montpensier* (younger brother of the *Duc d'Orleans*); and a little later a messenger came to me from the duke carrying a letter in which his highness informed me of the object of his visit, namely, his desire to become a candidate for the throne of Albania. There followed an invitation to lunch on board the yacht. I accepted, and after luncheon the Prince and I had a long conversation. He confided to me his intentions very frankly. I assured him I was happy and flattered, both for myself and on behalf of my country, that a Prince of the French Royal house should aspire to the difficult but honorable task of reigning over Albania. But I was forced to add that, as the blockade had kept us in total ignorance of what was our exact situation vis-a-vis the European Powers, we regretted we were not able to take the decision, even if it were one in conformity with our wishes. Next day his highness came to pay us a visit at Vallona. He made a tour of the town, in which he was able to notice the excellent impression he himself made—a sympathy which later caused all the more regret to the people and myself. I left with the Prince on his yacht on April 1, 1913, for the purpose of conferring with the Powers. He left me at Brindisi, and continued his voyage to Venice. I went successively to Rome, Vienna, Paris, and London. No understanding had been come to, and no decision taken on the question of this candidature, which would have been so welcome to the Albanians, and there the matter ends.

My object in making this journey was to fight the cause of the territorial integrity of Albania with the Powers, but especially in London, where the Conference was deliberating on the settlement of the Balkan question. I also wanted to hurry on the selection of the future Sovereign, which would help to ensure the stability of the National Government and remove all internal difficulties, which the continuance of provisional conditions necessarily engendered.

In Vienna, Count Berchtold, in our first interview, allowed me to perceive how slight was the hope that Albania would be permitted to preserve her territorial integrity, in spite of her rights, and in spite of the efforts he had himself made. It was the first painful blow to me, but worse was to come, for on the day when I left Paris for London came the news of the surrender of the town of Scutari by Essad Pasha to the Montenegrins. This disaster, which took place while the fleet of the six Great Powers was manœuvring before this port in order to force King Nicholas to raise the siege, jeopardized the integrity and almost even the existence of Albania. The question of the candidature to the throne was by this fact necessarily relegated to a secondary place; and all my effort had to be devoted to the territorial question.

On my arrival in London the same evening, I was happy to find myself again in the sympathetic atmosphere to which I was accustomed there, and I gathered renewed strength for my political struggle for the rights of the peoples of the East. The sincere sympathy shown by the British-press and people towards our national cause, and the kindly welcome extended to me by Ministers and Statesmen of this great country led me to hope that our indisputable rights, which were in no way incompatible with the political interests of Europe in general, or of our neighbors in particular, would be acknowledged by the Conference. Never was a nobler task offered to the Great Powers; never was a solution so necessary; and never had we such hopes of obtaining it, as at that moment, when the Powers were for the first time called on to form a Congress, whose task was not only to conciliate opposed interests, but also to act as an International High Court of Justice.

Of all the Balkan questions treated at this conference, in my view, the foremost, the most interesting, and above all, the most eminently European, was that of Albania. We thought it possible to hope that a people so worthy of interest by reason of its antiquity, its valor, and the services it had rendered to Europe, first by defending it against the invasion of the Turks, and then by resigning itself to a docile submission when it had become the pivot of European equilibrium, might have been allowed to become master in its own house, and to retain its national independence. The Albanians, delivered from the Turkish yoke, of which they had for centuries been less the instruments than the victims, would have been happy to recover their liberty and independence, and therewith the repose of which they stood in such great need. They had no other claims to make, no other pretensions to put forward. They desired that the work of restoration should take place for all the Balkan peoples as for themselves, that hatred and envy should cease, that all legitimate rights should become sacred, and every unjust ambition or enterprise meet with its condemnation in a guarantee of solidarity on the part of the Great Powers. Sure of the justice of our claims, we awaited with entire confidence the verdict of the Conference of the Powers.

But the sympathy shown to me in my mission was the only consolation offered to Albania's broken heart when we learned the decision which the Conference of London had taken. More than half my country's territory had been attributed to Serbia, Montenegro and Greece. The most flourishing towns and the most productive parts of the country having been taken away, Albania was reduced almost to its most arid and rocky portions. Thus plunged again into deep depression at seeing the future of our reborn country so darkened, we were comforted by being told that we had to be sacrificed to the general interests of Europe. Resigned but not despairing I returned to Albania buoyed up by the single hope that more favorable conditions would at some future time permit Albania to realize her legitimate desires.

On my return to Vallona in June 1913, the Provisional Government redoubled its efforts to organize the country and maintain order. It was a task which might well have seemed impossible, but was facilitated by the Albanian character, whose patience, foresight, and unflinching patriotism in the midst of all these complications and anxieties cannot be too highly praised. It was thanks to the virtues of this race in a country of which the frontiers were still undetermined, where the political statutes promised by Europe were awaiting their fulfillment, and where a frantic propaganda was carried on with the object of provoking trouble. . . . It was thanks to these virtues that my Government succeeded in bringing stability to the State and assuring it a normal administration.

But despite the satisfactory results in the present, the future was dark and uncertain so long as the question of the future

Sovereign remained unsettled. I therefore addressed a pressing appeal to the Powers in the following terms:

"If the Provisional Government of Albania, which has for eleven months been struggling with innumerable difficulties, has been able to maintain order and relative tranquility in a country harrassed on all sides by enemies who have sworn its destruction, it does not claim for itself the merit which in fact is due only to the patriotism and the resignation of the Albanian people.

"But this provisional state of affairs cannot be continued indefinitely without encountering insurmountable difficulties. We believe we have reached the extreme limit of the people's patience, and we hasten to submit to the consideration of your Government the unanimous wish of the people and the Government for the designation and enthronement of the Sovereign, whose mere presence will suffice to unite all classes of the population in the work of consolidating Albania and organizing her administration.

"In the hope that the guaranteeing Powers will take our request into serious consideration, the Provisional Government would be ready to take any steps necessary to hasten the happy result which Albanians await with such impatience."

It was a short while after this telegram had been sent that the name of the Prince of Wied was first mentioned in connection with Albania, vague rumors concerning his candidature being spread about. These rumors soon became more definite, in a way that recalled a curious campaign started on behalf of Prince Ahmed Fuad, of Egypt, by the "Zeit" of Vienna; in this case, the propaganda was launched in the form of a highly dithyrambic article in the "Oesterreichische Rundschau" (also published at Vienna), over the famous pseudonyme of the Queen of Roumania. "*Carmen Sylva*," more poetess than ever, after having evoked Albania vainly clamoring for a Sovereign, in the style of a recitative of the "Nibelungen Ring," proposed to her as guide the scion of an ancient race dwelling on the Rhine. She then gave the genealogy of the Prince of Wied, and his history since childhood. The prospect of confiding the destinies of Albania to this unknown celebrity did not particularly enchant me, but what troubled me more was the propaganda that began openly in favor of this candidature, in which money and presents were distributed with cynical effrontery. I asked for official information as to this candidature, and being informed that it was not under consideration, I no longer hesitated to take rigorous measures against the propaganda or to expel the agitators. But, though the reply to my question was so emphatically in the negative, destiny had doubtless willed otherwise since I was officially notified a little later that the six Powers had come to an unanimous decision regarding the choice of Prince William of Wied, and that nothing remained except to ratify it by the formality of a popular election. The Albanian people, unshakenly confident in the decisions of Europe sent their votes at once to the Provisional Government, which communicated the result to the Powers.

However, though all was arranged, the Prince of Wied gave no sign, at any rate in the direction of Albania. We expected him to arrive every day. His departure was announced, but he did not arrive. These inexplicable delays were utilized by the young Turks, who recommenced with even greater energy than before their campaign in favor of a Turkish Prince. I then appealed to the Commission of Control, begging them to draw the attention of the Powers to the urgent need for the enthronement of the new Sovereign. In case particular reasons were delaying the arrival of the Prince, I asked that a Commissioner should take over the Government in his name, or that the Powers should instruct the Commission itself to assume authority on their behalf. In my opinion, some such arrangement was the only way of straightening the intrigues which tended to cause disorder in the country. My request was at last approved by the Powers; and the delegates came to notify me that they were authorized by the respective Governments to assume the Power if I maintained my view on the advisability of this step. The following protocol was signed on the spot:

"This 22nd of January, 1914, the International Commission of Control has met in the presence of his Excellency, Ismail Kemal Bey. The President of The Provisional Government being persuaded that the only means of terminating the condition of disruption and anarchy ruling in the country is to constitute a single Government for the whole of Albania, and that in the present circumstances this end can only be attained if he placed the power in the hands of the International Commission of Control, representing the Great Powers, has repeated the request that he has already made to the International Commission of Control, in the presence of the Ministers, to take over the task and accept the placing of the power in their hands. The International Commission of Control pays homage to the patriotic sentiments which have dictated the actions of his Excellency, Ismail Kemal Bey, accepts this delegation of power, and, duly authorized by the Great Powers, assumes the administration of Albania in the name of the Government it represents.

"Vallona, Jan. 22, 1914.

Signed: "*Ismail Kemal, Nadolny, Petrovic, Krajewski, Harry Lamb, Leoni, Petriaew.*"

X.

EUROPE BEGINS TO PLAY HER TRAGEDY IN ALBANIA.

SIX weeks after Ismail Kemal Bey Vlora had handed over the power to the International Commission, William I, who had been appointed *Mbret* of the Albanians by the Great Powers, made his solemn entry into Durazzo, on March 7, 1914. He was accompanied by the Queen, his wife, and their children. His court consisted of a marshal and a doctor, both Germans, a private secretary, an Englishman and two ladies of Honor. On board the vessel which brought him, the *Mbret* had the two million dollars, which Italy and Austria had advanced in anticipation of the fifteen million dollars, which the other four Great Powers had not yet decided to pay. He was received with enthusiastic acclamations by the population, while salutes of welcome were fired in the port.

His first act was the nomination of Essad Pasha as Minister of war and first general of Albania, which of course was a fatal mistake for Essad, to say the least, was undesirable to his compatriots and his nomination met with unpopularity and contempt.

Once in possession of this important office, under the guidance and assistance of the greedy neighbors of his country, Essad Pasha began organizing a *coup-d'état* against his own Government, his ambition being to become himself the Sovereign of Albania. He was caught in *flagrant d'élit,* his house bombarded, and he himself was allowed to depart from the country, giving his word that he would never return to Albania.

KEY TO THE NEAR EAST

But with his departure, "The Essad Movement" did not cease; on the contrary it grew, assuming a threatening character, for now, it was even better fed by the neighbors, his own parents, lest it should fail.

While Essad was getting ready for his *coup d'état* in the capital of Albania, the Greeks gave the *coup-de-main* in Kortcha, the cradle of the Albanian National and educational movement, on Thursday morning, at 2.30, April 2, 1914. The following is the story of this attack, just as it was written on April 25th, 1914, by the author, who was an eye witness, for his American friends. It is the typical illustration of the general policy adopted by the neighbors of Albania for its dissolution and partition, in a disguised form, since they were vetoed to accomplish their purpose openly.

The attack began Thursday morning, April 2nd (new style), at 2.30 A. M. Fortunately the Albanians were not off their guard. On Wednesday evening, April 1st, Mrs. Dako had gone to call on a neighbor. While there, the boy of the house came in with the news that he had seen several Andarties (an andarty is a Greek revolutionist or irregular soldier), enter the house of *Dr. Polena,* nearby. Mrs. Dako at once went and notified *Major Snellen.* The Albanian garrison was very small; seventy gendarmes, one hundred twenty scattered Christian volunteers and twenty police. However, twenty volunteers were called out as police reserves and the house of Dr. Polena was surrounded.

Unknown to the authorities, an andarty, *"Captain" Sullo,* disguised as the Bishop's kavass, had gathered about one hundred and fifty men from the surrounding Christian villages and had placed them on the hills to the north, east and west of Kortcha. These men were induced to fight by the promise that the farms of the wealthy Albanians would be divided among them if the Greek autonomy was successfully declared.

Then *"Captain" Sullo* himself at about midnight entered the town and went at once to the Bishop's residence, and at half past two the villagers on the hill started firing. The Andarties in the house of Dr. Polena fired upon the police at the same time. The Bishop then sent for the two buglers of the "Sacred Regiment" and ordered them to call the assembly. At the same time he had the bells of the three churches rung.

At dawn we saw from our windows Andarties walking on the streets, members of the "Sacred Regiments" in uniform and the Greek officer *Papadakis,* accompanied by a bugler, giving orders. All the Christian quarter was forced to put up the Greek flag. We took down the Albanian flag and Mr. Spencer put up the American. Mr. Spencer, Zarif, our kavass, Miss Kyrias and two of the teachers, took rifles and guarded the school. Firing continued most of the day. The school was often threatened.

The Greeks captured the City Hall and all the schools and the churches. The Albanians kept the Government house and the telegraph station. In attempting to get to the police station, only three hundred yards from the telegraph office, *Major Snellen* was wounded a little above the heart by a Greek school teacher from Arta. The Greeks then attempted to take possession of the telegraph office. The line to Elbassan and Durazzo had been cut by the Greeks, but the line to *Bilishta* and *Florina* was working. This the Greeks wanted to capture and use. Leading the attack was *"Captain" Sullo* and the Greek archdeacon. "Captain" Sullo was wounded and the archdeacon, gun in hand, was killed by an Albanian Dervish. Holy orders claimed their own.

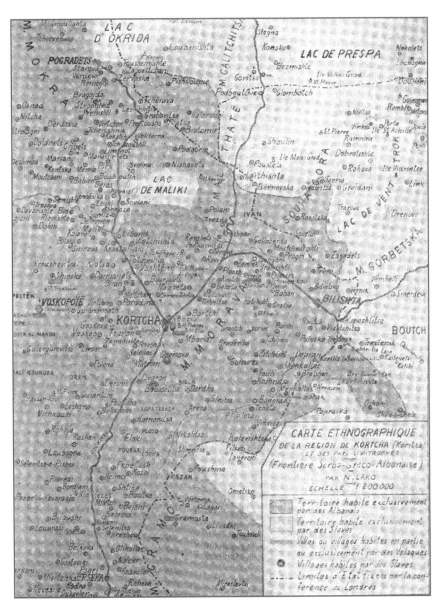

Ethnographic map of the district of Kortcha.

Blank in the original

All this time we were surrounded in the school. Our quarter was in the hands of the Andarties. Several times they requested the pleasure of hanging me, but Mr. Spencer and Miss Kyrias told them that I was at the Government house with *Major Snellen.* That night Mrs. Dako, the children and I went to my sister's who lives across the street. Mr. Spencer was left in charge of the school with his "army." Miss Kyrias and the three teachers stayed up the whole night watching the back wall from where an attack was expected. At two in the morning the scoundrel who lives behind us, Constantine Shosho, led two andarties to the top of the school wall. The moon showed them our army of five, with rifles pointed blank at them, and they, like "Humpty Dumpty," took a great fall.

The next morning the Greeks were in a panic. The expedition from the regular army (600 strong with three machine guns), had been repulsed in the defile of *Mboria,* three miles east of the city by a force of Albanian villagers. The Greeks now had only 150 regulars and a part of the "Sacred Regiment" with which to hold the city, until help could come from *"the natural frontiers"* of Mr. Venizelos. Meanwhile, the Albanians were pouring in from the west. The third day, Saturday, April 4th, there was a hard fight around the school. Although wounded, *Major Snellen* had tried to reach us several times, but was repulsed. At last *Emin Bey,* of Poiani, a young lieutenant of gendarmes from Pogradetz, and a local policeman reached us with a command of twenty men. Mr. Spencer and the "army," Miss Kyrias, two teachers and the kavass marched back to the government house. Major Snellen welcomed them and sent back seven men to help guard the school. Mr. Spencer did not return. Next morning we were awakened by machine guns. The Greek soldiers under Colonel

Mavranza had come from the north and had occupied the hill of *St. Elijah,* just above the school during the night. Our guard of seven men left at once to fight. After locking the school, we and everyone in the school took refuge at my sister's. All Sunday the fighting was terrific. My sister's house was constantly hit and we all came near being killed. Then, thinking the school was stronger, we all returned to the school. All the neighbors came with us. Late that evening, Rev. Tsilka, one of our teachers, who had come from Elbassan, reached the school. Early the next morning, Monday, April 6, after a good breakfast, Mr. Tsilka with Zarif, my kavass, and the fifteen men started fighting from our gate. They slowly advanced. Soon Greek flags and rifles were sent to the school as they were captured by these men. The Andarties had gone into the houses and were firing from the windows; but finally they were surrounded and offered to surrender. On coming out, their *Captain P. Papamihail,* tried to escape and was killed by Zarif, the kavass.

Late that night, Mr. Spencer returned to the school, after being gone two days. As Major Snellen was wounded, there were not enough officers, so the regular gendarmes, together with those who had come from the south were divided into four parts. Fifty men stayed at the Government House, then 150 men were taken to attack the Metropolis, and capture the Bishop. These were divided in three companies. *Capt. Doorman,* of the Dutch Mission, made the attack from the east; *Capt. Ghilardi,* from the south, and *Mr. Spencer,* who had been an officer in the American Navy, from the west. Mr. Spencer ordered his men to ignore the firing from the surrounding houses and to take charge directly from the Bishop's residence. His men, however, were held up for two hours where two streets met, but at

Greek regulars at Kortcha April 6, 1914.
After the failure of the Greek disguised attack on the coveted city.

last they reached the Metropolis. The Bishop gave up his arms and surrendered. As the Albanian villagers who had followed in Spencer's rear wished to hang the Bishop, Mr. Spencer placed a guard of 40 of his men around the residence and he himself entered with 10 soldiers. After half an hour, Capt. Doorman and Capt. Ghilardi arrived. The three commanders then placed the Bishop between them for protection and took him to Major Snellen. At midnight, for his own safety, he was sent to Elbassan.

With the arrest of the Bishop, the Hellenic attack was checked for a while; but the Greeks did not give up hope. Soon new regiments of the Greek army appeared on the scene and kept on *"the Epirotean Movement"* for four months. It is impossible to depict the horrors, through which the Albanian women passed during the most disastrous fight, which took place in *Kolonia*. It included a large number of villages. Bodies of young women, who had been strangled to death and outraged by Greek soldiers were found in many places. The young women had fought for their honor until they were dead of strangulation; then, their corpses were outraged. Many were the victims of this criminal invasion, and, not a small number of wounded. At this time the Kyrias school was turned into a hospital.

Taking possession of *Kodra*, a village near *Tepeleni*, the Greeks invited all the villagers, men, women and children to gather in the Church. When all were assembled, *two hundred and thirty* in number, the Greek officers ordered the soldiers to fire on them with machine guns. All were killed; their heads cut down and hung on the Church walls. *General De Weer,* of the *Dutch Mission,* went himself to this village, saw this terrible Greek cruelty and took the picture of this horrible sight. His report to the International Commission of Control says:

All through the villages the atmosphere was infected by corpses—all of them in advanced state of putrefaction. South of the village of *Kodra*, I found a little church, which was undoubtedly used as a prison. In the interior, the walls and the floor were washed in blood, everywhere caps and clothing soaked in blood. The doctor, member of the Commission of Investigation, saw himself human brains. At the altar, we found a human heart, which was still bleeding. A hundred and ninety-five bodies were dug out because the ditch they were thrown in was too shallow, so as to bury them in deeper graves; all the bodies were without heads.

In the latter part of June *"the Essad Movement"* joined the Greeks, and a general attack began, and on July 6, 1914, the Albanians, on account of lack of ammunition had to give up. Together with Government officials, three hundred and fifty thousand people fled for their lives. Fifty thousand crowded in *Berat,* a town of 15,000 population; a hundred thousand took refuge in *Elbassan,* and the rest wandered for a good while and then went for shelter under the olive trees of Vallona.

Speaking of the work of destruction of the neighbors of Albania, the Hon. *Aubrey Herbert,* member of the British Parliament, says:

It is my conviction that these people were systematically exterminated in various frontier areas of Albania, by those who had sworn to befriend them. In addition to all her misfortunes, Albania has suffered this great calamity, that the world-at-large is ignorant of what is happening in that corner of the Balkans. The Albanians are starving in silence, because they are not able to complain or to advertise the direness of their sufferings, they are left to die of famine without help.

Albania has been abandoned to its fate. The five Powers, who created it and pledged to it protection and help have withdrawn their moral support, and she collapsed as a result of the attacks, which were organized, supported and carried on by those who had *solemnly* sworn to befriend her!

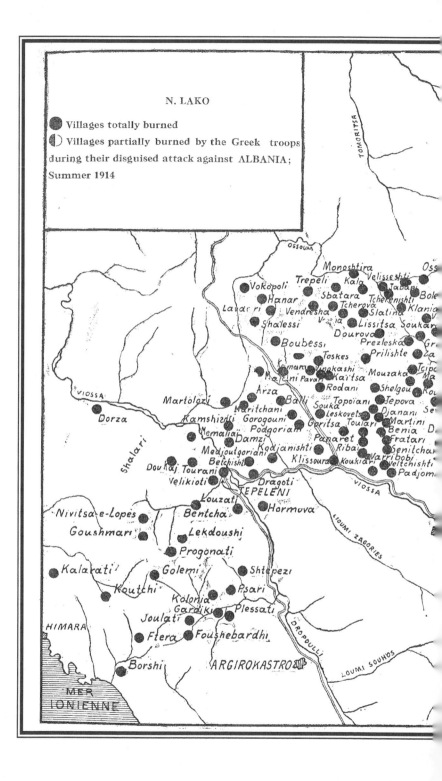

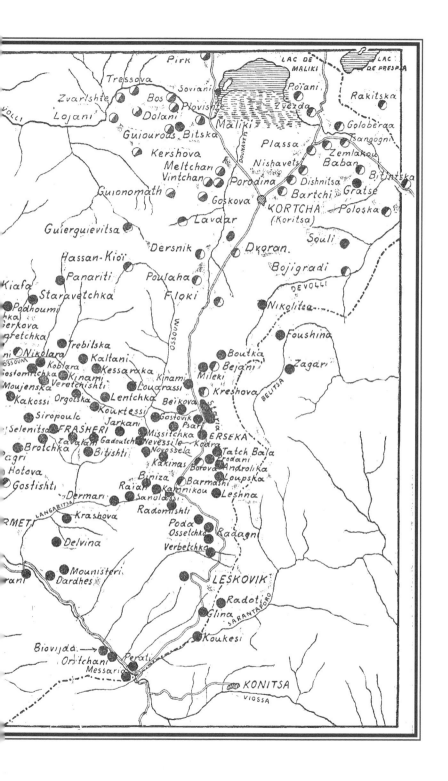

Blank in the original

XI

FUTURE PROSPECTS

THE vital questions upon which depends the national existence of Albania are *the question of its boundaries, and that of its status.*

The boundary drawn by the London Conference (1912-1913) is arbitrary and unjust. It was impelled by motives alien to the welfare of our country and of the other Balkan States. Large districts inhabited almost exclusively by Albanians were handed over to Montenegro, Serbia and Greece, depriving her of two important provinces and of many market centres, such as Ipek, Jakova, Prizren, Uskup, Dibra, Ochrida, Monastir, Janina, etc.; thus creating an *irredenta Albania,* almost twice as large in territory and population as the independent Albania itself. With such a boundary, Albania has no chance for national existence. The imperative necessity of establishing new frontiers for Albania, based on the ethnographic principle, is acknowledged today by every impartial student of the Balkan problems. And the Albanians hope that the representatives of the Allied nations assembled at Paris, will restore to Albania the provinces of Kossova and Chameria, and the clans of Hoti and Gruda, as well as the district of Gusinje and Plava, without which Albania cannot possibly exist.

Regarding the future status of the country several suggestions have been already been advanced, of which worthy of notice is the following. It is said, that on account of the aspirations of her neighbors Albania must be put under the protectorate of some Great Power. And since, it is added, neither the United States of America, nor Great Britain would be likely to wish to undertake the task, the duty of managing Albania's Affairs would naturally fall to Italy. This suggestion, however, independent of the source from where it comes, has been reluctantly rejected by the Albanians themselves. They know too well that the protectorate scheme is but a step towards definitive annexation. They realize that under an Italian protectorate the Albanians will disappear as a nation within a few decades.

On the other hand, it has been amply proved that a mixed Commission of Control is not only useless, but even embarrassing, not to say dangerous, as the Commissioners work for their respective countries and not for Albania.

The restoration of Albania cannot possibly have another political status except that of a sovereign independent state, politically and economically, for only under such a status will she be free from all foreign intrigues, able to develop and progress and become an element of good order and peace in the Balkans.

So far, none has been able to prove in spite of the fact that much brain energy and immense quantity of gold have been spent, and all systems of intrigue exhausted, that Albania is incapable to govern herself. Moreover history testifies to the contrary. Indeed, setting aside their heroes of antiquity, Alexander the Great, Pyrrhus the king of Epirus, the Ptolemies of Egypt, Emperor Diocletian of Rome, Constantine the Great, etc.—the modern Albanians have shown in Turkey, Italy, Greece, Roumania and elsewhere, that they can produce statesmen. They have given the reigning dynasty to Egypt founded by Mehmet Ali, the famous soldier and statesman, who played, in the nineteenth century, so great a part in the history of Egypt and indeed of Europe. The Küprüli family, who furnished the Sultans with three Grand Vizers, was from Albania. The troops with which

Mustapha Bairactar opposed and quelled the Janissarries were principally Albanian. The famous Galip, commonly called Patrona, was Albanian. This man, though a common seaman and a pedlar, headed the insurrection of 1730, in which Sultan Ahmet III was dethroned, and with a success of which neither ancient nor modern history can furnish another instance, remained for three weeks absolute master of Constantinople.

The fact that for fifteen months the Albanian people, struggling with innumerable difficulties, had been able to maintain order and tranquility without any organized police force, during the Provisional Government, in a country harassed on all sides by enemies, who have sworn its destruction, speaks loudly that they are capable of self-government. Miss M. E. Durham, who has traveled widely in Albania, in her recent book, "The Struggle for Scutari," speaking on the subject says, "The Powers were now treating Albania badly. They neither appointed any Government, nor recognized any local one, and people knew not to whom to look. They were for the most part terrified of offending Europe by recognizing any native as head of Albania. But the local headman was keeping excellent order. The patience with which a whole people, placed in a most difficult and almost unprecedented position, went on with their daily affairs quietly, has not been sufficiently recognized. While I was riding about the burnt districts I was always unarmed, was frequently with men I had never seen before, and everyone knew I had at least Lt. 200 in gold in the bag at my belt. Men by the wayside would call out to me: "Where are you taking the money today? Come to our village next." But no attempt of any sort was ever made, either to take it from me, or to force me to change my route. I often wondered whether similar sums could be safely carried through England, supposing all police withdrawn, and the Government entirely done away with."

The above instances show that there need be no fear that capable men will be wanting in Albania. Under a wise and strong national constitutional government, with a good system, of education,[1] the Albanians are capable of great development, and their strongly marked racial and linguistic unity would give them a strength, which not all the other races of the Balkan Peninsula possess.

The Albanian nation has given sufficient proofs of its liberal conceptions in the field of public and political affairs. Amongst us, the national interest has always predominated our religious considerations. In Albania, people are ranged, ranked and valued not according to their creed, age or birth, but according to the depth of their patriotic feeling, for an Albanian is before all else *proudly* an Albanian. In their view the highest nobility and the best religion is to love and write and cultivate their tongue and their nationality.

The best instance to illustrate his liberal attitude towards his neighboring races is the confidence shown from time immemorial, by the Wallachs, which confidence was expressed by them during the London Conference, to associate their political life with that of the Albanians.

The Albanian question is a comparatively simple problem for the Peace Conference to solve. The country is inhabited almost exclusively by Albanians; and, if the statesmen assembled at Paris throw overboard the old diplomacy, striving only to seek the interest of the Albanians, if they apply impartially the sacred principles of nationality and self-determination, as they are announced in the 14 points of President Wilson, then it would be easy to determine fair

---

[1] At the end of the volume, the reader will find a scholarly presentation of the educational system to be introduced in Albania.

frontiers, that would take in all territory inhabited by Albanians, and to confirm the recognition of the London Conference, which gave Albania a place of a sovereign state amongst her sister states of the world. Whatever the peacemakers will decide, they will do it with the full knowledge of the situation.

Coming now to the problems which must receive the immediate attention of the Albanian Government, they are as follows: There is the important problem of building up an administrative machinery, together with that of providing measures for the improvement of agriculture; that of creating a national industry; that of developing the commerce; that of building roads throughout the country and faciltating the exchange of products; that of giving Albania a money system and putting the public revenue on a sound and fair basis; that of eliminating all foreign schools of propaganda and establishing a national educational system for the whole country.

Let us consider them now one by one and state *briefly* how these problems can be approached and in due time solved.

At present the country is administered by local Councils, under the supervision of the military authorities of Italy and France, which have occupied Albania *temporarily* for military reasons. The boundary problem of Albania as well as that of her status, will be decided by the Peace Conference, and then the country will be handed over to the Albanian Government, which will do well to maintain the present organization of the local Councils with their respective police and gendarm force of natives, and work gradually for the establishment of the permanent system of administration.

The agriculture of Albania is primitive and backward. The country although eminently mountainous has rich and productive valleys, the most important of them being that of *Muzekea*. It is a mistake to say that the working hand is wanting. The population of Albania which numbers, as we have already seen, about three million people, is strong enough to make the land give the full rate of products. It is true that the Albanian is primarily a soldier; but it must be borne in mind that he was compelled to be a soldier by political events, defending his country from the greed of his neighbors. The Albanian, however, can easily accommodate himself to all kinds of labor. Those who have watched him during the short periods of peace know that the Albanian finds great pleasure in tilling his land. And the fact that he so far had to do his work with a primitive plough shows how deep is his love for agriculture. The Albanians living in Constantinople have proved that they are as good gardeners as the Bulgarians. With the introduction of modern machinery and increase of civilization, the agricultural situation can be greatly improved, her products sufficing not only for its inhabitants but will leave a good margin for exportation. Albania produces all kinds of cereals, fruits and vegetables of the moderate climate. In the south coast where the climate is warmer, there are olive and orange groves in abundance; also cotton, rice and sugar cane, etc., are raised.

The Albanians are as good tradesmen as they are agriculturalists. Not only all the commerce of their country and that of Montenegro are in their hands; but some of the leading tradesmen of Salonica, Constantinople, Roumania and Egypt are Albanians. The very fact that there are very few Jews in Albania, speaks loudly that they cannot be beaten in trade.

So far there is practically no industry in Albania in the modern meaning of the word; still there are plenty of instances showing what its inhabitants are capable of produc-

KEY TO THE NEAR EAST

ing in this field of activity. The little hand work which the Albanians are doing especially at Prizren, Jakova, Ipek, Tirana and Elbassan in gold, silver and iron, manufacturing articles of ornament, cutlery as well as good pistols and rifles, amply prove their inheritant inclinations towards the mechanical arts. Moreover the Albanians who live in America have demonstrated that they are skilful workers in manufacturing the most delicate work of the present century.

The country is rich in natural resources—coal, near Kortcha, bitumen, near Vallona, and petroleum, copper and sulphur elsewhere; and with the exceptional abilities that has been already shown to abound in the Albanian stock, it will not be long in making up arrears of industrial development.

Although the Albanians have paid taxes for roads, the Turkish Government did not spend even a cent to build them in Albania. It was the program of the Turks to leave our country without any roads; for they knew that facilities of travel bring enlightenment and civilization, and their very purpose was to keep the Albanians in darkness as long as possible.

During the Balkan war as well as during the great world war, it is reported that a number of roads have been built in Albania for military purposes by the interested parties; still the country is far from possessing the roads which are absolutely necessary for its economical devlopment. The Albanian Government must as soon as possible take all measures to build railroad lines connecting all important market centres of Albania. There are in existence three different projects, which deserve to be carefully studied, and out of them a fourth one could be easily outlined, bearing in mind, of course, first the interest of the country itself, and then proceed at once to build the main lines, without which the economical movement of Albania cannot possibly make even one step forward.

Albania has no money system of its own. The Provisional Government of 1912-1914, as well as the regime of the Mbret William had hardly any time to do any constructive work for the country. At present all kinds of foreign coins are in circulation in Albania, and this, of course, is a great hindrance to its trade as well as a great loss. It is imperative, therefore, that the Albanian Government should see that this problem is solved at once, and solved satisfactorily. A good beginning has already been made by the Albanian Council of the district of Kortcha, which has issued recently a series of Albanian bank notes, and has already begun to eliminate the circulation of all foreign coins from the market. Besides, the Albanian Government must abolish at once the Turkish system of favoritism and inaugurate a just system of taxation instead, in proportion with the income of each inhabitant.

The next important business which requires the immediate attention of the Albanian Government is that of eliminating once for all all foreign schools of propaganda, and that of establishing a national educational system for the whole country. The Albanians are very eager to learn. All of them understand that as in the past the *sword* was the symbol of power, so today education is the main supporting column of a nation, and they have already decided to hold fast to it. The progress made by the Albanians residing at present in America is a good illustration to show the rate of the speed with which the Albanian people are capable of advancing in this important field. In the last ten years, the Albanians of America, men between 20 and 55 years of age, the great majority of whom could neither read nor write their

KEY TO THE NEAR EAST 205

own language when they came to this country, as the teaching of it in Albania was forbidden by the Turks, today 85% of them can read, and quite a number of them have proved to be capable of such progress as to write newspaper articles.

These are in brief the problems upon which the future of the country rests; and, if wisely handled there is every hope to believe that Albania will get on its feet in a short time; and will be able to develop and progress and become an element of good order and peace in the Balkans.

XII.

REMINISCENCES.

EVEN in these days when practically the whole world has become a student of European affairs, conditions and peoples, when the maps of the Near East —constantly changing in the remaking process to which Europe has been subjugated during the past decade—have been studied more diligently perhaps than ever before, comparatively little is known of Albania and its *"Forgotten Race."*

Edward Gibbons, the eminent historian of the preceding century, writing more than 100 years ago of this earliest of *Aryan* peoples has said, "Albania is a country of which less is known than the interior of America." True as that remark was then, it would be equally as true today were comparison made with the interior of Africa. Yet the events of the past decade have demonstrated that Albania holds a place of considerable prominence in the affairs of the Balkan Peninsula and of Europe.

Concerning its geographic and political importance, as well as the outstanding features of its history, the author has gone into some detail in the foregoing chapters. It is his purpose here to relate briefly and from a personal viewpoint the trend of recent events among his people.

If the personal note seems to be over-emphasized, will the reader remember that the incidents narrated are all very real and vivid to the writer and that through these concrete illustrations he is endeavoring to portray the vicissitudes of his people.

My first active association with the Albanian National Movement came, *not* in Albania, as might readily be supposed, but in *Bucharest*, where with my brothers I attended school, having left my native home in Kortcha in 1890.

In Bucharest there was a large Albanian colony and a strong national organization. It was from Bucharest that the first literature in the propagation of the national movement for Albania was issued. The year that I became of age I was accorded the honor of being elected secretary of this organization. For several years I filled this post, learning the history of my *"forgotten race"* and becoming imbued with the principles of Albanian freedom and national independence.

Logically enough, holding such a position in the organization, which had for its avowed purpose the liberation of Albania from the Turkish yoke and its freedom from under the dominance of the Greek clergy, I came into contact and intimate association with many of the sturdy pioneers of the Albanian National Movement.

It was under these circumstances that I first met Miss Sevasti Kyrias, a young woman who was even then prominently identified with the movement which had for its purpose the education of the Albanian children in the written language and history of their country. With our ambitions and interests so closely allied, it was but natural that we should correspond frequently and the association thus begun quickly ripened into romance. Meeting in the work which to both of us had come to mean life's great ambition; our hopes, ambitions and longings for the future identical, it was inevitable that the personal element should enter and from this pre-destined meeting in the common cause of liberty I won my bride. Of the courtship conducted under as unusual circumstances as any in which man ever courted a maid, attended by hazards and hardships, sorrows and fears, I will make but passing reference here.

At the time that I first met her, the present Mrs. Dako had succeeded her brother to the head of the first Albanian school for girls to have been founded within the territorial limits of Albania. The story of the Kyrias School for Girls, its founding and the many vicissitudes that attended its progress from year to year has already been outlined in another chapter.

An outgrowth of our romance was a more vivid realization and comprehension on my part of the real underlying importance of the educational factor in the emancipation of Albania, and I felt the irresistible call to enter upon this field with its bright prospects for the future of my country. For even then, in the days of my youth, I felt that my life should be consecrated to the work of freeing my people from the Turkish yoke.

Even following my graduation from the University of Bucharest I did not feel myself adequately fitted for this work, and I came to the United States to complete my educational training with this sole motive: That I should be able to return to Albania and give my all to the cause of her emancipation. I entered Oberlin College in the spring of 1907.

In the summer of the following year, while I was working among my countrymen in New England the wire brought the news that 100,000 Albanians had gathered at Ferizovik and demanded that the Sultan of Turkey grant constitutional government to all nations under his rule. With the situation developing so rapidly, I felt that I could not stay away from my own country, in whose cause I was even then working, longer than could possibly be avoided, and in the spring of 1909 I interrupted my studies at Oberlin and returned to Albania.

Then began what was destined to prove the most trying period of my life and the most critical period in Albania's struggle for freedom of thought, education and daily living.

I found upon my return that my countrymen were working very actively in the furtherance of the organization of schools which should teach the Albanian language.

Up to this time the Turkish laws and the Greek church had forbidden the teaching of Albanian to her children. Schools were forbidden unless they were established under Turkish direction and unless the textbooks were published in Turkish. The consequence was an absolute dirth of Albanian textbooks during this early period of Albania education. One means of circumventing the Turks in this respect was the hectograph and many of our lessons were prepared at night, hectographed, distributed among the pupils the following day during class and then destroyed.

On the 20th of August, after the young Turks had invited the Albanians to join them in the uprising against Abdul Hamid, as a result of which the coveted constitution was granted and freedom of education promised, the first Albanian congress was held. Three others followed and the national movement thus started progressed steadily, even though subsequent developments threatened to undermine all the beneficient results thus achieved. Among other developments was the establishment of the first Albanian newspapers to be published in the Albanian language.

But in our approach to seeming independence we had reckoned without the inconsistency of the Young Turks. For, after all, their real purpose was *Pan-Islamism* and intolerance of any development of independence in national thought, education or religion among the subjugated peoples. Consequently it was but a comparatively short period of time before we were again subjected to persecutions as violent as before, and our budding nationalism was frost-bitten before the blossom had really begun to unfold. A vigorous campaign of oppression was instituted in which the educational features of our short-lived emancipation were the first to suffer. All of the schools were closed one by one, excepting the *Kyrias* school, and only the *Iradé* of the deposed Abdul Hamid saved that.

The Young Turks, following in the footsteps of the deposed ruler, issued through the *Shiek-ul-Islam* a *Fetfa* forbidding Albanians to write their own language in Roman characters and commanding that only the *Arabic Alphabet* be used. This was tantamount to suppressing the written language of Albania and was one of the causes of the Insurrection of 1909. During this period the heroic women of Albania fought side by side with their husbands, sweethearts and sons for the sweet cause of liberty. It was then that Albania developed her own *"Jeanne d'Arc,"* one of the most striking characters in all of Albania's modern history.

Indirectly this modern *Jeanne d'Arc* brought to me my first experience with the cruelty of the Turkish government.

It was in May that matters reached their crisis. I was seated in my study one morning when a young man came running in greatly excited and wrought up. Tears stood in his eyes and his voice trembled with emotion as he cried.

"How long must we stand this heavy and cruel yoke? How much longer must Albania bow beneath the heel of the oppressor and suffer from their cruelties!"

"Why what is the matter now?" I asked in some surprise at his heat.

"Don't you know?" he exclaimed, and then went on to tell me how the Young Turks had met and defeated a small body of Albanian revolutionists in which our brave *"Jeanne d'Arc,*" her husband and sons having fallen, took their place at the head of her clan and led the fighting against the Moslem despoiler of their homes. He told me how she had been surrounded by the Turks and taken prisoner; how, without even the formality of pretence of a trial, she had been horribly mutilated and then brutally murdered in cold blood.

My blood ran cold at the tale he had unfolded. It seemed to bring home to me closer than ever before the barbarity, the treachery and unreasoning cruelty of the Turk. I could not, myself, avenge the murder of this brave woman with deeds of arms, and could but resort to my pen. But so greatly had this crime against all moral or international law affected me that I could not allow it to rest. I secured all the information available and prepared an article of protest which was published in the Albanian papers.

It was this article that ultimately brought down upon my head the wrath and vengeance of the Turkish authorities. At the time of its publication no immediate attention was paid to it and I thought, after two or three weeks had elapsed, that it had passed unnoticed. But I had reckoned without the wide publicity which it received. Almost immediately after its first publication it was reprinted by the press of Europe, and caused a great furore. It came to the attention of officers and prominent men of the Young Turks government, principally those in Germany, with the consequence that an order was despatched to *Torgout Pasha,* military governor of the province, for my arrest.

This came six weeks after the article had first appeared. I was in my study when an unexpected visit was paid me by government officials, who notified me that the Governor of Elbassan desired to see me. Somewhat mystified, I courteously agreed to accompany them, but protested against any attempt to seize and confiscate personal papers. Three letters lying on my desk were taken, however.

Owing to the relative strength of Albanianism in Elbassan at that time the Turkish authorities apparently did not dare place me under arrest there. Upon being brought before the Governor I was merely informed that the Governor-General of the Monastir vilayet had demanded my presence. Accordingly, while nominally a free man, yet accompanied by a strong escort, I started on my three-day journey. On the second day out, as we broke camp, I was officially placed under arrest and heavily chained. Manacled as I was, it was no longer possible for me to ride my horse as formerly, and I was obliged to walk the rest of the distance to Monastir.

An old man who was accompanying his son, like myself a prisoner in chains, walked frequently by my side and sought to give me courage. As we approached the town which was to be our stopping place the second night, I asked that he seek out my friend *Hamdi Bey,* and one of the foremost leaders of the nationalist movement, state to him my plight and request that he send me food for the next day's journey.

I did not see the old man again until the following morning when he joined me and pressed surreptitiously into my hand a packet of lunch wrapped in a newspaper. While I enjoyed the food thus brought to me, the contents of the paper interested me even more. I had but chance to read the headlines, but through them learned that the editor of the paper in which my article first appeared had likewise been arrested, but did not even then appreciate its significance.

At Monastir, instead of being taken before the Governor-General as I had expected and learning the cause of my arrest, of which I was still in ignorance, I was thrown into prison, surrounded on all sides by guards, through whom I procured food and some comforts. Just as I was about to throw myself down on the straw pallet to get what sleep I could, an officer came to me with the information that I was to start the following morning for *Ferizovik*.

This information partly solved the mystery which confronted me. Ferizovik was the seat of court-martial at that time, and I realized that my offense had been political and that I was to be given military trial.

Before we started the next morning the American missionary at Monastir, Rev. William Clarke tried to see me, but failing in this, sent and received messages from me through the friendliness of my guards who were secretly in sympathy with my cause and were even members of the national organization, although wearing the Turkish uniform.

Through him and one of my guards I sent messages to my friends and to *Miss Kyrias* who had become my fiancée and to whom I had been about to be married, when I was arrested. At the depot while waiting for the train to Ferizovik, a number of my friends gathered around me as closely as possible and began talking among themselves in English of the causes of my arrest and the events leading up to it. In this wise I received much knowledge on matters that hitherto had been dark to me.

It was indeed fortunate for me that almost to a man the gendarmes who guarded me were secretly in league with the cause of Albanian freedom, for after we were aboard the train and locked in our compartment my handcuffs and chains were removed and I was given a certain amount of freedom that I had not up to this time enjoyed. Nor were the manacles replaced until just before we reached Ferizovik, three days after leaving Monastir.

My trial by court-martial lasted two days, and a large part of the time was occupied by attempting to force me to disclose the name and identity of the soldier who had given me information regarding the murder of *"Jeanne d'Arc,"* and subsequently the cause of my arrest. I refused persistently, and was finally thrown into prison, where for two weeks I remained. Feeling against my arrest and imprisonment waxed high and seemingly the Turks came to the conclusion that I was less of a menace free than in prison, for at the end of that time I was set at liberty.

I returned to Monastir, where my marriage to Miss Kyrias took place almost immediately, and we at once left the country. We went to Bucharest intending to remain there three weeks, but stayed three months. During that period I devoted myself to journalistic work and from Bucharest I sent many protests to the European Powers against the cruelties and oppressions of the Young Turks.

In October we returned to Monastir. Soon after our arrival I learned that another uprising had occurred at Kortcha. Leaving Mrs. Dako in Monastir, I proceeded to the disturbed region to do what I could for the protection of the Kyrias school. I found that, on the allegation that it had been converted into an arsenal and that arms and munitions had been stored there by the insurgents, the school had been seized and searched.

This action on the part of the Turks was wholly without legal authority even under Turkish laws, which prohibited the invasion or search of all buildings wholly occupied by women, as was the case of the Kyrias school at that time. Many of the books had been confiscated, together with the seal of the *"Order of the Morning Star,"* a society of patriotic young women in which Miss Paraskevi D. Kyrias, Mrs. Dako's sister, was the leader.

Although the confiscated articles were of comparatively little intrinsic value, the circumstances surrounding their seizure were such that we brought every effort to bear upon the Turkish authorities. When, as a result of our representations the Governor of Kortcha attempted to return them, we declined to accept them, and as a consequence of our stand he was ultimately dismissed from office.

During the next six months matters *simmered* along quietly. Our representations to the European Powers seemed to have had their effect and I availed myself of this period of comparative rest to return to Monastir, where we worked on the development of some text-books for use in the Albanian schools.

It was while I was thus engaged that I first met and came into close personal friendship with *Hon. Charles R. Crane, of Chicago.* Too much importance cannot be attached to the work that Mr. Crane has done toward the intellectual and political freedom of Albania and the powerful influence he has exerted in our behalf. We really owe more to Mr. Crane than to any other individual outside of our own nation. It is very largely through his efforts and personal representation of the situation that the Province of Kortcha was included, by the London Ambassadorial Conference, within the territorial limits of independent Albania.

Always a student and authority on Balkan matters, a close observer of conditions in the Near East, one of the best informed men in the United States in Russian affairs, Mr. Crane had, strangely enough, never visited Albania in person. At that time Mr. Crane was and still is president of the Board of Trustees of the American College for Girls at Constantinople, and was passing through Paris on his way to the commencement exercises when he met Professor E. I. Bosworth, D. D., of Oberlin College, president of the Board of Trustees of the Kyrias School. It was but logical that at such a meeting the talk should turn toward their respective school interests in the Near East and as a result of Mr. Crane's expressed desire to visit Albania in person, Dr. Bosworth brought up my name and address.

A comparatively short time after this meeting in Paris, Mrs. Dako and I were pleasantly surprised by a call, at our home in Monastir, from Mr. Crane. As a result of this visit Mr. Crane and I started on a tour to Albania, May 30, 1911, a journey that was destined to mean much for the future of Albania.

Through the courtesy of the Governor of the Vilayet we were furnished with an honor-guard of 24 *souvaries,* and thus escorted, we rode out of Monastir. Our first stop, after crossing the *Diavati Mountains* was at Resna, where we were the guests of *Niazi Bey,* one of the heroes of the Turkish revolution of 1908. That night we slept at Ochrida, at the northern end of the lake of the same name. Our arrival at Ochrida caused no little excitement, attended as we were by a guard of souvaries, particularly as the last time I had passed publicly through the town I had been a prisoner in chains. My old friend *Hamdi Bey,* he who sent me the newspaper on the occasion of my passing through Ochrida under arrest, was our host and many of the prominent leaders of the Albanian national movement were presented to Mr. Crane at this time.

The following evening was spent in a little *han* in *Kukes* and the next morning, before renewing our journey, I conducted Mr. Crane to the *Rocks of Scanderbeg,* where the Albanian hero of the 15th century defeated the mighty armies of Turkey.

As we crossed the bridge of *Hadji-Bekari* over the Shkumbi river, two hours' distant from Elbassan, the most important city of Central Albania, we were met by patriots who had heard of our coming, and who welcomed us with acclaim. Rifles were fired in the air and we were greeted as though returning from the dead. In fact, many had believed me to be dead, for the Young Turks after my arrest, had given out that I had been hanged. During our brief stay in Elbassan banquets were given in honor of Mr. Crane by *Dervish Bey, Akif Pasha* and *Shefket Bey,* leaders of the place.

Although there was the choice of two roads leading out of Elbassan, the one a comparatively easy one, the other a rough arduous passage over the *Kraba Mountain.* Mr. Crane selected the latter, stating that he had had enough of good roads and wanted to see the real mountain fastnesses of Albania of which he had heard much.

For nine hours we climbed straight up the mountain side, much of the way having to walk, as riding was entirely out of the question. But it was worth it! We arrived at Tirana 18 hours after leaving Elbassan and were entertained at the castle of *Fuat Bey Toptani,* one of the oldest feudal castles of Albania. Mr. Crane found much to interest him in Tirana, not only in the antiquity of the place, but in its famous silk works, as well, for Tirana has long been celebrated for its silk.

The Governor of Tirana, *Hysen Bey Vrioni,* son of *Aziz Pasha Vrioni of Berat,* did his best to dissuade Mr. Crane from continuing the trip, explaining that Albania was now in full revolt and that further progress would be fraught with much danger. Mr. Crane was persistent, however, in his determination to finish his visit in Albania and see for himself conditions as they actually existed. To this determination we owe a great deal, for it showed Mr. Crane, and through Mr. Crane, the world, just what those conditions were.

At this point in our journey we came within rifle shot of the Albanian insurgents and heard heavy firing off toward *Lesh* (Alesium). Word was brought to us that the Albanians had captured this place and were preparing for a further advance. Consequently we changed our plans and headed for Scutari, via Durazzo.

Because of the uprising Scutari was under martial law and immediately upon our entry into this city of Northern Albania, our books and papers were confiscated and on our awakening the following morning found our hotel completely surrounded by troops and an armed guard at our door.

Mr. Crane was not molested, but I was informed that I was under arrest, despite the protest of the resident Consuls, on the accusation that I had brought the *"American millionaire"* to Albania to encourage the revolution against the Turkish Government.

Mr. Crane immediately set about procuring my release, wiring his influential friend at Constantinople a strong protest which ultimately secured the desired result. In the meantime my enforced stay in the place gave him the opportunity of studying conditions more closely than he probably would have done.

Some little side light into the character of Mr. Crane can be found in the account given by *Miss M. E. Durham*.

In the baking hours of midday, under a wet towel, writes Miss Durham, I was drowsing heavily one day from sheer exhaustion, when the usual hammering began on my door. "A man wants to see you." "Tell him to go away." A short pause, then bang, bang, bang!

"He is an Englishman. He says he wants to see you at once." "Tell him he can't." I supposed he was a journalist, and I was sick of them. Bang, bang, bang! again. "The gentleman's card, and he cannot wait." Sleep was hopeless. I crawled miserably downstairs, and, under the white mulberries, found a tall man, who apologized very much for disturbing me. He was Mr. Charles Crane, of Chicago.

He said he wanted to see the condition of the refugees, and had been recommended when in Constantinople to apply to me. He wished to leave early next morning. It had to be now or never. I cursed my luck, but could not afford to lose a chance, however small so put on my opanke and clambered with him from cave to cave along the river-bank. He was quite imperturbable. I asked if he had seen enough. He said he had. We returned, I miserable at an exhausting afternoon for nothing.

It is darkest before the dawn, however. I had despaired too soon. When I was seeing Mr. Crane off next day, he said he was sorry he had not more to give me, and put a little bag into my hand. I did not open it till I was back in my room, and then found, to my amazement, it contained nearly eighty pounds in gold. It was a miracle. A quantity of people could now be helped; and as if in response to the influx of wealth, came an urgent message next morning early, from *Cattapani* at *Triepshi*, reporting that the misery was worse than ever, and begging me to come at once with various necessities. I at once bought 200 *kilos* of bread, and as soon as it was loaded on two pack-horses, started to ride up with about forty pounds in small coin in my pocket. Arriving late, there was time only to deal out bread to the nearest houses and turn in.

At midnight came a violent knocking on the schoolhouse door. I was awakened suddenly by cries that a telegram had come by military wire, and jumped out of bed in alarm. It was from Mr. Crane, to say that he had paid 10,000 *kronen* into the Bank of Podgoritza for me.

It seemed too good to be true. I should not have been more surprised had the skies opened and rained down gold. Nor was it the end of Mr. Crane's kindness. From that day onward he sent most generous aid, and many are the people who have to thank him for roof, food, and clothing.

But to return to my own story.

The political prisoner under Turkish rule is treated the most miserably of any in the Near East. This was my second experience, and while I did not myself suffer so badly, thanks to Mr. Crane's influence, I saw many who were most inhumanely treated. My greatest misfortune, or perhaps it was my fortune, was that I was ill at the time. But through Mr. Crane's influence I received a bed and some consideration—consideration that I would never have received otherwise.

As fellow prisoners with me were many representative Albanians: business men, professional men and men of all walks of life, held on trumped up charges. I saw many sights which I shall never forget. Sights which are seared upon my brain and which flash before me even to this day.

Near me was one of my countrymen who must have been nearly 100 years old. He had been wounded twice in the breast during a recent action against the Turks. Yet old as he was, and wounded as he was, he was shown absolutely no attention. Instead he was compelled to lie on the bare floor, his legs chained, and with a heavy iron collar around his neck connecting by a heavy chain to the floor.

I saw two women brought in, both wounded fighting, after their husbands and sons had fallen, and their home threatened. One had had her arm broken. Both legs of the other had been fractured. They were not only refused medical and surgical aid, but, as though their suffering were not enough, were subjected to the bastinado.

Had it not been for Mr. Crane's influence there is no doubt in my mind, but that I should have been subjected to similar treatment and probably sentenced to life imprisonment if not summarily executed. I owe my freedom today entirely to him.

Following my release from prison, Mr. Crane and I proceeded almost immediately to Cetinje. After a very brief stay there we continued to Vienna and there we parted, he to continue across Europe, I to return to Albania and my work there. Before we separated, however, Mr. Crane issued a statement, the significance of which cannot be over-estimated when it is understood that this was the first report from a responsible and unprejudiced eye-witness to be given to the world concerning the true situation in Albania and the Albanian revolt against Turkish domination. The substance of this statement was as follows:

"Under cover of an apparent amnesty and armistice, the Turkish troops are systematically destroying every human habitation and every crop and all means of sustenance in the territory of the Albanian highlanders. The work of devastation is proceeding pitilessly and no lives are being spared. Such of the old men, women and children, who have not made good their escape to Montenegro have been butchered. The women have been frightfully outraged. At the present moment some hundreds of women and children are cut off from the Montenegro and encircled by the Turks. Their escape is considered impossible."

Mr. Crane's statement was substantiated and confirmed by similar statements from *Miss Durham, Baron Siat Yoost de Kruyff,* president of the Foreign Press Association of Constantinople, and *Signor Zoli,* correspondent of the *Secolo.* As a result of these representations and the wide publicity given to them, *Torgout Shevket Pasha,* commander of the Turkish troops in Albania, was recalled and his resignation ordered.

Another outgrowth of Mr. Crane's visit to Albania has been his magnificent support of the Albanian educational movement. When he left me at Vienna, Mr. Crane offered to support six boys at the Robert College and six girls at the American College at Constantinople. To me was accorded the privilege of selecting the candidates for these schools and it has been one of my greatest pleasures. I have endeavored to be absolutely impartial and to select boys and girls best fitted for advanced study irrespective of religious beliefs or the province from which they came. Frequently I have been told by my colleagues that this has been one of the strongest factors in strengthening among all people the Albanian National Movement.

Many events of importance in the development of Albanian independence have occurred in the three years which elapsed between Mr. Crane's visit and the period in which it is my purpose to renew my narrative. During this time I had returned to the United States to resume my interrupted education at Oberlin. In the meantime the Balkan war had brought about the independence of Albania from under Turkish rule.

But while Albania recovered its independence at that time, the situation at Kortcha, if anything, went from bad to worse. While nominally included within the limits of independent Albania, Kortcha was nevertheless a disputed point and claimed by both Greeks and Albanians. But of all this I have written at some length in the chapter devoted to historical data. It is my purpose here, as stated earlier in the chapter, to confine myself almost exclusively to my own personal experiences and those of my own household.

Following the completion of my studies I spent the summer of 1913 actively engaged in the work of advancing the interests of my country from this side of the Atlantic. A part of the summer I spent in Boston, where I began work on my history of Albania, and where I worked in close association with the New England members of the Albanian societies of America. In July I attended the general assembly of the Federation and was then elected to the presidency and to the editorship of "Dielli" (The Sun), the official organ of the Federation.

As one result of our activities there came from the London Ambassadorial Conference this message quoting *Sir Edward Grey* of the London Foreign Office:

"Tell the Albanians not to spend so much money in cables. We know that the city of Kortcha, and its district—so much coveted by the Greeks—is Albanian."

On the tenth of August we were notified by Mr. Crane that our voice and the voice of the Albanian people had been heard with the result that Kortcha had been included within the territorial limits of independent Albania.

One month later, September 10th, Miss Kyrias and I sailed from New York on our way back to Albania. Our journey was quite uneventful until we reached Bucharest and started on the last lap of our journey to Monastir. The logical route was by rail to Salonica and thence to Monastir. But we were so strongly advised at Bucharest to avoid Salonica because of the hostile attitude of the Greeks toward Albanians in general and natives of Southern Albania in particular, that completely changed our plans and followed the Belgrade route.

From Bucharest, then, we went directly to Belgrade and thence to Uskup and Veles, where Mr. Kyrias met us with an auto and took us over the road to Monastir. In this manner we completely avoided Salonica and the fate of four or five hundred of our countrymen who had been clapped into prison solely because they were Albanians.

From Belgrade to Uskup we had to take a military train. Our passports were rigorously examined everywhere. At Uskup we were held up for 24 hours and were obliged to present ourselves to the police authorities and be subjected to a rigid examination before being allowed to proceed. Even then our trunks were detained and we were obliged to leave without them.

We arrived at Monastir at 3 o'clock in the morning. We had of course expected to find Mrs. Dako there and so were not surprised when she met us, but we were surprised indeed to learn of her distressing experiences while we had been gone.

With the Greek authorities still occupying Kortcha, despite the edict of the Ambassadorial Conference, which placed Kortcha where it rightfully belonged,—within the limits of independent Albania—our school was as much in jeopardy as it had been under Turkish rule and Mrs. Dako had been subjected to all manner of persecution, finally being compelled to flee from Kortcha for her life.

These were indeed dark days for the Kyrias school and the advancement of Albanian nationalism in Kortcha, or anything savoring of Albanianism in this city contended for by Greeks and Albanians alike. For the Greeks, despite the London Ambassadorial Conference decree, persisted in claiming Kortcha as a Greek city, as a part of that portion of Albania which they delight in calling *Epirus*. A sample of their policy is found in Miss Kyrias's statement of experiences in Salonica while waiting for her permit to be vised enabling her to return to Uskup and get our trunks.

"While in Salonica," Miss Kyrias says in her report, "I had the opportunity to both see and hear many of the cruelties enacted by the Greek authorities against the native Albanians. Passing to and fro in the public buildings while getting my permits vised, I saw many Albanians returning to Kortcha from America treated in a most barbarous manner. They were neither prisoners nor free men. They were permitted to go neither to Kortcha nor back to America. They were literally a people without a home, without a country, for the Greeks would not admit them to be Albanians, nor would they admit themselves to be Greeks. And there they had to remain, as mournful and dismal lot of men and women as it has ever been my misfortune to behold."

Some idea of the alternate hope and dread that the residents of Kortcha experienced in those days, between the termination of the Turkish rule and the coming of the Greeks, is contained in the letter written by Mrs. Dako while we were still in Monastir waiting opportunity to return to Kortcha. In this letter, from which I have already quoted freely, Mrs. Dako goes back over a period of one year to the time when the triumphant Greeks, bearing the banner of the Cross, drove before them the routed Turks and entered into Kortcha a triumphant, victorious army.

It was not until the first week in March that Mrs. Dako and I deemed it wise to attempt to return to Kortcha. In the interim the Greek evacuation scheduled for December 30th was postponed to January 7th, then for the end of January and again for February 25th. All this time Miss Kyrias was in Kortcha, where she remained cooped up in the school, hardly daring to go abroad and practically isolated from our neighbors and friends who feared to visit her because of the hostility of the Greek authorities.

But at last came the end of the Greek domination and the return of Kortcha to at least a semblance of Albanian independence. Speaking of this period, Miss Kyrias says in a letter to friends:—

"The second of March was a very happy day for Nationalist Albanians. At 3 P. M. the Albanians entered the city, quietly and without ostentation. The Greek bishop, who had not yet ceased his intrigues and who was still to be reckoned as a thorn in the side of Albanian advancement, had given strict orders to his flock to remain within doors and to avoid anything that might seem a welcome to the Albanian flag.

"The two foreign officers, *Major Snellen* and *Captain Doorman* of the Dutch army, who have been stationed here by the London Ambassadorial Conference, arrived the other day. They were cordially received, and Kortcha began to really comprehend its independence.

"A week ago yesterday (March 3, 1914) while I was resting in my room I heard the sound of carriages. A premonition of what that sound of wheels meant swept over me and I ran to the window. When I saw the Albanian banners fluttering bravely in the breeze, I knew who it was. With Mr. Dako here our troubles are over for the time. We shall open the school on Monday, March 16th with the prayer that the days of persecution are over."

This brings my narrative up to that period in March, 1914, when Kortcha, after five centuries of subjugation, again stepped forth into the world a part of independent Albania. Almost immediately upon my return to Kortcha I was plunged into a busy round of governmental duties.

But we still had the Greek bishop to contend with and in every way possible he attempted to frustrate all our advance toward independence of thought and deed. We were in constant conflict and in April matters reached the crisis. Under the able direction of *Major Snellen* we had established a small force of gendarmes, but it was pitifully small, numbering about 100 men, and while sufficient for ordinary police duty, was hardly equal to the bigger task of combatting Greek intrigue, accompanied by authorized attacks organized and instituted by the Greek military authorities.

Just when fair promises of the right to be a nation were filling all our hearts with hope and joy, to have these hopes shattered and even the prosperity which was still the lot of many absolutely swept away is indeed heart-breaking.

At 2 o'clock after midnight, April 2nd, 1914, I was roused by the sounds of church bells, followed by gun shots. Half awake, I suspected that something unusual was happening. We all got up and went around trying to peep through the window and see what was going on; but nothing visible, as it was too dark. Shots, hurried steps, whispers was what we heard. Waited impatiently until the dawn, when to our greatest surprise, we heard cheers to the Greek rule. At once we comprehended the greatest danger in which we were found. Like mad men we saw people up and down in confusion, shooting any way and which ever way they could, and screaming, "Long live Greece."

After a five days' severe fight in the streets, the leader of the Greek disguised movement, the Bishop, was arrested, and soon after his arrest the Hellenic *coup-de-main* for the possession of the coveted town failed, and the repetition of the *Bartholomian massacres* was avoided, at this time.

Thus ended the attack upon Kortcha which the Greeks claimed was a civil uprising against the inclusion of the province within the limits of independent Albania. Yet there is conclusive proof that the attack was engineered and executed by officers and men of the Greek army operating in conjunction with the Greek Bishop. The failure of this attack demonstrated the futility of the Greek argument that Kortcha is a Greek city, for the attack was repulsed by the civil population and not instigated by them.

The failure to prove Kortcha a Greek province by this means did not deter the Greeks from continuing their attacks, however, and for several months the Greek army hammered at the frontier, bombarding the whole province from three sides with long-range field pieces. About the middle of June "the Epirotian Movement," joined with the Essad movement and a general attack was begun all along the border, and on the sixth of July, 1914, Mrs. Dako, Miss Kyrias and I, together with all of our associates and many of the townspeople, were forced to flee for our lives. Our ammunition had been exhausted and it seemed suicide to remain. Time and again it seemed as though we had met with certain death. For sixteen hours we struggled onward, our ears filled with the cries of dead and dying, the shrill shriek of rifle bullets as they sped by and the deafening explosion of long-range projectiles. Thrice we met detached bodies of Essad Pasha's troops and were only saved by the presence of the escort furnished us by Mr. Gregg, the British consul at Monastir, who had sent a body of his own kavasses to aid us in our flight.

Appendices

APPENDIX A.

THE ALBANIAN LANGUAGE.[1]

I was not a little puzzled, when you asked me to write something for *Yll' i Mengjezit*, for I felt utterly unable to tell anything that might interest your readers. Your readers are, no doubt, asking for political information, and on the political domain I am rather an ignorant. I feel only at home on the domain of the scientific study of languages, especially of the Indo-European languages. But interesting as are the great lines of the result of linguistics, none the less the details of linguistic exploration are not a fit matter for a periodical intended not for the narrow circle of professionals, but for the broader public. So it might seem the wisest thing to me to keep silence and leave the word to men with greater political knowledge.

But on the other hand the destiny of your nation has always been the object of my sincerest wishes, especially during these years of war, and the dangers which threaten your race are so immense that I should not like to keep silence, if my word could do even the slightest good to the Albanian cause. And this is perhaps not quite impossible. For though the great services which your nation has done to civilization, struggling against the Turks, are well known to everybody, nevertheless many educated people in Europe, and perhaps in America, too, do not seem to object to sacrificing Albanian interests to Slav and Greek interests. The explanation of this strange phenomenon must, I think, be sought in lack of exact ideas of the language of the Albanians. And therefore it may not be useless to repeat some elementary facts concerning this language. These facts are well known and have been told scores of times. But even known things may take a new appearance when told by new persons. And the linguistic facts I allude to may to many ears take a special weight when told by a foreign linguist whose impartiality is out of the question, a linguist who has absolutely no prejudice against the neighboring languages and nations, but takes the same interest in Slavonic and Greek as in the Albanian language.

First, then, let me say that the Albanian language is a lan-

---
[1] See "The Morning Star," vol. 2, page 165-167.

guage of its own type; it has no nearer affinity to Slavonic or Greek than to Danish or Persian. The Albanian language is therefore the only medium of enlightenment and moral progress that can be successfully applied in Albania. To force foreign schools and foreign church language on the Albanian nation or on a part of it is the same thing as murdering the soul of this noble and gifted race.

Nor does any of the objections against the Albanian language hold good. It is often urged that there is no linguistic unity in Albania, the northern dialects differing radically from the southern dialects so as to render the mutual understanding impossible. But this is an absolutely wrong statement. The difference between the two Albanian dialects is much smaller than the dialectal differences found within most other languages; from a practical point of view they are quite insignificant. A foreigner who has learned one of the dialects does not find any serious difficulty in understanding the other dialect. The difficulties that may occur on some occasions are due exclusively to lacking intercourse; they have no roots in a real deep linguistic difference. Of course the Albanians will have for the present to use both dialects as written languages; but this is no great inconvenience, especially if they take care to acquaint the growing generation with both dialects, admitting texts in both dialects into the school readers. It is further urged that there is no settled orthography for the Albanian language. This was true a decennium ago; but since the Congress of Monastir of 1908 the statement is an anachronism; the Albanian orthography is now well settled as any other orthography.

It may be called for to add some remarks on the alleged mixed character of the Albanian language. I regret to say that the German linguist, *Gustav Meyer*, has done much to propagate false conceptions in this respect. In the preface to his meritorious etymological dictionary of the Albanian language (1891) he gave some misleading statistics as to the origin of the Albanian vocabulary. His dictionary, he said, contained 5,140 word-families; out of these 1,420 had a Roman origin, 540 a Slavonic origin, 1,180 a Turkish, 840 a Geeek origin; only 400 could be shown to be the genuine Albanian continuation of old Indo-European words, whilst 730 were etymologically obscure. These statistics have been repeated very often, and are known to a great many people, who know nothing else about the Albanian language, and consequently are unable to add the necessary commentaries. Of course these people do not realize the very important fact that the number of foreign words occurring in the dictionary of Gustav Meyer is necessarily greater than the number really existing in any definite Albanian dialect. For the different Albanian dialects have different neighbors, and have adopted different loan words; a very good deal of the Italian words adopted by the Albanian in Italy or the Greek words adopted by the Albanians in Greece have nothing to do with the common Albanian vocabulary. But they are contained in the dictionary of Gustav Meyer, and counted in his statistics. Moreover, the statistics do not tell us anything about the relative importance of the borrowed elements. It is true that a good deal of common Albanian all-day words are of Roman origin, to a less extent of Slavonic or Greek origin; but the Turkish element is not so important as the mere number given by Meyer make us believe. A very good deal of the Turkish words have no deep roots in the language; they are quite dispensable and could easily be removed and expelled. In an especial manner misleading is the repetition of the number given by Meyer for the words belonging to the original stock of the old Albanian language; for the number of recognized genuine words has ever since been continually augmenting. Words taken by Meyer as foreign, words that were obscure to Meyer, and words whose existence he did not even suspect, have proved to be indigenous. As an illustration of the growth of our knowledge I may mention that one of the youngest scientifically trained Albanologists, Dr. *Norbert Jokl*, in one of his numerous papers (*Studen zur Albanesischen Etymologie*, Vienna, 1911), has proposed more than a hundred Indo-European etymologies of Albanian words.

A revision of the statistics of Gustav Meyer, extended to the whole existing Albanian vocabulary, would no doubt yield a result that would be very similar to what may be seen in other European languages.

And nobody who is familiar with the Albanian language in living use and has a scientific knowledge of its structure, can approve of the description of it as a mixed language. As all other languages in the world it has absorbed a certain amount of foreign materials; but it has had a development of its own, and it is now a beautiful and powerful language that should be the pride of its speakers and a sacrosanct vehicle of the intellectual and cultural growth of the old Albanian nation.

HOLGER PEDERSEN.

APPENDIX B.

An Interesting Debate.

(Extracts)

Dear Mr. Editor:

I have read with great interest in *The Orient*, Mr. Dako's article about the Albanians, and I quite approve of it as a whole. In its details, however, and in some ethnological axioms, *i. e.*, "that Philip and his son Alexander the Great, as well as all the Macedonians were not Greeks, but the forefathers of the Albanians," I disagree altogether because of plain historical reasons.

Let it be known from the beginning, that the Greeks of today have at last come to understand that historical and hereditary rights have least weight in the realization of their national ideals. Today's policy is, unfortunately, one of brutal military force and violent might; so that historical rights if any may be brought forward only as a polite pretext for the strong to accomplish their greedy desires and political views. Thus, whether Macedonians and their kings were Greeks or not matters little for the present or future destiny of Macedonia; but the question changes aspect at once, as we approach the ground of science and the impartiality of the historical facts; here we must stick to the scientific truth, and get rid of the racial interests. Mr. Dako sustains his ideas about the Macedonians with the testimonies of the Greek writers, Herodotus, Demosthenes, etc. Would he then allow me by quoting passages of these authors, to come to the contrary conclusion?

Herodotus (5:20) presents Alexander, Amyntas' son—at the time of Xerxes' invasion—saying to his Persian guests about himself, "You may report to the king, who sent you that a Greek (ἀνὴρ Ἕλληνν) the prince of the Macedonians gave you a good reception . . ." and (9:45), "For, I am both myself a Grecian originally, and would by no means wish to see Greece enslaved, instead of free"; and (5:22) Herodotus himself reports, "that these princes, who are sprung from Perdiccas, are Greeks, as they themselves affirm, I myself happen to know, and in a future part of my history, I will prove that they are Greeks." See also Herod. (8:137-139) and especially about Macedonians, as being Dorians see Herod. (1:56) "Dorians in the time of Dorus, the son of Helen, inhabited the country at the foot of Ossa and Olympus, called Histiaeotis; when they were driven out of Histiaeotis by the Kadmaeans, they settled on Mount Pindus, and were called Macedonians . . ." See also Herod. 8:43. "Lacedaemonians contributed sixteen vessels, Corinthians . . ., Sicyonians . . . Epidaurians . . . Troezenians . . . all these being of Doric and Macedonic extraction, having come from Enineum and Pindus."

It is true, however, that Demosthenes calls Philip, the father of Alexander the Great, a *barbarian*, but this word in ancient times has no racial meaning whatever. Demosthenes is as furious as he can be against Philip, the threatening usurper of the Athenian state; so in his political passion uses many bad names against Philip, but without a shadow of ethnological meaning. [Consider what the German historian Otto Abel thinks in his book *Makedonien vor Konig Philip*, page 116. "The expressions of Demosthenes, against Macedonians, due to striving partyism, have little meaning to the historical ground; but as to ethnological research none." See also Beloch, Greek hist., p. 25-26. "We must always bear in mind the subjective nature of such testimonies, and not believe any advocate like Demosthenes, in what he says about his opponents, or the clients of his opponents."]

Curtius, the great German historian, says in his Greek Hist., vol. 3: 397, "The Greeks in the height of their civilization were strongly displeased at the crudeness of the language and the manners of others . . . so that they considered as foreign and barbarious those of kindred race . . . This crudeness resulted from the difference of civilization and accordingly this feeling cannot be taken as a true criterion of the ethnological relations."

Moreover, it is well known to all historians, that quite early the words Hellas, Hellenes, became rather synonymous with the "civilized country, refined people," and so it was more opposed to "barbarians, ignorant, rude people." See Isocrates' Panegyricus, 50, "Our city Athens, is so much ahead of the other people in thought and speech that she caused the name Hellenes to mean not simply the nation, but the spirit and Hellenes are called those who participate in our education rather than those of the same origin." See the opposite meaning of the word "barbarian." Aristoph. Neb., v. 492, "ignorant and barbarian." etc., etc. For this reason, all those who were not followers and imitators of the Athenian civilization, those who were not living in civilized liberal countries, were named barbarians, even if they were of the purest Greek blood. Let me give some examples of this.

Thucydides 3:94 speaks about the Eurytanians, "as one of the largest population of Aetolia, who spoke a dialect more unintelligible than any of their neighbors and are believed to eat raw flesh." See also Thucyd. 2: 80 about the Hasnians of Epirus "of barbarians a thousand Hasnians"; and 2:81 "the Chaonians and the other barbarians." But it would be absurd to suppose that these inhabitants of Epirus were not Greeks because the inscriptions of those times excavated by the Greek scholar, Mr. Karapanos, at and near the famous oracle of Dodona proclaimed abroad undoubtedly that the language of the Epirotes was one of the northern Greek dialects. The German linguist, August Fick, after a profound study of the inscriptions, wrote in Beiträge von Bezzenberger, vol. 3, p. 266, as follows, "The misunderstanding of some passages of Thucydides, who in regard to the learning of the Epirotes called them barbarians, misled some historians to suppose that Epirotes were not originally Greeks, but were lately Hellenized. It was also supposed that the old Illyrians, that is the Albanians of today and the Epirotes were the same people. All these confused thoughts are now dissolved, and the cradle of Hellenism (Epirus) is purged from any suspicion of barbarism. The inscriptions of Dodona show us the ancient dialect of Epirus, as one of the northern Greek dialects, which alike to each other extended from the Akrokeraunian mountains down to Boeotia and to southern Thessaly."

Now, I think it has been made most clear that what Mr. Dako says, "the term barbarian was applied by the ancient Greeks to all who spoke a different language from their own; the Pelasgians, the Epirotes and the Macedonians spoke not Greek but a different language, which there is every reason to believe is the same as the Albanian now spoken by their descendants," is improbable. The Macedonian language as it is represented in the inscriptions has all the chief and important characteristics of the Greek language. These inscriptions show us the popular dialect of Macedonia, because we possess no representative literature of that country, and indeed the vocabulary, declension, syntax, phonology and so forth are identical with the Greek language. The greatest German linguist Paul says in his "Principien der Sprachgeschichte p. 44, "phonology especially is the strongest basis of the identity one dialect has to another. Surely Macedonian dialect has its peculiarities, its own development; but is it not the same exactly with the Greek dialects, Doric, Aeolic, Ionic? I remember that once a student reading Sappho's poems told me that they sounded to her like Chinese!! but, who would attempt to prove that the Aeolians (of Lesbos) were not Greeks, for their language differs so much from the Attic dialect of the classical period? Why then, not to deal with the Macedonian and the Epirotes on the same principles exactly?

ROBERT COLLEGE. M. G. MICHOELIDES.

Dear Mr. Editor:

In answer to Mr. Mihaelides' article, criticising a statement of a previous article of mine on the Albanians, published in *The Orient* of the 17th of January, I would say the following:

First. According to the best authorities, the Greek word βάρβαρος barbarian, in classic Greek, means one *not* a Greek, a foreigner; or one that did *not* speak Greek, without having any reference to civilization. The ancient Egyptians had an analogous word for all τοὺς μή σφισιν ὁμογλώσσους, those who did *not* speak the same language that they did. See Hdt. 2: 158. The Jews had the word *Gentiles*, which they applied to all but themselves. Even the primitive people called *barbarians* all those who did not speak or understand their language. The Latin poet Ovid, in his book, "Tristium," written at Tomis (Constanza), where he was banished, says, "Barbarus hic ego sum, quia non intelligor ulli," I am a *barbarian* here, because I am understood by none. Prof. Max Müller, in his book, "Lectures on the Science of Language," says, "The Greeks never thought of applying the principle of classification to the varieties of human speech. They only distinguished between Greek on the one side and all other languages on the other, comprehended under the convenient name of *"barbarians."* It is true that the word βάρβαρος means also uncivilized, ignorant, rude, etc., but this is a later meaning given to this word. (See A. Chassang, Nouveau Dictionaire Grec-Français; Liddell and Scott's Greek-English Lexicon; Standard Dictionary, etc.) I think it has been made clear, by the above statement, that to say that the word βάρβαρος "has no racial meaning *whatever*," is extreme.

Second. In regard to the Greek inscriptions, I do not think that they necessarily prove that the Epirotes and the Macedonians were Greeks. The reason why these inscriptions were written in Greek is because, at that time, Greek was the language figuring in civil papers, on coins, in treaties, etc., as Latin was in the middle ages. Even today it is so in some parts of Albania. For instance, in Kortcha, all commercial affairs, all civil documents, all epitaphs on tombstones, etc., etc., are in Greek; moreover, Greek is the official language of the Greek Orthodox Church and of the schools under her control, while the seal of the Orthodox community of our city is in Greek and reads: "the Greek community of Kortcha," but this does not prove at all that Kortcha is a Greek city. Therefore, if Mr. Mihaelides wishes to prove that the Epirotes and the Macedonians were Greeks, because of the inscriptions found in these regions, he has to prove first, that the language of these inscriptions is identical with that spoken by the Epirotes and the Macedonians. But we have proofs to the contrary, and I shall mention some of these further on.

Third. It is true that the Macedonians were Dorians; but who were these Dorians? Were they Greeks? Herodotus tells us that the Dorians were Pelasgians, and these Pelasgians were *not* Greeks; and they did *not* know any other language except the Pelasgic; (See Hdt. 1: 56-59). The reason why Alexander the First, Amyntas' son (and *not* Alexander the Great), called himself a Greek is simply because his forefathers, the Pelasgians, came from Argos to Macedonia. It is well known to all historians that the first inhabitants of Greece were these Pelasgians. (See L. Benloew, La Grêce avant les Grecs; also Dr. Hahn, Das Albanesische studien; also the *Greek* writer, Dr. Cleanthes Nicolaïdes, Macedonia, Chap. 5.) So when Amyntas' son called himself a Greek, he meant that he was originally from Greece, rather than from Greek blood. Our argument is strengthened, if we note the fact that the Greeks themselves called him a *"Philo-hellen,"* for the services he rendered them in seeking to make peace between Persia and Greece.

In my former article on the Albanians, I did not mention the historical reasons, which led me to believe that Philip and his son Alexander the Great as well as all the Macedonians, the Epirotes and Illyrians were the forefathers of the Albanians; but I am more than glad to give some of them. Those who have read history thoughtfully know that from the first the Pelasgians and their direct descendants, the Macedonians, the Epirotes and the Illyrians were distinct from the Greeks. Their form of government, laws, customs, military organization and language were distinctly different from those of the Greeks. Moreover, neither the Macedonians, Epirotes and Illyrians on the one side, nor the Greeks on the other, have shown any mutual sympathy

KEY TO THE NEAR EAST 237

in one another's interests. Two great historical events illustrate this. When the Persians started to fight Greece and when all the tribes of Greece united to fight the enemy, not only did the Macedonians, Epirotes and Illyrians refuse to join them, but they even became allies of the Persians in their war against Greece. Again, when the Romans came, under Paul Emilianus (168) to fight the Macedonians, Epirotes and Illyrians, the Greeks made no effort to aid our forefathers. Another important fact is that while the Macedonians, Epirotes and Illyrians intermarried among themselves, they never did so with the Greeks.

The only thing in common between the Greeks and our forefathers was their pagan religion. Let us not forget, however, that these gods were originally the gods of the Pelasgians and that the Greeks borrowed them later from our forefathers. This fact, of which history speaks, can be easily proved by considering the names of these gods. Indeed, $Z\epsilon\acute{u}s$ comes from Zaa, Zee, which in Albanian language means *voice;* the modern forms Zaan, Zoon, Zoot, all mean God. And $P\acute{\epsilon}a$ (Rhea), probably derived by metathesis from the Albanian erë, *wind,* from which $Z\epsilon\acute{u}s$ was born, in Albanian means *cloud.*

Another historical instance in our favor is the fact that the Macedonians, the Epirotes and the Illyrians were not members of the Amphictyonic council, which was the political and religious centre of the Greek tribes. Every one who has read Greek history knows that Philip the Great entered into this council only by force, the reason why he was so anxious to enter it being because he wanted to know all the political plans of Greece.

But we have still another series of proofs in favor of our opinion. Plutarch tells us that when Alexander the Great quarreled with Clitus and before he killed him, he summoned his army in the *Macedonian* language. Other important historical instances, which show us that the *Macedonian* language was *not* identical with Greek, are the following: Philotas, one of Alexander's Greek generals, was rebuked by his sovereign because he spoke to his countrymen in Greek. Again, when Alexander the Great sent Philotas before the court to be tried, as one who was implicated in a plot against his life, he asked Philotas to speak in *Macedonian,* so that his judges, who were Macedonians, might understand him; but the Greek general refused, saying, "I shall speak in Greek, because I want to be understood by my own countrymen, the Greeks." Again, we read that Ulpianus rebuked Cinulquus, for using Latin words in his writings. He, in order to defend himself answered, "I know writers who have used in their works Persian words; moreover, I know *Athenians*, who many times have used *Macedonian* words in their writings." Again, Plutarch tells us that Alexander the Great was born in July which in the *Macedonian language*, was called "loos." To the present day, in some places in Albania, *loonar* means July.

Our opinion that Philip and his son Alexander the Great, as well as all the Macedonians, the Epirotes and the Illyrians were not Greeks, but the forefathers of the Albanians, is sustained by a large number of impartial European scholars, as well as by the ancient Greek writers. Let me quote some of these. Mr. E. M. Vogüe states, "L'Albaniais, c'est *l'Epirote* de Pyrrhus et de la phalange *Macedonienne*, Alexandre l'a menè jusqu' au fond de l'Asie; c'est l'Arnaut de Mehmet Ali et d'Ibrahim Pasha . . ." Mr. Clark says, "*The Epirot* or the *Albanian* is as unlike the Greek, as his fathers were in the time of Pyrrhus" (see Clark's Turkey, p. 80). Baker assures us that "the Shkipetars (the Albanians) are the descendants of the Illyrians and the Epirots, Chaonians, Thesprotians, Molossians." (See Baker, Turkey in Europe, p. 363.) Our hero Scanderberg, writing to the prince of Taranto, said, ". . . you do not know my Albanians; we descend from the *Epirotes* who begat Pyrrhus, the victor over the Romans; we descend from the *Macedonians*, who bred Alexander the Great the conqueror of India."

For Strabo and other Greek writers, Greece went as far as Sallahora; from thence on, the land belonged to the *barbarians*. For Demosthenes, "Alexander the Great not only is *not* Greek, but neither has he any connection with the Greeks, and that I might be better understood," says Demosthenes, "not even a good barbarian comes out from thence (Macedonia), but he is a *Macedonian pest*, whence you cannot obtain even a good slave." (Phillippic III, 31.)

Christo A. Dako.

APPENDIX C.
Russian Official Statement.

St Petersburg, April 10, 1913.

The following communication has been issued by the Ministry of Foreign Affairs:

The principal object pursued by the Russian Government at the time of the military successes of the Balkan Allies was to assure for the victors the fruits of their victories in the largest

KEY TO THE NEAR EAST

possible measure. This object has been attained as the result of complicated and difficult negotiations, for the Allies could not look for success except by virtue of non-intervention of the Powers. To appreciate at its just value the importance of the service rendered by Russia towards the Balkan States, the complexity of the international situation with the collision of opposing interests must be fully taken into account. The localization of the war was only possible on two conditions—first, the renunciation by the Great Powers of individual territorial and other advantages; secondly, by renunciation of any individual action on their part.

These negative conditions implied a third and positive condition—namely, the revision of the situation created by the war and its reconciliation with the interests of the Great Powers, interests which they could not renounce, and the adjustment of which could be effected only by the European Court, whose decision should be rendered in the name of the whole of Europe. Hence individual action could not be taken by any of the Powers except on condition of the unanimous recognition by them that the decision of Europe had compelling force.

In these circumstances the Conference of Ambassadors in London was convoked.

That Conference has just completed the heavy task of determining the frontiers of North and Northeastern Albania in opposition to the interests of Montenegro and Serbia with their very natural tendency towards expansion.

On the other hand, there were the interests of the Albanians protected by Austria and Italy, who considered the *Status-Quo* in the Adriatic of such vital importance as to admit of no argument on the subject. The maintenance of this *Status-Quo* implied also the existence of the Albanian province, and from this naturally followed the effort to widen as far as possible the frontiers of an Albania having a homogeneous population of Albanian origin.

As the result of long and persistent negotiations, a compromise was reached on the basis of mutual concessions. Having preserved Prizren, Ipek, Djakova and Dibra for the Slavs, Russia thought it necessary to concede the annexation of Scutari to Albania. This concession was made in order to preserve peace, the rupture of which for the above cause would have been manifestly absurd, Scutari being a purely Albanian town and the seat of a Catholic Archbishop. This has been fully confirmed by reports from the Russian Vice-Consul in Scutari, who has adduced facts to show that the Montenegrins play an essentially military *role* and have proved incapable of assimilating several thousand Catholics and Mussulman Albanians who have been established in Montenegro for 35 years.

Consequently the annexation of a portion of the Sandjak of Scutari would only weaken Montenegro considerably, as it would swell the scanty Montenegrin population with an influx of 100,000 men foreigners to them in religion, blood and language, and Montenegro would thus be threatened with the fate of becoming a Montenegrin Albania. Our representative further believes that the union of a considerable number of Roman Catholics with Montenegro might furnish an opportunity for strengthening of foreign ties and thus render easier the penetration of foreign influences.

King Nicholas broke the understanding into which he had entered to warn Russia in the event of war and to obtain her consent. Nevertheless, the Tzar magnanimously came to the aid of Montenegro by supplementing the resources of her population. When the question of Scutari was settled a friendly notification was sent to King Nicholas, and he was at the same time warned of the grave responsibility which he would assume if he continued his resistance. He was afterwards advised to desist from all recrimination which would condemn his people to useless massacre. These representations to King Nicholas have proved to be without effect. It has become clear that he bases his calculations on embroiling Russia and the Great Powers in a European war. The Russian Government could not, therefore, oppose the taking of measures which had become necessary since the refusal of King Nicholas to submit to the decree of the Powers. The Imperial Government cannot abandon the hope that Montenegro will cease her obstinate efforts, and will consider it sufficient for her *amour propre* to submit to the will of Europe, supported by an imposing display of naval force. In this case Europe will be able to find means of alleviating the lot of the Montenegrin people, who have been overwhelmed by the excessive sacrifices demanded by the siege of Scutari.

The Imperial Government cannot lose sight of its formal responsibility to the Russian people, a responsibility which involves the duty that not a drop of Russian blood shall be shed unless the interests of the Fatherland demand it. Russia, a great Slav and orthodox Power, has never been sparing of help and sacrifice on behalf of her brothers, but on the latter, in their turn, is imposed the duty, which our press has not always been urgent in recalling to them, of respecting the counsels which Russia cannot be accused of giving to excess, and of remembering that if we are proud of their successes these would not have been achieved without Russia, which gave them life and which continues to be necessary to them in their joy, as in their grief, especially for the purpose of mutual reconciliation, without which these people cannot acquire power or vigour. These relations of Russia towards the Slav peoples exclude any idea of hostility towards other states and nations. Racial differences do not lead inevitably to racial antagonism. It is difficult to admit that the cause of peace would gain by the clash of arms. Conscious of her right and of her strength, Russia has no need to pass from uneasiness to threats which do not express the strength of a people. (London Times, April 11, 1913.)

APPENDIX D.

A MEMORANDUM ON ALBANIA'S RIGHTS, HOPES AND ASPIRATIONS.

Presented by the Albanian National Party to the Allied Powers, October 12, 1918.

It is admitted today as an historical fact that the Albanian people is the most ancient, the most compact, the most homogeneous, and the most important factor of all the Balkan nations. His origin and his strong national consciousness, that of being Albanian by race, language, customs and feeling, distinguish him entirely from the neighboring races, and give him that proper individuality, which enabled him to resist for centuries all endeavors of being denationalized and assimilated.

The history of Albania is a long record of chivalrous struggle, not only to safeguard her integrity and independence, but also to hinder the barbarians from carrying on their invasion any farther into Europe. Two great historical events illustrate this. In ancient times, Alexander the Great saved Europe from the Persian invasion; in medieval times Scanderbeg fought the Turks for 40 years, when they were in the climax of their conquering power, thus insuring peaceful times for the western nations and enabling them to reach their present stage of civilization and learning.

It is true that during certain periods of its history, Albania was forced to acknowledge a certain amount of foreign, nominal domination, but she never consented to renounce entirely her sovereignty, never consented to give up her national aspirations; her submission being only temporary and apparent. This is evident from the many revolutions which followed one after another, at very short intervals, with the purpose of regaining her complete freedom; but the European Powers, for selfish motives refused to recognize her independence more than once. In 1876, when it became evident that the Ottoman rule was to leave the Balkan Peninsula, the British Government strove to create a strong, independent Albania, including within her boundaries Kosova, Scutari, Janina, and part of Monastir vilayet. Lord Goschen and Lord E. Fitzmaurice, both foreseeing the importance of the Albanian question, worked hard for this end. Had they succeeded, many of the recent complications and much blood and misery would have been obviated. But unfortunately the Powers could not come to an agreement, so they contented themselves merely with a recommendation for certain administrative reforms for the Turkish Provinces, which were never put into practice.

In 1878 Albania presented her legitimate claims to the Congress of Berlin, asking that her territorial integrity be safeguarded and her independence recognized; but Bismarck with his brutal disregard of facts which did not suit him, rejected to consider them, saying—what Metternich had said a few decades before in regard to Italy—"There is no Albanian nationality!"

The frontiers drawn by the Treaty of Berlin were impossible; in some place they could not be defined, in many other places they floated on blood. The Albanian League proved, even while the representatives of Europe were still sitting around the table of peace, that they were wrong; and a few weeks later, after thousands of lives had been wasted, they receded from the position they had taken in ignorance and acknowledged that both Scutari and Janina, the first coveted by Montenegro, and the latter by Greece, were Albanian territories, as well as Monastir and Uskup.

Nobody can fail today to see that the common action undertaken by the Balkan Allies against Turkey in 1912-1913 was a continuation of the Albanian uprisings of 1909-1912, and that their success *undoubtedly* was the fruit of a struggle for liberty

KEY TO THE NEAR EAST

in which the Albanians by their continued insurrections, and by their indefatigable *irredentisme* distinguished themselves most valiantly. We naturally expected, therefore, a fair treatment at the Peace Conference of 1913, where the national rights of Albania were stoutly defended by Sir E. Grey, but in spite of all these, the Powers drew a rough and most unjust and unfortunate frontier, by which the gallant people who had borne the brunt of the fight for freedom in 1909-1912, were awarded to Montenegro, Serbia and Greece, and the guilt of handing over these Albanian districts to be butchered and exterminated, rests primarily with Tsarist Russia. But this was not enough. Some of the Great Powers, just when they were putting their signatures for the recognition of the Albanian nationality and for the independence of their country, advised the Serbian and Greek Governments to defy the decisions of the European Concert. Greece, encouraged by this advice, refused to evacuate southern Albania and at once organized the disguised movement, which they like to call Epirotian, against the Albanian Government. This criminal movement, supported in every way by our neighbors, and carried on by the unscrupulous Essad Pasha, was the chief cause of the dissolution of the newly born Albanian state. Incidentally we wish to call the attention of the Governments of the Allied Powers, that Essad Pasha, to every right-minded Albanian, is as dangerous a man to united Albania, as another Pasha was to France, because of his persistent efforts toward a division or separation of our country for personal ambition, to the effect of creating a limited state out of central Albania and becoming its ruler, while alowing the northern and southern parts of the country to be sucked in by the greedy neighbors, the Serbians and the Greeks.

Soon greater events followed, washing in blood the boundaries drawn by the London Conference and by the Bucharest Treaty, thus showing once more that it is not safe to underestimate the weight of the ethnographic element in drawing the frontiers of any country.

Albania's earnest desire is to become an element of order and peace in the Balkan Peninsula; but for this it is absolutely necessary that her national unity, which was sacredly safeguarded and conserved during so many centuries of struggle, must be consecrated by the restoration of Albania, and by such a readjustment of her frontiers—and the necessity for such a readjustment is acknowledged today by everybody—as will insure her future existence and her free development. The restoration of Albania cannot possibly have another political status, except that of an independent state, politically and economically, for only under such a status will she be free of all foreign intrigues. It has been amply proved that a mixed Commission of Control is not only useless, but even embarrassing, not to say dangerous, as the Commissioners work for their respective countries and not for Albania. Greece and Bulgaria when first liberated, were given *strong*, moral assistance and financial aid till they were able to stand alone. "Impartial justice" requests that Albania should receive similar treatment.

The Albanian people inspired by local necessities, by sentiments of friendship towards the neighboring nations, and being assured that this great war, on the part of the Allies, is not a war of conquest, but a war of liberation, and that all issues involved will be settled by definitely and unequivocally accepting the principle that "the interest of the weakest is as sacred as the interest of the strongest," asks, for the sake of tranquility and peace, that the future boundary must rest upon geographical and ethnographical considerations, impartially applied for all the parties concerned. To leave or put Albanian territory and people under foreign domination is to perpetuate the germs of discord and of trouble in the Balkans. It is for these reasons that the Albanian nation claims her natural boundaries, which are imposed not only by ethnographic and geographic reasons, but also by the right of being the first inhabitants of the country. We are convinced that the vigilant goodwill and the sense of "impartial justice to all nations," which animate the Allied Powers will see that this fundamental principle is scrupulously applied. The boundary which we legitimately claim includes, with the respective hinderlands, the following towns: Scutari, Ipek, Mitrovitza, Prishtina, Uskup, Monastir, Metzova, Janina and Preveza, and the highlands of Plava, Gusinja, Hoti and Gruda.

The Montenegrins and Serbians have been forced in this direction through the fault of Austro-Hungary, which has debarred them from their lawful outlet to the south Slavonic coast. Had the Montenegrins and Serbians been at liberty to reach the sea through Cattaro and Dalmatia, they would never have tried to reach it through Shkodra, San Giovanni di Medua and Durazzo, by subjugating an Albanian population almost as numerous as their own. The thoroughly non-Slavic character of Kosovo, "Old Serbia," can be seen by the following impartial testimonies.

KEY TO THE NEAR EAST

Miss Durham says, "Kosovoplain is now by a very large majority Moslem Albanian . . . Albanian predominance is proved by the fact that so far as my experience goes, and I tried repeatedly, the Albanians are almost solely Albanophone, whereas the scattered Serbs usually speak both languages, and when addressed in Serbian, *often* replied *at first* in Albanian."

Mr. N. H. Brailsford speaking on the same subject says, "In the two districts of Prizrend and Ipek there are no more than 5,000 Serbian householders, against 20,000 or 25,000 Albanian families. In all 'Old Serbia' there are as many Serbian families as there are Albanian families in Ipek and Prizrend alone."

Mr. Gabriel Louis Jaray, speaking in his book "L'Albanie Inconnue," of the ethnography of Northern Albania says, "Prizrend, Ipek and Jakova are *par excellence* Albanian towns."

Besides, there is a traditional feud between the Serbians and the Albanians which would render the peaceable administration of the country under a Serbian hegemony impossible. Far from considering them as his superiors in culture, the Albanians have learned to despise and to exploit them as his villeins.

It is said that the famous plain of Kosovo must be given to Serbia, for the Serbs have a sentimental claim, as it was there that the Serbian kingdom was finally defeated, and the Tzar Lazar slain by the Sultan Murad on June 15, 1389. But the Albanians have also a sentimental claim to the field, for not only did a contingent of them fight against the Turks, as allies of the Serbs, but Kara Mahmoud Pasha of Shkorda, the semi-independent ruler of northern Albania, defeated the Sultan's army there in 1786.

The Hellenic Kingdom is at enmity with Albania because European diplomacy deprived her of her islands and of her Asia Minor coast; so she has been forced to lay claims upon a land which neither geographically nor ethnographically belongs to Greece. The fact that "Epirus" geographically belongs to Albania can be easily verified by everybody who can examine a map. The rivers of Epirus all empty into the Adriatic on the Albanian coast. Besides, the majority of the population is Moslem Albanian, while the Christian minority, though members of the Orthodox Church, is Greek neither by race, language or sentiment. The Christian inhabitants of southern Epirus are "Greeks" only in the sense that the Romanians, the Bulgarians, and the Serbians were Greeks a century ago, when they had the misfortune too, of being under the jurisdiction of the Orthodox

Church of Constantinople. In fact, all of them are Albanian by blood, language, customs and feeling, and for centuries have proved to be impossible of assimilation.

The thoroughly non-Greek character of Epirus can be seen by the following testimonies: Edward Brerewood, writing in 1625, says, "But at this day the Greek tongue is very much decayed, not only as touching the largenesse and vulgarnesse of it, but also on elegance of language. For as touching the former, the *natural languages of the countries* have usurped upon it so, that parts in which Greek is spoken at this day are, in a few words, but these: First, Greece itself—excepting Epirus and the part west of Macedonia . . . likewise in the isles west of Candie, and along the coast of Epirus and Corfu."

Viscountess Strangford, traveling in 1863, states, "We started on June 1, intending to make Janina, the capital of Southern Albania, our farthest point. . . . As we had divided upon the plain into three or four different parts, the first thing to be done when we had reached Delvino, was to find each other; but this was not accomplished until we had wandered far and wide, loudly shouting and inquiring from every man, woman and child we could see. We were decidedly in difficulties, for it was the hour of the midday sleep, and our inquiries were made in Greek, while the seeming answers were given in Albanian, neither party in the least understanding the other."

Greece is trying to lay claims to Southern Albania, just as she has tried in the past to acquire wide tracts of Slavonic lands by classing all members of the Orthodox Church as "Greek." Rome with equal justice might claim all English, French, and American Catholics, as Italians.

Another objection mentioned against the Greek unjust claim upon Southern Albania is the following: It would rob Albania of its most progressive and enlightened element. Mr. N. H. Brailsford speaking on this point says, "An Albania, which included Epirus would already contain a considerable population on a relatively high level of civilization which might be trusted to leaven the whole mass."

Setting aside their heroes of antiquity, Alexander the Great, Pyrrhus, the king of Epirus, the Ptolemies of Egypt, Emperor Diocletian of Rome, Constantine the Great, etc.—the modern Albanians have shown in Turkey, Italy, Greece, Roumania and elsewhere, that they can produce statesmen. They have given the reigning dynasty to Egypt founded by Mehmet Ali, the famous soldier and statesman, who played, in the nineteenth century, so great a part in the history of Egypt and indeed of Europe. The Küprüli family, who furnished the Sultans with three Grand Vizers, was from Albania. The troops with which Mustapha Bairactar opposed and quelled the Janissarries were principally Albanian. The famous Galip, commonly called Patrona, was Albanian. This man, though a common seaman and a pedlar, headed the insurrection of 1730, in which Sultan Ahmet III was dethroned, and with a success of which neither ancient nor modern history can furnish another instance, remained for three weeks absolute master of Constantinople.

The fact that for fifteen months the Albanian people, struggling with innumerable difficulties, had been able to maintain order and tranquility without any organized police force, during the Provisional Government, in a country harassed on all sides by enemies, who have sworn its destruction, speaks loudly that they are capable of self-government. Miss M. E. Durham, who has traveled widely in Albania, in her recent book, "The Struggle for Scutari," speaking on the subject says, "The Powers were now treating Albania badly. They neither appointed any Government, nor recognized any local one, and people knew not to whom to look. They were for the most part terrified of offending Europe by recognizing any native as head of Albania. But the local headman was keeping excellent order. The patience with which a whole people, placed in a most difficult and almost unprecedented position, went on with their daily affairs quietly, has not been sufficiently recognized. While I was riding about the burnt districts I was always unarmed, was frequently with men I had never seen before, and everyone knew I had at least Lt. 200 in gold in the bag at my belt. Men by the wayside would call out to me: 'Where are you taking the money today? Come to our village next.' But no attempt of any sort was ever made, either to take it from me, or to force me to change my route. I often wondered whether similar sums could be safely carried through England, supposing all police withdrawn, and the Government entirely done away with."

The above instances show that there need be no fear that capable men will be wanting in Albania. Under a wise and strong national constitutional government, with a good system of education, and an iron discipline, the Albanians are capable of great development, and their strongly marked racial and linguistic unity would give them a strength, which not all the other races of the Balkan Peninsular possess.

The Albanian nation has given sufficient proofs of its liberal conceptions in the field of public and political affairs. Amongst us, the national interest has always predominated our religious considerations. In Albania, people are ranged ranked and valued not according to their creed, age or birth, but according to the depth of their patriotic feeling, for an Albanian is before all else *proudly* an Albanian. In their view the highest nobility and the best religion is to love and write and cultivate their tongue and their nationality.

The best instance to illustrate his liberal attitude towards his neighboring races is the confidence shown from time immemorial, by the Wallachs, which confidence was expressed by them during the London Conference, to associate their political life with that of the Albanians.

These are in short Albania's rights, hopes and aspirations; and today the civilized nations of the world, who are fighting for the great and sacred principle of nationality, have a chance to pay their indebtedness to the oldest nation of Europe, by rendering unto her what, by all tokens of history and nationality, is hers for more than 4,000 years. This measure of "impartial justice" accorded to us, will be of advantage, not only for ourselves, but also for those who sought for their own aggrandizement in our destruction.

(Signed) SEVASTI K. DAKO,
President of the Albanian National Party.
DIMITRI BALA, *Secretary.*

APPENDIX E.

THE DEVELOPMENT OF SCHOOLS IN THE TURKISH EMPIRE AND AN IDEAL SYSTEM OF EDUCATION FOR ALBANIA.

One would perhaps naturally expect the condition of that place which is known by the name of the Turkish Empire, to be flourishing in education and civilization, especially being so near the place whence the greatest educational ideals have sprung. But unfortunately, as is well known, the Turkish race could never assimilate the education and civilization of Europe, and the fate which they suspected for a long time has come upon them as a result of the present Balkan War. The different races under its rule were suppressed by them and not allowed to work for their enlightenment until the time when it was for Turkey's political

KEY TO THE NEAR EAST

interest to allow considerable freedom of education and schools to all different nationalities except to Albania—her purpose being to arouse jealousy and rivalry among the races who would in that case fight among each other and would leave Turkey free.

It is the aim of this paper to trace the development of the different educational institutions in this country and also to outline an ideal system of education for the Albanians, that "forgotten race," as a well known French author likes to call them.

Three kinds of Turkish schools may be distinguished, viz., *ward schools*, *rushdiyés*, and *mosque schools*. Each ward or *mahallah*, has a small school founded by special request, where the *imam* teaches the Turkish alphabet and reads the *Koran* in Arabic with his pupils in a parrot-like way. All the children attend these schools for five or six years and pay a small fee. On leaving the ward schools at the age of ten or twelve, they are admitted as day pupils to the rushdīyēs schools of higher grade, where instruction is given gratuitously. Here they learn the reading and writing of Turkish, some arithmetic, and the history and geography of Turkey. The course at these schools last five or six years, and on leaving them the students return to their families. The mosque schools are of a higher grade. The course of study embraces Turkish, Arabic, philosophy, theology and history. It does not include any of the natural sciences. The professors of these schools are highly esteemed and their directors are called "rectors." Pupils enter these mosque schools at the age of 16 or 18 and attend them for about fifteen years; they are free and lodged in special houses called *medreses*, where forty to one hundred students live. There are in Constantinople 500 medreses, in Adrianople 17, and several in each capital of a province, and at least one in each large town. They leave the mosque schools at the age of 30 or 36, and many of them become *cadis* (judges), *myftis*, or *rectors*. Most of the leading men of Turkey have been students at the mosque schools.

During the most flourishing period of the Turkish Empire, the mosque schools were of very high reputation; at present, the only important studies at these schools are Arabic and religion, so that they might actually be considered as theological schools.

Besides the above mentioned schools, which are open to all Mohammedan children, there are a number of special schools, which are under government control. The more important of these schools are the military academy, the naval academy, the artillery and the medical school. Each of these has a preparatory school or *idadyé*. In the Idadiyés, the scholars remain three to six years according to whether they have attended the *rushdiyés* or not, where the principal thing is the study of the three R's, elements of Turkish geography and history, and occasionally the rudiments of some foreign language, such as German or French. These courses embrace all such knowledge as may be useful in future life to the students of such needs, but the ignorance of the pupils, the poor preparation they get in the idadiyés, unfortunately paralyzes even the most laborious efforts. These young people, who know nothing but the R's, are in six years' time to become doctors of medicine, and in four years officers in the army. If they are to begin any reorganization at all, they should begin with the idadiyés.

Instruction in the medical schools has for about forty years been given in French. This has been justified on the basis of the absence of scientific terms and medical works in the Turkish language.

In the year 1869, they made a school law which contains the following provisions:

1. Each ward or village or mahallah should have at least one primary school; in towns of 500 houses, primary schools of a higher grade should be established.

2. Each town containing more than one thousand houses must have a preparatory school; and the capital of each province must have a lyceum.

3. At Constantinople there is to be a Imperial University and a great council of education.

The excellent provisions of this law have never been carried out and neither new primary nor preparatory nor lyceums have been established. The funds gave out and there was a most deplorable want of good teachers.

The administrative system is more or less an imitation of that of Germany, but not as elaborate as in Germany. The ministry of public instruction has nothing to do with the special schools, the mosque schools, the rushdiyés, nor the ward schools. The schools founded by the rayahs (the subjects of the Sultan, who are non-Mohammedans), and by the foreigners are supported and managed exclusively by them; so that the functions of the ministry of public instruction extend to only a small number of schools, viz., the normal school at Constantinople and some small schools in the provinces.

KEY TO THE NEAR EAST

In no other place of Europe have the different nationalities and creeds preserved their distinguishing features to such a degree as in Turkey. Education, which in other countries unites the children of all classes, has in Turkey tended to widen the distance between them, because each nationality supports its own educational institutions, where instruction is given in the mother tongue by their best educated leaders and where religious traditions are preserved and political prejudices fostered not only against the Turks, but also against all the other nationalities.

Christians of different denominations, as well as Jews, support a large number of schools. The most important ones are, The Greek Patriarch's schools, the Armenian schools, the Hebrew schools, the Italian schools, which are under the management of the Jesuits; the French schools of the Lazarists and of the Christian Brethren; the German, the English, the American Missionary schools, the Slavic (Serbian and Bulgarian), the Roumanian, and the Austrian schools. The French Jesuits, who were at a later date succeeded by the Lazarists, founded boys' schools at Constantinople more than 350 years ago. They were later on followed by the Sisters of Charity and the Christian Brethren. The course of study includes Latin, Greek, the vernacular, history, geography, philosophy and natural science.

All the above mentioned nationalities had some kind of secondary schools, while the Turks had none, and the consequences were that the public offices were filled with incapable and insufficiently prepared men. Special efforts were made to remedy this state of affairs and an attempt was made to found in this country schools with such literary and scientific courses as are indispensable to every person of every nationality. *Mr. Bourée*, the French Ambassador in Constantinople, in 1864, urged the Turkish government to establish lyceums for secondary education in the principal cities of the empire. He succeeded in convincing Sultan Abdul Aziz and his ministers, and at once a beautiful building at Galata Sarai, Constantinople, erected originally for military purposes, facing the Bosphorus, was appropriated for a model lyceum.

The administration and the greater portion of the instruction were confided to Frenchmen, chosen by the Turkish government, and the French minister of public education, and these were held responsible to the Turkish minister of education. The chief language was to be French, and the course consisted of literature, history, geography, elementary mathematics, natural sciences, Turkish, Arabic and Persian. Latin and Greek were only used so far as was necessary for the understanding of scientific terms.

It is difficult for any one outside of Turkey to get an accurate idea of the varieties of opposition that were made against this institution. The Greeks complained of the little attention given to the study of their language and professed to be exceedingly disappointed. The Jews said they would not allow their children to attend a Mohammedan institution which was under the control of Christian leaders. The Catholics refused to sympathize with such an institution where all creeds were to be equally protected. Before the opening of this lyceum, the Pope forbade all the Catholic families to send their children to this school under the penalty of being excluded from the church. Besides this, way, fearing this lyceum, if allowed to develop, might interway, fearing this lyceum, if alolwed to develop, might interfere with their political plans, and so they all tried to prevent its growth.

All the different kinds of schools in the Turkish Empire number about 36,230, and have an attendance of about 1,331,200 pupils.

The different nationalities in the European Turkish Empire were almost never at peace; but the bitter struggle has been more active since the middle of the 19th century. Until that period, the Greeks, because of their superior culture, had a great influence over all the population that belonged to the Greek Orthodox church. Their schools all over the Empire were numerous. In 1896 there were 2,914 primary schools with 3,465 teachers, attended by 129,120 boys and 29,119 girls. By a law passed in 1905, the primary schools which had reached the number of 3,359 in that year were reduced to 2,604. Support was provided partly by the community, partly by the government, and partly by benevolences. The Greek schools all over this coutnry are mostly primary and secondary. The course of study cannot be compared either with the French or with the German secondary schools. Their chief purpose, as well as that of all other nationalities, is to organize the strongest possible propaganda for denationalizing the people.

The course of study consists mainly of the three R's, the study of Greek literature, Greek history, mythology and the elements of natural sciences.

A few years ago they began choosing the brightest pupils and sending them to the University of Athens, where they have a chance to become better Greeks, at the expense of the Greek Government. After graduating they are sent back to fill different positions upon promising to work for the interests of the Greeks. In 1905 the University had 537 foreign students, mostly from Turkey. The intellectual culture acquired here is too often of superficial character, and this is due to their neglecting the useful branches of knowledge and aiming at a showy literary proficiency.

The first opposition made against the Greeks, came through the Bulgarians. Before this movement all the education of the Bulgarian population was under the control of the Greek clergy, and the peasantry even to this day is ignorant. This was due to their literary revival in the 19th century. For a long time they struggled to free themselves from the Greek Partriarchate, and in the year 1871 they obtained the first Exarch. Soon after that they founded schools all over the country. In 1893 they had 554 schools with 30,267 pupils and 853 teachers. In 1900 they had 785, including five gymnasia, and 58 secondary schools, with 39,892 pupils and 1,250 teachers. A great many of these schools were closed after the insurrection of 1903 and were not opened until 1909. Many of their teachers were imprisoned or exiled.

At present the Bulgarians have an organized educational system which is centralized and dates from 1891. In nearly all the villages they have a primary school and the course consists of reading, writing, arithmetic and some catechism in the principles of their religion. These primary schools are all connected with the church and are supported by the community.

The secondary schools are founded on the same basis as the European, and they have one in each important city. For the support of the gymnasia they receive special grants of funds from the Bulgarian government in Sofia.

The Serbians constitute another nationality which must be mentioned. History says that while they were under the Turkish rule (1350-1815), there was no attempt made towards education. But immediately after their liberation from the Turkish yoke, the people made special efforts to raise the standard of education. Twenty years later, in 1836, the Serbian National Assembly for the first time gave attention to the subject of education and passed the following resolution:

1. In every district the inhabitants are to support two schools.

2. Every community which has a church must also support a school.

At that time there were in Serbia only 72 schools, with 2,514 pupils. Sept. 11, 1844, the first Serbian school law established elementary schools, a business college, gymnasia, and a lyceum. This is the first beginning of a system of education in Serbia and was soon applied among the Serbianized population of the Turkish Empire.

Their primary schools are of two sorts: village schools, having three classes (a course of three years), with only one teacher; and the city schools having four classes with four teachers.

Their secondary schools are of three kinds: 1. small real gymnasia, with two classes; 2. pro-gymnasia, with four classes; 3. gymnasia with six classes. The course of the real gymnasia is the same as that of the lower classes. The course of the real gymnasia is the same as that of the lower classes of the pro-gymnasia, so that the students on leaving the small real gymnasia can enter the third class of the gymnasia. Each of these schools has at least four teachers.

The subject matter of the gymnasium curriculum is, Religion, the vernacular, Slavic language, German, French, arithmetic, geography, Serbian history, elementary algebra, natural philosophy, geometry, natural history, drawing, vocal music and gymnastics. Higher institutions of the different nationalities do not exist here, their universities are usually in the capitals of their own countries. Most of their teachers receive their training in German universities.

The support of all these institutions is chiefly that of the state.

The Roumanian Movement makes its appearance later. The Vlachs were under the Greek influence for a long time, and although they tried to withdraw from the Greek church in 1855, they were not able to do it until after the union of the principalities of Wallachia and Moldavia in 1861. From this time on there awakened in them a strong national sentiment. Their great leader called *Apostol Margarit*, who was a priest, founded in 1886 the first gymnasium in the city of Monastir. This movement was encouraged by the French Catholics and also by Austria. There are now forty Roumanian schools in the country, including two gymnasia, whose well-qualified teachers are provided from the university of Bucharest.

Their primary schools are of the same character as those of the other nationalities which have been mentioned. The sec-

KEY TO THE NEAR EAST

ondary schools are more or less an imitation of the German Gymnasium and the French Lyceum, with a course of eight years. Great attention is given to the study of Greek and Latin and the modern languages, French, German, English and Italian.

The education of all these different nationalities is free, and the cause for this is a political one. Each nationality tries to get the largest number of pupils so that through educating them and providing them, for many of them, even the daily needs, it can make them sell their own nationality and adopt that for which the school stands.

All these different nationalities have Agricultural and Commercial schools in their own countries, but not in the Turkish Empire, with the exception of the Greeks, who have a commercial school in Salonica.

All schools in this country are non-coeducational. The program of the course of study in the girls' school is very poor. If a girl knows how to read and write, with some arithmetic and the elements of other fields of study, it is quite enough. A great deal of time is given to needlework of all kinds. But now they are trying to do away with this idea and are sending as many girls as they can to higher institutions for a more thorough education. Everybody begins to realize that "The hand that rocks the cradle is the hand that rules the world."

There is another little nation which comes "last but not least." Its name of Albania is so little known because of its being forced to keep silent. To be able to understand who these people are we must go back to their origin.

Long before the invasion by the Greeks of the country now called Greece, this place was settled by several races, chiefly nomadic, of which the greatest in number and most important in civilization were the Pelasgians, the forefathers of the present Albanians. They became largely an agricultural people and were eminently distinguished as architects; almost all of the most ancient and remarkable monuments of architecture in Greece are being ascribed to them. They were acquainted with the higher styles of pottery, with work in metals, and with other arts. But the most important of all, according to the opinion of Dr. Hahn, the great authority on this matter, is that the people possessed the Phoenician alphabet, which they had enlarged and adapted to represent the copious sounds of their own language, and which the Albanians appear to have preserved to our own times.

Through our forefathers, not only the Phoenician alphabet passed to the Greeks, but also their myths, logical conceptions, etc.

Undoubtedly our forefathers with such inclinations toward civilization as those which we have mentioned briefly, would have developed a system of education of their own, but unfortunately for us they were forced, sometimes by events, sometimes by their eagerness for military glóry, to spend all their energy and all their time in fighting their neighbors. Several hundreds of years afterward, different races emigrated from this land, the union of which resulted in the present Greeks. The Albanians did not oppose this emigration but allowed them to occupy part of their territory from which they themselves withdrew, and they called that part *"Elene,"* which means deserted place *Hellene*, and ever since then these people have called themselves, *Hellenes*. The proper names of almost all places which we consider Greek, have an Albanian meaning which we use to this day. As an illustration, we may take Sparta, which is a modification of *Spata*, meaning a spear. This took its name because of the ability of the people to use the implement so well. Even in Asia Minor (for all that region as well as the Balkan peninsula was first settled by the Pelasgians) the name Troya is a modification of Kroya, which means *Springs*, because of the many fine springs that they found there.

While these people busied themselves with fighting with other races, the Hellenes took from them their Alphabet, their educational as well as architectural ideas, which they developed to the extent which is so well known to all the world. But it must not be forgotten that some of their greatest men who took advantage of these educational developments, were not Hellenes, but pure Albanians. The Greeks boast of the glory of *Homer*, but who was he? A poor blind Albanian who every time he sang, exclaimed, *"Un' i mjeri!"* poor me! (which meaning we use to this day), and which the Greeks modified into Homer.

It soon came to pass that the Greek, being the diplomatic language, and education being limited to the officials, the Albanians were educated by Greek instructors, up to 168, A. D. At that date Macedonia, Epirus and Illyria became provinces of the Roman Empire, and by this fact the Latin language took the plac' of the Greek, which continued to be the language of enlightenment throughout Europe during the middle ages.

In 1486 Albania, after a long struggle, became a province of the Turkish Empire, and the Albanians were forbidden to use their language not only in schools and churches, but even in private correspondence. All those who dared trespass the order of the Ottoman administration found their fate in prison, exile, or the depths of the Bosphorus.

While we were forbidden to educate ourselves in our own language, our neighbors, the Greeks, the Bulgarians, the Serbians, the Roumanians, the Austrians, and the Italians had full freedom to come to our country, to establish schools of their own and to work to make us Greeks, Roumanians, Slavs, etc.

The Slavic propaganda is championed by the Serbians and Bulgarians, each of whom separately claim certain districts of our country. Although the Serbians in their propaganda lacked the funds of the Greeks, and were less able to carry on their plans than the Bulgarians, yet for some years the Albanians and the Serbians in the north of Kossova Vilayet have lived in a continual state of feud. So strong has been the strife between the two races that many of the Serbians of "Old Serbia" have been forced to emigrate to Serbia, while some of the Albanians formerly in the district that were ceded to Serbia by the treaty of Berlin have been obliged to withdraw to the vilayet of Kossova.

The Bulgarian propaganda, through schools and churches extends as far south as Kortcha.

The Greek propaganda extended along the western side of Albania as far north as the town of Elbassan. The object of the Patriarchate of course is to establish schools and open churches with the purpose of "Hellenizing" the Albanians, rather than of educating them.

The Austrian propaganda in northern Albania has been pretty strong. They have founded many schools which are of the same character as the cattecummenal schools of the period of early Christianity. In the past the education of the Christian Albanians in this part of the country has been carried out almost entirely under the protection of Austria and Italy. Soon afterwards the arrival of the Jesuits in Scutari, about the middle of the last century, the first Austrian supported school was opened in that city. About the same time Austria was recognized as the protector of the Roman Catholics in Albania. At first instruction was supposed to be given only in religious subjects, but later on the education provided a more general course. Besides this school, which is still in existence, the Franciscans have recently started a school for mountain boys, most of whom are sons of the famous men of the Mirdita tribe. The same order has established separate schools for orphan boys and schools. In addition to this they have recently founded an infant school in the same city. The education of all these Austrian schools is old fashioned. Only book work is taught; there is no instruction in any practical subject. The boy that leaves the school is fitted only for some office work. The Italian propaganda is perhaps of less importance, but must not be ignored. They have established several schools in Scutari and Vallona. In Scutari they also have a house for the aged people and orphanages. The Italians have made their schools more attractive by introducing different industries for the boys and different arts for the girls, according to their needs.

While speaking of these different propaganda we must not think that the Albanians were indifferent. They did not approve of these foreign schools, but they could not help it. Being as they were surrounded by so many strong and different influences one of the most wonderful thing about them, says again Dr. Hahn, is the way they have preserved their individuality, language and customs for 6,000 years. The Albanians made several attempts while under Turkish rule to open their own schools and organize an education in their own language, but no sooner were they found engaged in such an enterprise, than they were sent to be food for the fishes of the Bosphorus. The more important national attempt towards education was made in the year 1884. The greatest leaders of these attempts were *Naim Bey Frasheri* and Sami Bey Frasheri, who founded an educational society in Constantinople. They printed here the first Albanian primer. As soon as this was made known, these men and others with them were exiled, never to see their dear fatherland again. But exiled as they were, they contributed to their nation many valuable works which are generally prized by all. The Society was at once transferred to Bucharest. The first fruit of this society was the establishing of a boys' school in Kortcha in 1885, but no sooner was it started than the government stepped in and closed it, and the teacher paid for his service with three years of imprisonment in the White Tower of Salonica.

During this time, a young Albanian by the name of Gerasim D. Kyrias was being prepared in one of the American colleges for another national attempt. In the year 1890, Mr. Kyrias, after graduating, went to Kortcha (an important city in Southern Albania) with the purpose of establishing an educational institution, preaching the Gospel in the Albanian language; but unfortunately, on his way he was captured by brigands, and only at the end of six months, after paying a large ransom, was he released. This great trial, from the view it gave him of the social misery of his people, greatly deepened his resolution to labor for their uplift. Soon after his release, he started for Kortcha again, and the first Sunday after his arrival preached the Gospel for the first time in the Albanian language. Immediately after the service the Moslem and Christian Albanians, hungry for the hearing of their own language, begged him to stay there permanently and establish an Albanian institution. In the year of 1891 he founded the First Albanian Girls' School under the leadership of his sister, Miss Sevasti Kyrias, who had just graduated from the American college at Constantinople. The Government has been fighting this school for twenty-two years, but, thank God, has never succeeded in closing it. This is a secondary school, with a course of four years and an annexed elementary course of five years. It was started with absolutely no Albanian textbook of any kind, except parts of the New Testament. Year after year Mr. Kyrias and his sister translated the necessary textbooks, but nothing could be printed as the circulation of Albanian textbooks of any kind were prohibited. This school has been and still is in the centre whence all rays of national feeling and learning are spread over the country.

In the year 1908, with the establishment of the Turkish Constitution, the Albanians thought they had attained what they were so longing for, freedom of the use of their mother tongue. They set to work at once and in less than one year were able to establish twenty-four night schools with 1,753 pupils, thirty-four day schools with 1,850 pupils, and a normal school with 145 pupils and fourteen teachers. These schools were supported by sixty-six national clubs which had 10,000 members, at the head of which was the National Board of Education, founded by the National Congress held at Elbassan in August, 1909. At the same time, the Albanians founded four printing presses; 17 newspapers were circulated; ten literary and four musical and one ladies' society were also founded. This progress was too much for the young Turks, who decided at once to stop the Albanians. They sent against them Djavid Pasha, who arrested most of their leaders. This caused the revolution of 1910, when all our educational institutions were closed except the Girls' School of Kortcha. In the spring of 1911 another revolution took place, which was continued in 1912, and the result of which brought up the Balkan War.

Now one of the outcomes of the Balkan War is that Albania will hereafter be independent. Albania will soon be able to enjoy the treasures of learning from which she has been deprived in the past. In order to be able to attain them sooner she must have a well-organized educational system of schools.

To be able to introduce an ideal school system for this country, one must take into consideration the country, the people, their customs, and especially their characteristics and needs.

1st, Their firm independence. The Albanian as an individual or as a nation, will not permit any one to think for him or' dictate to him;

2nd, Their persistency. The constant persistency of the Albanian enables him to carry through all he has taken hold of;

3rd. Their strong sense of honor. Should the Albanian give his word of honor, *besa-besen* to do a certain thing, he will do it even though he must pay for it with his life;

4th, Their caution. Fortunately with the above mentioned qualities is combined a large measure of caution.

5th, The poetic sense of the Albanian is another of their prominent characteristics which enables them to appreciate the ideal."

The second element which should be taken into consideration is the needs of the country. If I should try to enumerate them all, there would be no end to it, but I will content myself by mentioning a few of the more important ones.

1st. The building of a National Educational System. A country with a population of three million people has only one Albanian school which has been struggling for its existence under the Turkish rule for twenty-two years; it has been tossed by waves of trouble many a time, but thank God, it has not perished and has not been swallowed up by them. The few schools that we have in our coutnry are those mentioned, foreign schools of propaganda, whose chief aim is to denationalize the people.

2nd. The establishment of some organization which will uplift the nation, and enable it to distinguish its real interests.

3rd. The unification of the nation and the elimination of Greek Orthodox, Roman Catholic and Moslem intrigues.

4th. The effort to maintain, after civilization is introduced, the present high moral standard.

KEY TO THE NEAR EAST

5th. The abolition of the feudal system, by allowing equal opportunities to all people of all classes, and by introducing the ideal of a democratic nation.

6th. The preservation of some of the present industries.

In view of these facts Albania must have a system of training, as far as possible adapted to its characteristics and its present needs and capable of development in such a way as to meet both present and future national needs. We must work for social equality and equality of the sexes in education (for otherwise we have it). Not only boys but girls, too, should receive a complete intellectual physical and moral training.

To be able to get the best results in the shortest time, it seems to me, we must have a centralized administrative system, very much like that of Germany. There should be a minister of education as the chairman of a committee of education, responsible to the Parliament. Each city should have both elementary and secondary schools and in the capital and two or three other of the most important cities should be universities. Country places can be supplied with elementary institutions and towns with both elementary and secondary schools.

There should be boards of trustees for each city with its district, which will be responsible to the minister. One of the members of the Board should be the Superintendent. A superintendent should be a man especially trained for his work. Mr. Stockton says: "No one should be thought of for the position of superintendent who is not trained in the aims of education, in certain sections of biology, sociology, and psychology (together with their pedagogical supplications), and who is not able to make courses of study, and intelligently to judge of their application in general or specific teaching situations."

The duties of the Board must be the following:

1. To consider the definite aim of each institution;
2. To use the best means to attain this aim;
3. To arrange the program of each institution.
4. To state the duties as far as necessary of each teacher;
5. To decide upon text books;
6. To arrange the course of study;
7. To fix the teachers' salaries;
8. To see that each institution is provided with the necessary equipment.

The Superintendent will be responsible mostly for the administrative work and will also recommend teachers.

The number of the institutions included in the system should be:
- A. Kindergarten.
- B. Elementary.
- C. Secondary.
- D. Higher.
- E. Normal.
- F. For defectives.
- G. Private school.

A. Kindergarten:
1. The purpose, "The kindergarten combines the home with the rational discipline of the school.
2. Course of study—two years 4-6.
    a, Manners and morals,
    b, Occupation—sewing, etc.,
    c, Nature study,
    d, Language,
    e, Physical culture,
    f, Religious instruction.
3. Special preparation of teachers in Normal schools.
4. A combined method of both kindergarten and the Montessori system for children that receive no attention at home, especially homeless children, the best thing for a child is to be with the mother until the age of six.

Most educators agree that the elementary course should begin when a child is six years of age, and continue for six years. The experience of the present great question of the relation of an elementary school to a High School, but help the Albanian nation to start right. Special care must be taken to see that these two institutions be not isolated, but that each one recognizes the aim of the other. A child that is through with the elementary course must be able without difficulty to enter the first year of High School. "The function of the elementary school," says Brown, "should be to teach all children the elements of morality, good health, and good citizenship, and to give them a mastery of the tools of intelligence and culture, wtih such elementary information concerning nature and mankind as may be taught during six years of child life." Its importance lay in that, "Here are laid the first foundation of cultural moral and physical development."

A good curriculum for this institution may be the following:
1. The study of the three R's.

The six years' course may be divided into two halves. During the first three years the greatest attention must be given to see that the child forms correct habits in reading, writing and arithmetic, and also acquaint the mind of the child with all he comes in contact with, in the world. This will be a good time to begin teaching them vocal music, too.

During the last three years the subjects that must be studied are:
1. History, in the form of stories.
2. Language.
3. Nature study.
4. Gardening.
5. Drawing.
6. Geography.
7. Vocal music.
8. Some exercises for physical development.
9. Poetry.
10. Some kind of occupation. (Like sawing, etc.)

The kindergarten and elementary school may be coeducational; but the high school courses must be given in separate institutions for boys and girls.

The elementary teachers must have at least full secondary education.

The aim of the secondary education, says Mr. Hunsaker, "is the development of intelligent, broad-minded and valued citizens."

The function of secondary education is:
1. "To promote pupils' normal physical development."
2. "To stimulate every individual to aim at intelligent self-support or some worthy form of life work."
3. "To promote the welfare of society of which he is a part."
4. "To prepare them so that they shall continue to study alone in their active life."

The best age to enter high school, psychologists as well as all educators agree, is the age of twelve. Mr. Machie, in an article in the "Educational Magazine," gives the following reasons:
1. "Young adolescents should be taught by men teachers."
2. "It will give the pupils the advantage of being taught by teachers specially trained for the different branches."

3. "It would mitigate the present abruptness of the transition from the elementary school and check the loss of pupils at this critical period."

4. "The high school curriculum is fully consistent with established principles of genetic psychology and pedagogy for the beginning of adolescence, which means according to genetic psychology that new matter and methods must be introduced."

Mention was made before that the high school should be non-co-educational. Some of the reasons for this separation are based:

1st. On the fact that this age is the age of character building and the boys must be under the direct influence of men teachers, who will understand them better, and girls should be under the direct influence of lady teachers.

2nd. This being the adolescent period, when children lack thought in most things, they, too, must be kept away from needless experiences and temptations.

3rd. Better results can be attained if the boy or girl give their whole time to reach the aim for which they attend school.

4th. The fact that in a country like Albania this will be the only way by which to reach the girls, especially Moslems.

This being the most important institution of a nation must consist of a course of eight years with a complete curriculum which will answer both the needs of a university and life. The course may be divided into halves, and the first four years may include the following subjects:

1. Language, and in connection with that, reading, grammar, composition and literature.
2. History.
3. Mathematics (arithmetic, elementary algebra and geometry.)
4. Modern languages (French and English).
5. Geography.
6. Botany.
7. Zoology.
8. Physics.
9. Drawing.
10. Music (vocal and instrumental).
11. Manual training (for the boys).
12. Needle work, domestic science, etc. (for the girls).
13. Physical training exercises for both schools.

14. Courses in education.

The second half of the curriculum may consist of the following subjects:
1. Rhetoric, composition.
2. Literature.
3. History.
4. Algebra, Geometry, Trigonor
5. Language study, Classical, Latin and Greek; Modern, French and English.
6. Physics.
7. Chemistry.
8. History of Philosophy.
9. Art.
10. Biology, Physiology.
11. Physical training.
12. Manual training for boys, and proper occupation for girls.

The course may be divided into two courses, the Literary and Scientific, and the subjects required may be arranged accordingly. Pupils must be directed in the second half of the curriculum what choice to make. During the first four years they will have shown what their inclinations are.

With a well-organized secondary institution, it is needless to establish colleges. Upon completion of this course the student must be able to enter the University, where he may specialize. The course of study here may be three years and will include philosophy, medicine, law, etc. This institution may be co-educational.

The normal school is not of less importance than the rest; its purpose being to prepare for teaching. There was a time when everybody thought that if there is anything easy to do, that thing is teaching. Even to this day most of the teachers in the country which has been our topic are ill equipped, their aim being chiefly to earn their living, instead of to promote social efficiency. A teacher bears on his shoulder one of the greatest responsibilities of this world and must not accept it unless he or she is well qualified.

The requirement for entrance to this institution should be high school graduation, and the curriculum should consist chiefly of
1. Pedagogy.
2. Educational problems, and
3. Practice teaching.

To better the conditions of society, the educational system must include schools for defectives. The blind and the deaf and dumb must be given something to do. A course for these defectives can be arranged with some cultural work, most of the rest being some kind of manual training.

At present, private schools, unless they be under government supervision, are dangerous for a place like Albania, especially those of the Greeks, Austrians, and Italians, for if these be allowed it would be difficult to save the country from foreign influences.

If a system like this be put into practice, Albania will soon be able to reap good fruit. The nation is waiting for a chance to train and utilize its abounding energies.

BIBLIOGRAPHY.

1. "Das Albanesische Studien," by Dr. Hahn.
2. "La Grèce avant les Grecs," by Louis Benloew.
3. Encyclopedia Britannica.
4. Official Reports of the Minister of Public Instructions of Roumania, Bulgaria, Serbia, Greece and Turkey of 1910.
5. The religion of the Ancient Alb. A. Siljani (Albanian).
6. The Statesman's Year Book, 1912.
7. Revue des deux Mondes, Oct. 15, 1874.
8. Books on education by Hanus, Buttler, Dewey, Davis,

P. D. KYRIAS,
Oberlin College, June, 1913.

Brown, Baldwin, and Mrs. Young.

BIBLIOGRAPHY

The chief authorities consulted in preparing this book, besides my personal experiences, are as follows:

I. Books and Booklets.

A.

Arrien, book I.
Athénée, book 13; 557.
Aubneau, J., Les Aspirations autonomistes en Europe; Paris, 1913.
Avril, Adolphe (d'), Négociation relatives au traité de Berlin et aux arrangements qui ont suivi; Paris, 1886.

B.

Baker James, Turkey; New York, 1877.
Baldacci Antonio, Die neue albanische Staat und seine Grezen; Gotha, 1913.
Baldacci, Antonio, Itinerari albanesi; Roma, 1917.
Baldacci Antonio, Bollettino Officiale del Ministero d'Agricolt.
Balkanicus, Le Problème Albanais; Paris, 1913.
Balkanicus, Les Serbes, les Bulgares dans la guerre Balkanique; 1913.
Barbarich, Albania; Roma, 1909.
Barletius Marinus, De Vita Moribus George Kastriota.
Beaven Murray, Austrian policy since 1867; London, 1914.
Bellaire (Captain), Précis des opérations générale de la division française du Levant; Paris, 1805.
Benloew Louis, La Grèce avant les Grecs, 1877.
Benloew Louis, Analyse de la langue albanaise; Paris, 1879.
Bertaux E., Les Français d'outre mer en Apulie, en Epire etc.; Revue Historique, tome 85, 1904.
Best J. J., Excursions in Albania; 1914.
Biemmi, Istoria di Giorgio Kastriota; Brescia, 1742.
Bianconi F., La Question Albanaise; Paris, 1913.
Bianconi F., Carte Commerciale des Provinces d'Albanie et d'Epire.
Bigham Clive, With the Turkish army.
Boehmer, Romanische Studien; vol. IV, page 431ff.

Bonaparte (Prince Louis Lucien), Albanian in terra d'Otranto, London, 1885.
Bopp F., Uber das Albanesische in seinen verwandtschaftliden Beziehungen; Berlin, 1855.
Boppe A., L'Albanie et Napoleon; Paris, 1914.
Boppe A., Le Régiment albanais; Paris, 1902.
Boucabeille (Lieut. Col.), La guerre Turko-balkanique; Paris, 1913.
Bore E., Correspondances et Mémoires d'un voyageur en Orient.
Boué Ami, La Turquie d'Europe; Paris, 1840.
Brailsford H. N., Macedonia, its races and their future.
Bubenicek J., An der Schwelle Albaniens; 1904.
Broughton (Lord), Travels in Albania.
Burigny (de), Histoire des révolutions de l'empire de Constantinople; Paris, 1750.
Buxton (Noel and Charles), The war and the Balkans.

C.

Caesar, Commentaires, guerre civile, book III.
Calviere P., Le vilayet de Kossova au point de vue industrial, agricole, commercial, en 1809.
Cantu C., Histoire Universelle; 1880.
Chalcocondylas L., De origine et rebus Turcorum.
Chalcocondylas L., Histoire de la décadence de l'empire grec et établissement de celui des Turc; 1662.
Chantepleure (Guy), La ville assiegée; Paris, 1913.
Cheradame A., Douze ans de propagande au faveur des peuples balkaniques; Paris, 1913.
Chopin et A. Ubicini, Provinces Danubiennes; 1856.
Choublier M., La question d'Orient depuis le traité de Berlin; Paris, 1897.
Clark E. L., The Races of European Turkey.
Conforti Gerardo, San Giorgio e la questione albanese; Napoli, 1903.
Constante C. S., Spre Albania; Bucharest, 1904.
Crispi G., Albania; 1836.

D.

Dareste, Anciennes coutumes albanaises; Paris.
Daru, Histoire de la république de Venise; Paris, 1826.
Davenport R. A., The life of Ali Pasha of Tepeleni; 1837.

KEY TO THE NEAR EAST 269

Debidour A., Histoire diplomatique de l'Europe; Paris.
Degrand A., Souvenir de la Haute Albanie; Paris, 1893.
Delare, Les Normands en Italie; Paris, 1883.
Deloche M., Du principe des nationalités.
Djuvara T. G., Cent projets de partage de la Turquie; Paris, 1914.
Densusianu Nicolae, Dacia Preistorica; Bucharest, 1913.
Descamps (Baron), L'Avenir de l'Albanie; Louvain, 1913.
Diefenbach L., Völkerkunde Osteuropas.
Diplomatist, Nationalism and war in the Near East; Oxford, 1915.
Diodor Sicilianus, book XVIII, chapter XI.
Dole N. H., History of the Turko-Russian war; (1877-1878).
Dora d'Istria, La nationalité albanaise d'après les chants populaires; Paris, 1866.
Dora d'Istria, Gli Albanesi; 1870.
Dozon August, Manuel de la langue albanaise; Paris, 1878.
Dozon August, Contes albanais; Paris, 1881.
Driault E., La Question d'Orient depuis ses origines jusqu'à nos jours; Paris, 1898.
Dugard H., Histoire de la guerre contre les Turks (1912-1913); Paris, 1913.
Duggan S. P. H., The Eastern Question.
Duhesme (Général), Précis historique de l'infanterie légère; tome III.
Dumont A., Le Balkan et l'Adriatique.
Dupoucet (le père), Traduction de Barlecio; Histoire de Scanderbeg; Paris, 1709.
Durham M. E., The Burden of the Balkans; London, 1906.
Durham M. E., High Albania; London, 1909.
Durham, M. E., The Struggle for Scutari; London, 1914.

E.

Eissner Chr. G., Die alten Pelasger und ihre Mysterien; 1825.
Engelhart E., La Turquie et le Tanzimat (1826-1832).
Epirote (Un), L'Epire et la Question grecque; 1879.

F.

Fallmerayer I., Das Albanesische Element in Griechenland; Munchen, 1860.
Faurres Rangatien, Scanderbeg the hero of Christendom.
Farley J. L., Turkey; 1866.

Feiling Keith, Italian policy since 1870; London, 1914.
Finlay G., Albanians in Greece, in his History of Greek Revolution.
Fisher H. A. L., The value of small states; London, 1914.
Fraser Foster John, Pictures from the Balkans.
Fribourg A., Les questions actuelles et le passé (1913); 1914.

G.

Galanti Arturo, L'Albania. Roma, 1901.
Gaudolphe M., La crise macédonienne; 1904.
Garnett L. M. J., Women of Turkey. Albanian Women and their folk lore.
Geblesco C. R., La Question d'Orient; Paris, 1904.
Geitler Lavoslav, Die Albanesiche und Slavischen Schriften Wien, 1883.
Georgevitch Vladan, Les Albanais et les Grandes Puissances; Paris, 1913.
Georgiadès D., La Turquie actuelle; Paris, 1892.
Ghika (Prince Albert), L'Albanie et la Question d'Orient; Paris, 1908.
Gibert Frédéric, Les Pays d'Albanie et leur histoire; Paris, 1914.
Glennie J. SS., On the Ethnography of Turkey.
Golovin J., Nations of Russia and Turkey and their destiny.
Gopcevitch S., Oberalbanien und seine Liga; Leipsic, 1881.
Gotha (1910), Albanien, eine militär geogràphischen Studie.
Gneux W. Le, An Observer in the Near East; London, 1907.
Grote, Histoire de la Grèce.

H.

Hahn G. J., Albanesische Studien; 1853.
Hamard P. J., Par delà l'Adriatique et les Balkans; Paris, 1890.
Hanotaux G., La guèrre des Balkans et l'Europe (1912-1913).
Hasdeu B. P. Cine sunt Albanezi; Bucharest.
Hasdeu B. P. Strat si substrat; Bucharest.
Hasdeu B. P., Genealogia Popoarelor Balcanice; Bucharest, 1892.
Hecquard (d'), Description de la Haute Albanie; 1859.
Hecquard Charles, La Turquie sous Abdul Hamid.
Henry R., Question d'Austriche-Hongrie et la Question d'Orient.
Hickens R., The Near East; London, 1913.
Higgins A. Pearce, The Law of Nations and the war; London, 1914.

Historicus, Bulgaria and her Neighbours; New York, 1917.
Hobhouse J. C., A Journey through Albania; London, 1813.
Hogarth D. G., The Nearer East.

I.

Ippen Theodor V., Scutari und Nordalbanesische Kustemebene; 1907.

J.

Jallifier R. et Vart H., Histoire contemporaine; Paris, 1913.
Jaray Gabriel Louis, L'Albanie Inconnue; Paris, 1913.
Jaray Gabriel Louis, Royaume d'Albanie; Paris, 1914.
Jokl Norbert, Studien zur albanesischen Etymologie und Wortbildung; Wien, 1911.
Jonquière A. Le, Histoire de l'Empire Ottomane.
Jouanin J., La Turquie, histoire et description géographique; 1842.
Justinian, book XIII: I.

K.

Knight E. F., Albania, a narrative of recent travel; London, 1880.
Knolles Richard, The General History of the Turks; London, 1621.
Kolin Jacquemyns G., Le droit international et la Question d'Orient.

L.

Lafout Emile, Trois mois de chasse sur les côtes albanaise; Paris, 1899.
Landemont (Comte De), L'Europe et la politique Orientale; Paris, 1912.
Leake W. M., Researches in Greece; London, 1814.
Legrand Emile Louis Jean, Bibliographie albanaise; Paris, 1912
Lejean G., Tour du Monde (1860-1873).
Lejean G., Ethnographie de la Turquie d'Europe.
Lear's, Illustrated Journal in Albania.
Levy S., Le declin du Croissant; 1913.
Loiseau (Captain), La guerre des Balkans; Paris, 1913.
Loiseau Charles, L'Equilibre Adriatique.

Lorecchio A., Il Pensiero politico Albanese in rapporto agli interessi Italiani; Roma, 1904.
Lyde L. W., Some Frontiers of tomorrow; London, 1915.

M.

Malte Brun's, Universal Geography, vol. 6, book 99.
Manandian A., Beiträge zur albanische Geschichte; 1897.
Marchiano S., Studii filologici svolti con la lingua pelasgo-albanese; 1822.
Meyer Gustav, Albanesische Studien; Wien, 1883-1897.
Meyer Gustav, Ethymologisches Woerterbuch der albanesischen Sprache; Strassburg, 1891.
Miller W., The Balkans; London, 1899.
Morgan F. and Davis H. W. C., French policy since 1871; London, 1914.
Muir Mackenzie G., and Irby A. P., Travels in the Slavonic Provinces of Turkey in Europe; 1866.
Muir Ramsay, The National Principle and the war; London, 1914.
Müller M., Lectures on the Science of languages.
Murray W. S., The Making of the Balkan States; London, 1912.
Murray's Hand Book, Greece, etc.; London, 1884.

N.

Neigebaur J. F., Albania; 1851.
Newbigin M. J., Geographical aspects of Balkan problems, etc.
Nicolaidès C., La Macédoine; 1879.
Nicolaidès N., L'empire Ottoman; Paris, 1909.
Nopcsa Franz, Im Katholischen Nordalbanien; Wien, 1903.

O.

Odysseus (Sir Chas. Eliot), Turkey in Europe; London, 1908.
Offeicoff, La Macédoine au point du vue ethnographique, etc.; 1887.
Outendirk F., La Turquie à l'exposition universelle de 1867 à Paris; Paris, 1867.

P.

Paganel C., Histoire de Scanderbeg.
Panthier G., Les Iles Ioniennes pendant l'occupation française; Paris, 1863.

KEY TO THE NEAR EAST

Pausanias, book 12:I.
Pernice Angelo, Origine ed Evoluzione Storica delle Nazioni Balcaniche; Milano, 1915.
Patsch Carl, Das Sandschak Berat in Albanien; Wien, 1904.
Peacock W., Albania, the Foundling State of Europe; New York, 1914.
Pears S. E., Türkey and its people.
Pedersen H., Albanesische text mit einen Glossar; 1895.
Perétié, Mouvement Commercial de Scutari en 1908-1909.
Petrovitch P. J., Scanderbeg; 1881.
Pinon R., L'Europe et l'empire Ottoman; Paris, 1908.
Pinon R., L'Europe et la jeune Turquie; Paris, 1911.
Pittard E., Contribution à l'étude anthropologique des Albanais; Paris, 1894.
Plato, Cratylus.
Plutarch, The Lives.
Polyvios P. J., L'Albanie et la Réunion d'Ambassadeurs à Londres; Paris, 1914.
Poujade E. Chrétiens et Turcs, 1862.
Pouqueville F. C. H. L., Grèce; 1835.
Pouqueville F. C. H. L., Voyage de la Grèce, 1826-27.
Pouqueville F. C. H. L., Histoire de la régénération de la Grèce; 1822.

R.

Rach H. C. Lu, The Fringe of the East; London, 1913.
Rada Girolamo de, Gli Albanesi.
Rankin (Reginald, Lt. Colonel), The Inner History of the Balkan war; London, 1914.
Reader M., La politique Russe dans la question d'Orient, Bibliothèque Universelle; vol. 8, 4e page, 1897.
Reclus E., Nouvelle Géographie Universelle. La terre et les hommes.
Reinhold, Noctes Pelasgicae.
René Moulin et Serge de Chessin, Une année de politique extérieure, 1908.
Report of the International Commission to Inquire into the causes and Conduct of the Balkan wars; Washington, 1914.
Ripley William Z., The Races of Europe; London, 1900.
Ruelle, Histoire du Moyen Age; Paris, 1842.

S.

San Giuliano (The Marquis of), Albania.
Schneider Edourd, Une race oubliée, les Pélasges et leurs descendants; Paris, 1894.
Schopoff A., Les réformes et la protection des Chrétiens en Turquie (1673-1904); Paris, 1904.
Siebertz Paul, Albanien und die Albanesen; Wien, 1910.
Slade A., Records of travels in Turkey, Greece, etc., 1833.
Seignobos Ch., Histoire politique de l'Europe contemporaine; Paris, 1905.
Steinmetz Karl, Eine Reise durch der Hochlandergaue oberalbaniens; 1904.
Steinmetz Karl, Ein Vortoss in die Nordalbanien Alpen; 1905.
Steinmetz Karl, Von der Adriatik zum Schwarzen Drin; Sarajevo.
Steur Ch., Ethnographie de l'Europe.
Strabon, Rerum Geograph. Book VII and IX.
Strangford (Viscountess), The Eastern Shores of the Adriatic; London, 1865.
Stratico Albert, Albanian literature.
Sulliotti A. Italo, In Albania, sei mesi di regno da Guglielmo di Wied a Essad Pascia da Durrazzo a Vallona; Milano, 1914.
Sulliotti A. Italo, Albania; Milano, 1916.
Svoronos, Les Réformes et les œuvres de l'assemblée Nationale; Athenes, 1911.
Szamatolski L., Albanien in Lichte neurer Forschun; 1910.

T.

Thalloczy Ludovicus De, etc., Acta et Diplomata Res Albaniae Mediae aetatis. Illustrantia collegerunt et disgesserunt; 1912.
Thomopoulos Jakob, Pelasgica; Athens.
Tite Live, book 33 and 44.
Toiani Francesco, History of Albania.
Tomitch, Les Albanais en Vieille Serbie et dans le Sandjak de Novi-Bazar; Paris, 1903.
Touchard, La maitrise de l'Adriatique; Paris, 1913.
Toynbee Arnold J., Greek policy since 1882; London, 1914.
Tozer H. F., The Highlands of Turkey.
Trubert M., Impressions et Souvenirs d'un diplomate; 1913.
Truhelka Ciro, Les Restes Illyriens en Bosnie; Paris, 1900.

KEY TO THE NEAR EAST 275

U.

Unquhart, Spirit of the East.
Unquhart F. F., The Eastern Question; London, 1914.
Upward Allen, The East end of Europe.

V.

Valaque du Pinde (Un), Les Grecs, les Valaques, les Albanais; Bruxelles, 1886.
Vellay Charles, L'irrédentisme hellénique; Paris, 1913.
Villari L., The Balkan Question; London, 1905.
Villehardouin, Conquête de Constantinople.
Vié L., Des principales applications du droit d'intervention des puissances dans les affaires des Balkans; 1900.

W.

Watson-Seton R. W., The Rise of Nationality in the Balkans.
Watson-Seton R. W., The Balkan, Italy and the Adriatique; 1915.
Weigand Gustav Ludwig, Albanesische Grammatik; Leipzig, 1913
Wilh L., Les Pélasges; 1856.
Woods H. C., The Danger Zone of Europe; London, 1910.
W. P., Grammaire albanaise; London, 1887.

X.

Xenopol A. D., Theoria lui Rosler.
Xenopol A. D., Histoire des Roumains de la Dacie Trajane.
Xylander Joseph Karl, Die Sprache der Albanesen oder Sckiptaren; Frankfort a Main; 1835.

II. ENCYCLOPAEDIAS AND DICTIONARIES.

Dechambres Dr., Dictionnaire Encyclopédique des Sciences médicales, M. G. Obedenaru, Les Albanais en Roumanie.
Encyclopædia Britannica, eighth, ninth and the tenth edition.
Knight Charles, Cyclopædia of Geography.
Larousse P., Grand Dictionnaire Universelle.
Universite (L') Catholique, tome XXII, 1846.
Vivien de Saint Martin, Nouveau Dictionnaire de Géographie Universelle.

III. STATES, PAPERS AND ACCOUNTS.

Austrian Red Book. Diplomatic documents concerning the relations of Austria with Italy; from July 20, 1914 to May 23, 1915.

France, Ministère des Affaires Etrangères. Négociations relatives à la rectification des frontières de la Grèce; 1879-80.

Great Britain, Accounts and papers; Turkey, 1878-1881.

Italy's Green book; August, 1915.

Italy, Min. degli Affari Esteri; Documenti diplomatici; 1876-81.

IV. PERIODICALS.

A. 1815-1911.

Adamidi G., Aperçu Général sur l'Origine des Albanais et de leur langue, Bulletin de l'institut Egyptien; Quatrième Série, No. 3, 1902.

Apostolidès B., Les Pelasges, les Hellènes, etc., Bulletin de l'Institut Egyptien; Quatrième Série, No. 7, 1907.

Bertaux E., Les Français d'outre mer en Apulie, en Epire, etc., Revue Historique; tome 85, 1904.

Best, Excursions in Albania (1841) Mo. R. 157:371.

Bourchier J. D., A Balkan Confederation; Fortn. R., London, Sept., 1891.

Brailsford H. N., Albanians, Turks and Russians; Contemp., September, 1900.

Caillord V. H. P., Albania and the Albanians; Fortn. R. 43:461.

Cvijic, Researches in Macedonia and Southern Albania; Geographical Journal, August, 1900.

Dillon E. J., Turkey rocks ahead, Contemp., Sept., 1911.

Dora d'Istria, L'ame albanais d'après les chants populaires; Revue des Deux Mondes, vol. 3, 1866. See also the same for 1859-1868, 1870, 1871 and 1873.

Dumont, Revue des Deux Mondes, vol. 6, 1872.

Durham M E., Serb and Albanian frontier; Contemp. January, 1909.

Fitzgerald, Question d'Albanie (1880); Macmil. 42:201.

Gibbons H. A., Albania in arms; Ind. September 25, 1912.

Gounot, Notes sur les mines de bitume exploités en Albanie; Annales des Mines; July, 1903.

Gravier G., Revue de Paris, November 15, 1911.

Green A. H., Albania and its People; Princ. 29:699.

Karaczy, Count de, Geographical account of Albania; The
    Journal of the Royal Geographical Society of London, vol. 12,
    1842.
Montegazza Vico, Il Mediteraneo; Questioni di Politica estera,
    1910.
Ohie J., Blood Vengeance and Pardon in Albania; Pop. Sci. Mo.
    35;529; Brown's Ath. 1888, 2:512; Chamb. J. 66:310.
Pinon René, Revue des Deux Mondes, December, 1909.
Pittard Dr., Contribution à l'etude anthropologique des Albanais; Revue de L'école d'Anthropologie, July, 1902.
Scotus-Viator, Austria-Hungary, Italy and the West Balkans,
    Contemp. March, 1908.
Wiet E., Itineraire en Albanie et Roumelie; Soc. de Geographie;
    Bull, 5e Serie, vol. 16, 1868.
Williams O., Jaunt to Janina; Blackw. R., June, 1909.
Wyon R., Roman Catholic Albania; Living Age, May 30, 1903.
Yemeniz, Revue des Deux Mondes, vol. 2, 1865.
............, Questions diplomatiques et coloniales, Revue de
    polique extérieure, 1899-1919.
............, Macedonia and the Albanians, Contemp. April, 1903.
............, Les Anciens Coutumes Albanais. Nouvelle Revue
    historique du droit Français et Etranger, vol.
    27, 1903.

............, Albania, Hon. and For R. 3:52.

............, Albania and Scanderbeg; Ed. R. 154:325.

............, Costumes of Albania; Penny M. 5:179, 187, 220.

............, Albanians in South Epirus; Blackw. 129:304.

............, In the Albanian Mountains; Chamb. J. 66:518.

B. 1912-1918.

A. H., La Commission financière internationale; Economiste
    Europeen; 4, 11 July, 1913.
Aubry E., The case of Albania, Asiatic Review; London, 1914.
Baldacci Antonio, L'Albanie économique et politique à la veille

de la guerre. Revue économique internationale, 15-20 November, 1912.

Baldacci Antonio, L'Albanie Reale, Societa geografica Bollettino; Roma, 1914.

Baldaccio Antonia, Nell' Epiro Turco. Itinerari albanesi del 1895. Reale Societa. Geografica Bollettino; Roma 1916. Serie 5, vol. 5, pages 164-200; 323-336; 368-384.

Bardoux J., Les Balkans et le Triplice; Opinion, Nov. 9, 1912.

Bardoux J., L'évolution de la crise diplomatique; Opinion, Nov. 23, 1912.

Bardoux J., La Conférence de Paris; Opinion, June 7, 1813.

Bardoux G. Louis, La reprise de l'incendie albanais; Opinion, Sept. 27, 1913.

Barnes J. S. (Captain), The Future of the Albanian State; The Geographical Journal of London, July, 1918.

Barth J., L'équilibre de la Méditerranée; Revue des sciences politiques; July and August, 1913.

Barth J., La France et la Triple-Entente dans le Méditerrnée; Revue des sciences politiques; February 15, 1914.

Berard V., La France dans le Levant; Asie française; February, 1912.

Blondel G., Les problèmes économiques des Balkans; Questions diplomatiques et coloniales, June 16, 1913.

Bonsel S., Sons of the eagle; North American Review, January, 1913.

Bourchier James D., The Final Settlement in the Balkans; Quarterly Review, October, 1917.

Brailsford, H. N., Albania and the allies; Contemporary Review, May, 1913.

Carus P., Albania; Open Court; February, 1913.

Cassanges C. P., Case of Epirus; Forn. Review, March, 1914.

Charmes Francis, La Chronique de la Quinzaine; Revue de Deux Mondes, 1912, 1913, 1914.

Cheradame André, L'Europe et l'Albanie; Correspondant, Paris 1914, tome 255, Nouvelle serie tome 219, pp. 969-1007.

Connard R. L'Autriche et la paix dans les Balkans; Revue des Français; December, 1912.

Cosmetatos Phocas S. P., L'Albanie; Monde Economique, January, 1914.

Christitch E., Powers and Albania; Catholic World, May, 1914.

KEY TO THE NEAR EAST

Damon T. J., Albanians; National Geographical Magazine, November, 1912.
Dell A., Some Recent experiences in Albania; The 19th Century and after; vol. 76, 1914.
Denis E., Le principe des nationalités et la paix des Balkans; Revue du Mois, June, 1913.
Dillon E. J., Albanian characteristics; Contemp. Review, October, 1913.
Dillon E. J., Alleged plan to extirpate the Albanians; Contemp., April, 1913.
Dillon E. J., The Albanian Tangle; Fortn. Review, vol. 96, 1914, July, 1914.
Dillon E. J., Albania's tribulations; Contemp. Review, July, 191´
Dillon E. J., Albania to be or not to be; Contemp. Review, June, 1914.
Dillon E. J., Albanian anarchy; Contemp. Review, August, 1914.
Dorobantz J., La Question albanaise; Questions diplomatiques et coloniales, May 16, 1913.
Duboscq A., La Question albanaise; Revue Bleüe; June 22, 1912.
Durham M. E., The Albanian Question; Contemp. Review, October, 1917.
Erickson C. T., The Truth about Albania; Asiatic Review, London, 1914.
Erickson C. T., The Making of a nation; Missionary Review, March, 1914.
F..........., Le Problème Albanais et les rélations entre Autriche et Italie.
Fribourg A., Les Albanais et la France; Opinion, November 30, 1912.
Gaulis G., La Russie en Orient; Opinion, April 20, 1912.
Ginistrelli E. P., Albania and Italy; Living Age, March 11, 1916.
Gravier G., L'Albanie et ses limites; Dec. 15, 1912; Jan. 1, 15, 1913.
Hanotaux G. Vers l'entente; Revue hebdomadière, November 16, 1912.
Hanotaux G., Fin de la crise orientale; Revue hebdomadière, February, 7, 1914.
Harpe F. De la, La crise et le droit des peuples; La Revue, Nov. 1, 1912.
Hogarth D. G., The Geographical Journal, April, 1913.

Imbrie R. W., Across Albania with an Ambulancier; Travel, April, 1918.

Interim, L'aréopage de Londres et les peuples balkaniques; Opinion, April 5, 1913.

Jaray G. J., L'Albanie et les Albanais; Revue politique et parlementaire, Paris 1913; vol. 75, pp. 239, 255.

Jaray G. J., L'Albanie autonome et l'Europe; Questions diplomatiques et coloniales; Paris 1914, tome 219, pp. 969-1007.

Johnston C., Land of the Blood feud; Harper's Weekly, January 11, 1913.

Kemal Ismail Bey, Albania and the Albanians; Quarterly Review, July, 1917.

Lamouche L., L'indépendance albanaise et le débouché Serbe sur l'Adriatique; Revue politique et parlementaire, Jan. 10, 1913.

Lamouche L., La naissance de l'Etat albanais; Revue politique et parlementaire, May 10, 1914.

Leroy Beaulieu Paul, Conjectures sur la crise; Economiste Français, Nov. 2, 9, et 30 et December 7, 1912.

Leroy Beaulieu Paul, Les enseignments des guerres des Balkans; Economiste Français, August 23, 1913.

Leune J., Grèce et Albanie; Grande Revue, May 10, 1913.

Marvand, A., Autriche-Hongrie et Montenegro; Opinion, March 29, 1913.

Metz, H., Un voyage en Albanie; Bulletin de la Société de géographie commerciale de Paris, June, 1913.

Montegazza Vico, The Relations between Italy and Austria and the Albanian Question; The British Review, vol. 2, p. 321-334, London, 1913.

Nevinson, H. W., Appeal in favor of the Albanians; Westminster Gazette, April 9, 1913.

Nevinson, H. W., Land of the eagle; Contemp. September, 1913.

Nicholas (King of Montenegro), On Scutari; Daily Telegraph, April 5, 1913.

Peacock W., Italy and Albania; Contemp. Review, March 1915.

Peacock W., The Future of Albania; Fortn. Review, vol. 93, pp. 920-932, 1913.

Peacock W., Wild Albanian; Fortn. Review, February, 1913.

Perrand R., Triple-Alliance et Triple-Entente; Opinion, January 10, 1914.

KEY TO THE NEAR EAST

Pinon R., L'Autriche et la guerre balkanique; Revue des Deux Mondes, Feb. 1913.

Politis N., Les Commission internationales d'enquête; Revue générale du droit international public, vol. 19, 1912.

Pontcray J. du, L'Albanie et la Question Albanaise; Nouvelle Revue, Serie 4e, tome 5, p. 59-68; Paris 1913.

Portalis G. Fefevre, Un héro albanais; Scanderberg; Revue hebdomadière, August 2, 1913.

Prince ......, Le Saint Siege et les Balkans; Revue, October 1, 1913.

Powell E. A., Making a nation to measure; Ind. September 4, 1913.

Recouly R., Les conférences de Londres et la guerre balkanique; Revue politique et parlementaire, January 10, 1913.

Recouly R., La question de Scutari; Revue politique et parlementaire; May 10, 1913.

Recouly R., La note anglaise et les affaires balkanique; Revue politique et parlementaire, January 10, 1914.

Recouly R., L'Albanie, les iles et les Etats balkaniques; Revue politique et parlementaire, February 10, 1914.

Rosati T., Osservazione politiche sull' Albania Redenta; La Vita Italiana, Anno 5, vol. 9, pp. 474-480, Roma, 1917.

Saint Blancard (L. de Saint Victor De), Six mois de crise balkanique; Revue des sciences politique, July and August, 1913.

Saint Blancard (L. de Saint Victor De), L'équilibre balkanique; Revue des sciences politiques, February 15, 1914.

Scriven G. P., Recent observations in Albania; National Geographical Magazine, August 1918.

Sokolovitch P. P., Albanian Question; Fortn. Review, September 1912.

Steppany Percy, La situation économique actuelle en Albanie; Revue Economique international, vol. 2, No. 1, 1914.

Stienon Charles, L'Albanie et la querre; Correspondant, tome 262, pp. 130-148, Paris, 1916.

Thomasson (Commandant De), Les prodromes de la crise diplomatique; Questions diplomatiques et coloniales, Nov. 16, 1912.

Thomasson (Commandant De), Le jeu de l'Autriche; Questions diplomatiques et coloniales, October 1, 1913.

Tzarigradski, La valeur comparée des acquisitions balkaniques; Questions diplomatique et coloniales, October 1, 1913.

Vaina Eugenia, Albania che nasce catania; La Giovane Europa, 1914.
Vaka D., In Wild Albania; Delin. July 1915.
Vaka D., Romantic Albania; Century, March 1917.
Viator-Scotus, Future boundaries of Albania; Spec. January 4, 1913.
Williams G. F., Shkypetars; Harpers Weekly, April 10-May 1, 15, 1915.
Woods H. C., Situation in Albania; Fortn. Review, March 1914.
Woods H. C., Situation in Albania and Macedonia; Fortn. Review, May, 1912.
Woods H. C., Albania and the Albanians; Geographical Review, April 1918.

............, La guerre des Balkans, les antécédents, les causes, les influences, le rôle des grandes Puissances; Correspondant, October 25, 1912.
............, L'Allemagne et la guerre des Balkans; Correspondant, Dec. 10, 1912.
............, La force menaçante de l'Autriche; Opinion, Dec. 21, 1912.
............, Albanian Macedonian Commission; Spectator, 1912.

............, Austria and the Albanian Question; R. of R., Dec. 1912.
............, Europe and the Problem of Albania; Living Age, Dec. 28, 1912.
............, Le conflit austro-serbe et la question albanaise; Economiste Européen, October 24, 1913.
............, Les suites de la guerre des Balkans; Correspondant, July 10, 1913.
............, Future of Albania; Spectator, March 8, 1913.

............, Albania between two fires; Lit. Digest, September 27, 1913.
............, Albanian policy of Austria and Italy; Outlook, May 24, 1913.
............, Albania's fate; Lit. Digest, January 18, 1913.

............, Albania's many friends; Lit. Digest, May 10, 1913.

............, Scutari and the Slavs; Outlook, May 10, 1913.

............, Who are the Albanians and what do they want? R. of R., February 1914.
............, Baby Balkan Kingdom; Lit. Digest, October 11, 1913.
............, Aegean and Albanian problems; Spectator, February 21, 1914.
............, Albania, the Adriatic and the Balkans; Spec., April 11, 1914.
............, Troubles of Albania; Spectator, May 23, 1914.

............, American hand in the new Balkan crisis; Current Opinion, August, 1914.
............, Roman road in mid-Albania; Living Age, April 11, 1914.
............, Insurrection in Albania; Nation, June 18, 1914.

............, Russia, Albania and Turkey; Living Age, June 27, 1914.
............, William of Wied's Thorny crown; Literary Digest, February 14, 1914.
............, Albania, Austria, Italy, Essad; Contemporary Review, August 1917.
............, Independence of Albania; Living Age, August 11, 1917.
............, Two offers of autonomy for Albania; Current History, July 1917.

Table of Contents

		Page
Preface		I-IV
Outline		V-X
List of appendices		X
List of plates, illustrations and maps		XI-XII
Chapter I.	The Unknown Country and Its People	1-37
Chapter II.	The Stumbling Block of the Turks	38-54
Chapter III.	Albania Defying the Congress of Berlin	55-79
Chapter IV.	The Mighty Power of the Spelling Book	80-94
Chapter V.	Albania the Cause of the Balkan War	95-116
Chapter VI.	The European Importance of the Albanian Question	117-133
Chapter VII.	Albania and the Great Powers	134-158
Chapter VIII.	Albania and the Balkan States	159-166
Chapter IX.	Europe Struggling to Save Her Checkerboard	167-189
Chapter X.	Europe Begins to Play Her Tragedy In Albania	190-196
Chapter XI.	Future Prospects	197-205
Chapter XII.	Reminiscences	206-228

APPENDICES:

Appendix A.	The Albanian Language	229-231
Appendix B.	An Interesting Debate	232-238
Appendix C.	A Russian Official Statement	238-241
Appendix D.	Albania's Rights, Hopes and Aspirations	241-248
Appendix E.	The Development of Schools in the Turkish Empire and an Ideal System of Education for Albania	248-266

Bibliography	267-283
Table of Contents	284
General Index	285

Index

A.

Abdul Assiz, Sultan, 251
Abdul Bey Frasheri, 56
Abdul Hamid, Sultan, 77, 92, 172
Abdul Medjid, Sultan, 46, 50
Abel, Otto, 233
Achilles, 34
Achilleus, king of Epirus, 17
Acropolita, George, 21
Ahmet III, Sultan, 199, 247
Akif Pasha Elbassani, 217
Alaric, 163
Alexander the Great, 17, 29, 122, 126, 198, 232, 233, 236, 237, 238, 241, 246
Alexander, king of Epirus, 123
Ali Pasha, 67
Ali Pasha Tepeleni, 7, 25, 41, 44, 81, 126, 152
Ali Riza Pasha, 110
Alphonse d'Aragon, 137
Andrassy, Count, 118
Andronicus, 20
Angelo, Isaac, 20
Angelos, Michael, 21
Antigonus, 123
Arcadius, 19, 124
Aristophanes, 233
Aristotle, 17
Arslan Bey, 43
Asquith, The Rt. Hon. H. H. 131, 135, 136
Assan, John, 164
Aubaret, 152
Azis Pasha Vrioni, 217

B.

Baker, James, 11, 238
Baldacci, Antonio, 141
Balzha, 23, 24
Barletius, Marinus, 40
Basil Bulgaroktonus, 166
Basil II, Emperor, 20
Bayazid I, Sultan, 38
Beaconsfield, Lord, 60, 71, 134
Becir, General, 102
Beloch, 233
Benckendorff, Count, 146, 150
Benloew, Louis, 2, 236
Berchtold, Count, 99, 118, 185
Bettollo, Admiral, 139
Bib Doda, 152
Bismarck, Prince, 57, 59, 154, 155
Bogdanus, Archbishop, 80, 81
Bohemond, 20
Boletini, Issa, 78
Boppe, August, 152
Boris, Tsar, 165
Bosworth, Prof. E. I., 215, 216
Botchari, 43
Bouree, Ambassador, 251
Brailsford, H. N., 3, 13, 83, 88, 128, 173, 245, 246
Brerewood, Edward, 173, 246
Bubulina, 43
Burney, Vice Admiral, 102, 103, 104
Bushat, Mehmet, 24, 41
Byron, Lord, 30, 41

C.

Caesar, 105
Cambon, Jules, 146, 150
Cantacuzenus, 23
Capodistrias, J., Count, 159
Carmen Sylva, 187
Catherine II, Empress, 156
Cecil, Lord, H., 135
Charles VII, king of France, 30
Charles, king of Sicily, 22
Christ, Jesus, 13
Christo, Rev. H., 53
Christoforidhi, C., 84
Clark, 11, 238
Clarke, Rev. W., 213
Clitus, 237
Comnenus, Alexius, 20
Comnenus, Theodore, 21
Corti, Count Lodovico, 67-68
Crane, Hon. Chas. R., 92, 215-216, 217-223
Crane, Mrs. Chas. R., 92
Crispi, Francesco, 138
Curtius, 233

D.

Dako, C. A., 3, 151, 226, 232, 234
Dako, Mrs. C. A., 85, 86, 90, 111, 191, 193, 214, 216, 224, 228
Damianos, General, 110
Dandolo, Dr. A. C., 160
Delcheff, Cotze, 72
Delyannis, Theodore, 58, 59, 62, 232, 233
Demosthenes, 17, 238
Dervish Bey Elbassani, 217
Dervish Pasha, 25
Descoin, Colonel, 28, 154
Dhone, 153

Diocletian, Emperor, 198, 246
Dino, Mesim, 116
Djavela, 43
Djavid Pasha, 78, 110, 259
Djuvara, T. G., 134
Doorman, Captain, 194, 195, 226
Dozon, August, 9
Durham, Miss M. E., 106, 172, 199, 218, 221, 245, 247
Dukaghini, Lek, 32, 40
Dushan, Tsar, 22, 164, 165, 168

E.

Edward VII, king of England, 75
Efthim, Miss Fanka, 87
Emilianus, Paulus, 18, 237
Emin Bey Pojani, 193
Emmanuel III, king Victor, 145
Essad Pasha Toptani, 97, 98, 100, 142, 190, 191, 228, 243

F.

Ferdinand, king of Naples, 137
Ferrero, General Giacinto, 145
Fick, August, 234
Finlay, George, 4
Fitzmaurice, Lord E., 26, 71, 134, 242
Fuat Bey Toptani, 217
Fuat, Prince Ahmet, 187

G.

Galip, Patrona, 197, 247
Galli, Signor, 109
Gennadius, Patriarch, 49
Gentius, 124

KEY TO THE NEAR EAST

Gibbons, Edward, 206
Giorgio, General De, 74
Gërmënji, Th., 145
Ghilardi, Captain, 194
Gibert, F., 46
Gladstone, William, 67, 120, 121, 131, 137
Gopcevitch, 76
Gortchakoff, Prince, 157
Goschen, Lord, 26, 71, 134, 242
Grameno, Mihal, 90, 91, 151
Gregg, Consul, 228
Grey, Sir Edward, 101, 108, 135, 136, 137, 146, 150, 177, 178, 223, 243
Grueff, Damian, 72
Guiscard, Robert, 20

H.
Hadik, Count, 118
Hahn, G. J., 9, 10, 80, 236, 255
Hamdi Bey Ochrida, 212, 216
Hannibal, 18
Hatzfeld, Count, 69
Heraclius, Emperor, 163
Herbert, Hon. Aubrey, 136, 196
Herodotus, 14, 17, 232, 233, 235, 236
Hilmi, Pasha, 73
Hirt, Herman, 9
Hodo Bey, 56
Honorius, 19, 124
Homer, 256
Hotzendorff, von Konrad, 99
Howard, W. W., 179
Hysen Bey Vrioni, 217

I.
Ignatief, General, 157
Ilia, Kristo, 145

Illyrianus, king of Illyria, 17
Imperiali, Marchese, 146, 150
Iphigenia, 34
Ipitis, Colonel, 117

J.
Jaray, Gabriel L., 173, 245
Jean d'Anjou, 137
Jeanne d'Arc, 210, 211, 214
John, Despot of Epirus, 23
Jokl, Dr. Norbert, 231

K.
Kantcheff, 76
Kara Mahmoud Pasha, 41, 171
Karanus, 16
Karapanos, 234
Karatheodori Pasha, 60
Kastriota, George, 24, 38
Kastriota, John, 38, 39
Kemal Bey Ismail, 26, 109, 117, 182-183, 188-189, 190
Kennedy, Rev. P. B., 113
Kiamil Pasha, 117
Knight, E. F., 57
Kosturi, Spiro, 54
Krajewski, 189
Kruyff, Baron Suat Yoost de, 221
Kyrias, George D., 91
Kyrias, Gerasim D., 85, 86, 258
Kyrias, Miss P. D., 90, 93, 151, 192-193, 214, 223-225, 228
Kyrias, Miss Sevasti D., 85, 88, 207, 213-214, 259

L.
Lamb, Harry, 189
Lascaris, Theodore, 21

Law, Bonar, 135
Lasar, Tsar, 168
Leake, 9
Lear, 131
Leoni, 189
Levine, Isaac don, 146
Longfellow, H. W., 39

M.

Mahmud II, Sultan, 25, 46
Malte Brun, 9
Manos, Colonel, 126
Margarit, Apostol, 162, 254
Maroulis, Dr. Demetrios, 53
Martinovitch, General, 95
Mavranza, Colonel, 194
Mavrommati, Consul, 174
Mehmet Ali Pasha, 66, 67, 126, 198, 246
Mentor, 14
Meyer, Gustav, 9, 230, 231
Miaulis, 43
Midhat Frasheri, 91
Mignot, Major, 152
Mihaelides, M. J., 235, 236
Mikloschich, 9
Mohammed, the Prophet, 13
Mohammed II, Sultan, 24, 39, 41, 42, 48, 156
Montpensier, Duc de, 184
Morley, Lord, 101
Murat I, Sultan, 24, 39, 168
Murat II, Sultan, 40
Mustapha Pasha, 25, 43, 44
Muller, Karl Otfried, 8
Muller, Max, 10, 235

N.

Nadolny, 189
Naim Bey Frasheri, 258

Napoleon Bonaparte, 30, 1ґ੧
Niazi Bey, 76, 77, 216
Nicephorus Bacilaces, 20
Nicephorous Botaniates, 20
Nicholas II, Emperor, 75
Nicholas, Emperor, 159
Nicholas, king of Montenegro, 95, 96, 98, 99, 100-102, 168, 185, 240
Nicholas, Grand Duke, 55
Nicolaides, Dr. Cleanthes, 236
Niebuhr, 123
Nossi, Lef, 91

O.

Orchan, Sultan, 45
Osman Pasha, Marshal, 77
Othman, Sultan, 45
Ovid, 235.

P.

Pachymer, 21
Palaeologus, Andronicus, 23
Palaeologus, Manuel, 24
Palaeologus, Mihail, 22
Papadakis, Captain, 192
Papamihail, Captain, 194
Paparousi, 129
Pauli, Carl, 9
Pasitch, 129
Peacock, Wadham, 164, 171, 180
Pears, Sir Edwin, 3
Pedersen, Dr. Holger, 231
Pelissier, Marshal, 152
Perdiccas, 232
Perseus, 18, 124
Peter the Great, 156
Petraew, 189
Petrovic, 189
Pharos, Demetrios, 18

Philip V of Macedonia, 18
Philip the Great, 16, 123, 233, 236
Philip Duke of Taranto, 22
Philotas, 237
Piccino, 144
Pinon, Rene, 3
Planz, 97
Plato, 14
Plutarch, 17, 237, 238
Poda Silehdar, 43
Polena, Dr. C., 191, 192
Polyxena, 34
Pompey, 105
Popovitch, 129
Pouqueville, Laurent, 152, 175
Prenk Bib Doda, 56, 153
Prometheus, 83
Ptolemy, 16
Pyrrhus, 16, 17, 29, 123, 126, 198, 238, 246

Q.

Qulli, Dr. Mutcho, 91

R.

Rada, Girolamo De, 10
Rangabe, 59
Reclus, Elisee, 2
Reshid Pasha, 25, 43
Roze, General, 152

S.

Safvet Pasha, 62
Saint Paul, 11
Salandra, Signor, 109
Sami Bey Frasheri, 82, 258
Sami Bey Pojani, 91
San Giuliano, Marquis of, 109

Sappho, 234
Sarafoff, Boris, 72
Scanderbeg, 12, 24, 29, 32, 38, 39, 40-41, 83, 119, 249
Schneider, Edouard, 10
Selim III, Sultan, 45
Semshi Pasha, 76, 77
Sheik ul Islam, 93, 210
Shafarik, 3
Shefket Bey Elbassani, 217
Seymour, Admiral, 69
Shpata, 23
Shishman, Tsar, 166
Sidismund, 19
Simeon, Tsar, 166
Snellen, Major, 191, 195, 226
Sonnino, Baron Sidney, 27, 28
Sapoundzakis, General, 114
Soutzes, General, 115
Spencer, H. S., 192, 195
Stambouloff, 72
Strabo, 238
Strangford, Viscountess, 174, 246
Sullo, Captain, 191, 193
Sylva, Carmen, 187

T.

Tahsim Philati, 82
Tell, Wilhelm, 93
Teuta, Queen, 17, 18
Theodore of Elbassan, 81
Theodoric the Great, 19
Theodosius the Great, 19, 124
Tittoni, 139
Tocco, Charles, 24
Topia, Arianiti, 24
Torgut Pasha, 79, 211, 221
Tottila, 163
Trotzky, Leon, 146

Tsilka, Rev. G. M., 54, 93, 194
Thucydides, 234

U.
Ulpianus, 237
Ulysses, 14

V.
Vasil, Rev. of Negovani, 53
Vehid Bey, 115
Vekilarxhi, Naoum, 81
Veli Bey, 43
Venizelos, Elefterios, 193
Victor Emmanuel III, 145
Vogüé, E. M., 11, 126, 238
Vokutitch, General, 97
Vreto, John, 82

W.
Waddington, William, 59, 153
Wasa Pasha, 17, 56, 57, 82
Weer, General De, 195
William, Mbret, 27, 143, 187, 188, 190, 204
Wirchow, 2
Wilson, President, 151
Woods, H. Charles, 3, 89

X.
Xerxes, 232

Y.
Yankoff, Colonel, 73

Z.
Zarif Zenel, 192, 194
Zoli, Signor, 221
Zonceff, General, 73

CHRISTO DAKO
circa 1905